Basic Statistics for Risk Management in Banks and Financial Institutions

Basic Statistics for Risk Management in Banks and Financial Institutions

ARINDAM BANDYOPADHYAY

Associate Professor (Finance), National Institute of Bank Management (NIBM), Pune

OXFORD
UNIVERSITY PRESS

OXFORD
UNIVERSITY PRESS

Great Clarendon Street, Oxford, OX2 6DP,
United Kingdom

Oxford University Press is a department of the University of Oxford.
It furthers the University's objective of excellence in research, scholarship,
and education by publishing worldwide. Oxford is a registered trade mark of
Oxford University Press in the UK and in certain other countries

Published in India by
Oxford University Press
22 Workspace, 2nd Floor, 1/22 Asaf Ali Road, New Delhi 110 002, India

First Edition published in 2022

Library of Congress Control Number: 2022931363

ISBN–13 (print edition): 978–0–19–284901–4
ISBN–10 (print edition): 0–19–284901–8
ISBN–13 (eBook): 978–0–19–266549–2
ISBN–10 (eBook): 0–19–266549–9
ISBN-13 (UPDF): 978–0–19–266548–5
ISBN-10(UPDF): 0–19–266548–0
ISBN-13 (OSO): 978–0–19–194426–0
ISBN-10(OSO): 0–19–194426–2

DOI: 10.1093/oso/9780192849014.001.0001

Typeset in Minion Pro 10.5/14
by Newgen KnowledgeWorks Pvt. Ltd., Chennai, India

In loving memory of my mother-in-law,
Late **Manjusree Nath**.
Her life as a teacher with extraordinary human qualities and selfless contribution to family and society has become the encouraging source of strength.
This has inspired and motivated me to complete this work.

Preface

Banking is a dynamic business where new threats as well as opportunities are constantly emerging. Banks are in the business of incurring, transforming, and managing risk. They are also highly leveraged. A major objective of bank management is to increase the organization's returns. However, higher return comes at the cost of increased risks. There is a need for risk management since financial institutions will have to react aptly to market developments including venturing into new business or launching new products and services for their own survival. There are important issues like business continuity, meeting the changing regulatory requirements make risk management, a dynamic exercise. Risk management is generally considered as a 'science' and then an 'art'. The science of risk management needs to be understood by the management to sharpen their business skills to take informed management decisions.

Risk management is the identification and evaluation of risks to an organization including risks to its existence, profits, and reputation (solvency) and the acceptance, elimination, controlling, or mitigation of the risks and the effects of the risks. The purpose of risk analysis is to assist the senior management and decision makers to better understand the risks (and opportunities) they take and evaluate the options available for their control so as to enable them to make a much better and conscious decision. Given the appetite for risk, if one uses accurate and relevant data, reliable financial models, and best analytical tools, then one can minimize risk and make the odds work in one's favour. This is the major challenge in risk management. An effective forward-looking integrated risk management framework can help banks and FIs to accelerate growth and enhance risk-adjusted performance on a continuous basis.

Data analysis, statistical modelling, and their applications are the fundamental requirements for measurement and managing the effect of risk in a financial institution. Commercial banks will have to necessarily develop a comprehensive self-understanding of the design and operation of a sound risk management system, including modelling, their business applications, and uses as well as their limitations. In order to achieve organizational objectives and enhance shareholders' value, FIs must be able to identify and measure the types of risk they face across their entire business. Measuring and understanding effect of risk are equally important as measuring returns. In this context, knowledge of basic statistical tools and their usage in banking in general and risk management in particular are very essential. The understanding of statistical methods is greatly facilitated through solving of real-life business problems. This book is designed to enable students as well as banking professionals to obtain a working knowledge of econometric/statistical techniques to gather and analyze datasets that are typically encountered in financial risk management research. A fairly large number of problems faced by financial risk analysts have been explored, and demonstration of their workable solutions has been worked out throughout this book.

The purpose of writing this book is to elucidate the statistical and quantitative techniques that are useful for identifying and estimating crucial risk parameters in the banking business. Understanding of consolidated credit risk, market risk, and operational risks through Value-at-Risk (VaR) measures is critical for management of organizational risks. Written in a lucid manner, this book demonstrates approaches of statistical risk modelling techniques using relevant applicable examples.

The book is specifically designed for the finance students and risk management professionals to get an easily understandable reference guide to know relevant and effective statistical applications in measuring and understanding risk in banks and financial institutions. The essence of statistical risk analysis is to provide insights for identification and assessment of key risks, performance evaluation, and setting risk limits. The chapters are designed to enable students as well as risk professionals to obtain a working knowledge of econometric/statistical techniques to extract and analyze relevant datasets that are typically encountered in financial research in the banking area. Attempts have been made to update the audience on the latest developments and techniques in the field of risk management including Basel III advanced approaches and ICAAP requirements. This book will also enable the reader to have hands-on knowledge to adopt sophisticated risk metrics to meet the current regulatory requirements (including validation and stress testing) as it demonstrates the benefit from the transition to risk-based oversight (economic capital and business forecasting). The miscellaneous problems and their solutions given in this book should test as well as enhance the understanding of the material presented in the text.

Acknowledgements

My gratitude goes to all those who have helped me in the process of drafting and finalizing this manuscript. The inspiration for this book came from my discussions and interactions I constantly had with my programme participants and students and their desire to know application of various statistical techniques in measuring and understanding risks in banking.

I specially thank Shri Dhiraj Pandey, my editor, for his help and support to complete this project. I am also grateful to Oxford University Press team for their continued support for this project. I sincerely acknowledge the constructive comments and suggestions provided by both the reviewers who have helped me to finalize the manuscript.

There are many people from academics and banking professionals whose continuous support and ideas deserve to be honoured and appreciated. I am grateful to my banker participants for their detailed interactions and suggestions in various executive training programmes that I have conducted. Special thanks to my PGDM students for their questions and discussions in my risk management and research methodology courses that I have taught them. It immensely helped me to create various numerical statistical solutions and applications for the book. I was also inspired by the work of my professors at JNU, Dr A. L. Nagar and Dr Sudipto Dasgupta. I am deeply thankful for the support that I have received from my institute: National Institute of Bank Management (NIBM), Pune. I am proud of this association and also deeply thankful to my institute.

This book project would not have been materialized if had I not been continuously inspired and motivated by my wife Mousumi. I am grateful for her patience and support to complete this assignment. I also owe to her family members, father Mukunda Debnath, and mother Majushree Nath and brother-in-law Mrinmoy for their constant support and inspiration. I thank my family members for their good wishes and blessings. I owe to my eldest sister Rajyashree Gupta and elder brother Apurba Kumar

Banerjee for their encouragements. I also express my deep sense of gratitude to my late parents Satyendra Nath Banerjee and Uma Rani Banerjee for their blessings and love bestowed on me. I wish that this book motivates many young professionals to carry out empirical research. I look forward to your comments at arindb@rediffmail.com

Contents

Book Summary

In this book, the author demonstrates how banks can apply many simple but effective statistical techniques to analyze risks they face in business and safeguard themselves from potential vulnerability. It covers three primary areas of banking risks—credit, market, and operational risk and in a uniquely intuitive, step-by-step manner, the author provides hands-on details on the primary statistical tools that can be applied for financial risk measurement and management.

Key Highlights of the Book

This book covers lucid explanation of applicability of important statistical techniques such as various descriptive statistics, hypothesis testing, probability distributions, predictive models, validation techniques, and diagnostic tests in the measurement and management risks in banking business. Monte Carlo simulation and VaR methodology, risk capital estimation and back-testing, time-series trend analysis and forecasting methods, and their usage in risk prediction are elaborated with numerous examples.

It emphasizes on specific risk measurement tools and techniques with data applications, templates required for data collection and analysis, numerous excel-based illustrations as well as analysis in econometric packages like STATA, EVIEWS, and @RISK.

It covers topics key to risk measurement and management such as probability theorems, descriptive statistics and distribution concepts, fitting probability distribution, multivariate techniques, Monte Carlo simulation techniques, and VaR.

1

Introduction to Risk Management

Basics of Statistics

Quantitative research is about measurements. Statistics and econometrics are the most widely used branch of mathematics in quantitative research. Quantitative research using statistical methods typically begins with the collection of data based on a theory or hypothesis, followed by the application of descriptive or inferential statistical methods.

Statistics is the methodology for collecting, analysing, interpreting data, and drawing conclusions from information obtained by the researcher. Since we cannot 'get away' from theory in scientific research, it should be made explicit to bring transparency in research. Theory provides us with a framework for the research. That is why we need to understand risk management subjects as well to apply these techniques. Theoretical formulation of research results enables generalization, benchmarking the study, and enhances the 'explanatory power' and acceptability of the results.

Econometric techniques utilize economic theory, facts (data), and statistical techniques, to measure and test certain relationships among meaningful (economic) variables, thereby giving these results to economic reasoning. Empirical finance provides analytical tools needed to examine the behaviour of financial markets, viz. estimating the dynamic impact multiplier of financial shocks, forecasting the value of capital assets, measuring the volatility of asset returns, testing the financial integration, assessing the determinants of non-performing assets (NPAs) in banks, and more.

Those who are likely to be successful researchers/analysts are more usually attracted by the problem-solving side of the work and the practical application of the mathematics and logic rather than the mathematics/statistical concepts per se.

This chapter provides a broad description of types of risks faced by the banking institutions. It introduces the reader with various types of risks and their interrelationships. We also discuss the role of statistical methods in measuring and monitoring the core risks faced by financial institutions (FIs).

What is Risk?

A risk is a random event that may possibly occur and, if it did occur, would have a negative impact on the goals of the organization. Risk refers to the chance of financial losses due to random changes in underlying risk factors. It is the probability of incurring loss due to unexpected and unfavourable movement of certain parameters. Risk is composed of three important elements: the scenario (or event identification), its probability of occurrence, and the size of its impact (either a fixed value or a range of values in distribution pattern). An opportunity is also a random variable which is the other side of the coin. But it has a positive impact on the goals of the organization. Risk managers are more concerned about the possibility of random events that would have negative influence of profitability (e.g. sudden increase in percentage of gross non-performing assets or rise in interest rate volatility).

In the business world, accepting risks is necessary to obtain a competitive advantage and generate profit. Introducing new product or expanding production facilities involves both return and risk. Risk taking is a natural part of banking transactions since without a willingness to take risk, there is generally very little expected reward. Banks typically create value for shareholders through their liabilities as well as their assets. The goal of risk management for banks is to determine the optimal level of risk that maximizes bank return subject to the constraints imposed by the regulators. A well-governed bank will have process and system in place to identify this optimal amount of risk and to make sure that its risk does not deviate too much from this amount. Risk management makes bankruptcy less likely, by making top management aware of the volatility of overall cash flows.

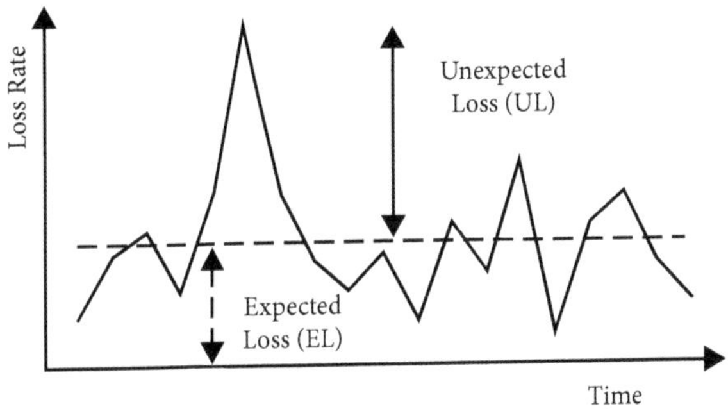

Figure 1.1 Expected vs. Unexpected Loss
Source: Adapted from BCBS illustration, BCBS (2005)

Risk implies losses. A bank needs to measure the impact of three kinds of losses:

Expected Losses: Anticipated losses borne in course of day-to-day business. This loss can be covered through pricing and provisions.
Unexpected Loss: Unanticipated, though predictable, losses to be absorbed under normal business/market conditions. The capital base is required to absorb the unexpected losses (ULs), as and when they arise.
Extreme Losses: Highly rare, though not improbable, losses under abnormal/distressed market conditions which must be overcome to survive and remain solvent. Stress tests study extreme losses.

It is the UL that creates the need for economic capital. Losses above the expected levels are usually referred to as UL as shown in Figure 1.1.

Essence of Financial Risk Management

Effective management of risk is a critical component of a comprehensive approach to risk management and essential to the long-term success of any banking organization. On the other hand, failures in the management of risk have contributed to episodes of financial instability and bad loan crisis. Consequently, capital adequacy of a bank has become an important benchmark to assess its financial soundness and strength. Over time, the techniques of risk measurement are constantly evolving and also the regulatory requirements.

Evolution of Basel Regulation

Capital is the cushion that protects the liability holders of a bank (depositors, creditors, and shareholders). Capital is required as a cushion for a bank's overall risk of UL. Adequate pricing and reserves should provide sufficient earnings to absorb Expected Loss. Regulatory Capital (Basel I, Basel II, and Basel III) is to ensure financial stability. The pitfalls associated with the regulatory capital requirements led to the development of more risk-sensitive or economic capital-based Basel II/III approach. Basel I accord mainly focused on credit risk. It ignored changes in financial markets and banking business. Hence, there was a wide gap between regulatory capital and economic capital as it was too broad brushed. Risk weight (100%) was same for all loans irrespective of credit rating of loan or borrower. Operational risk was considered as a part of credit risk. Under Basel II accord (introduced in 2006), focus shifted from Operational risk was considered as a part of credit risk to credit risk, market risk, and operational risk. The aim was to ensure that capital allocation is more risk sensitive. Basel III focused (introduced in 2010) on increasing the quality, quantity, and transparency of capital especially the core capital and ensures more risk sensitivity in estimating regulatory capital. It also introduced leverage ratio and emphasized on liquidity risk.

Risk taking is a natural part of banking transactions, and the regulatory agency is responsible for creating a sound financial environment by setting the regulatory framework where the supervisory agency monitors the financial viability of banks and checks compliance with regulations. Broadly speaking, the objectives of Basel II and III are to encourage better and more systematic risk management practices, especially in the area of core risks (credit, market, and operational), and to provide improved measures of capital adequacy for the benefit of supervisors and the marketplace more generally.

The introduction of Basel norms has incentivized many of the best practices banks to adopt better risk management techniques and to reconsider the analyses that must be carried out to evaluate their performance relative to market expectations and relative to competitors.

We ensure that regulatory capital requirements are more in line with economic capital requirements of banks, and by this, make capital allocation of banks more risk sensitive.

The focus of Basel accord is identification, measurement, and reporting of all material risks in a bank's portfolio. Basel Regulation has three pillar structures.

Pillar I: Making capital more risk-sensitive various risk measurement techniques are used to quantify major risk types (credit, market, and operational risk) through estimation of a set of (more or less sophisticated) risk parameters.

Pillar II: Focus on those risks which are captured inadequately, or not covered at all, under Pillar *I*. Credit concentration risk, interest rate, and liquidity risk in banking book and strategic and reputational risks, model validation (use test), and stress testing are part of Pillar II risks.

National supervisors are entitled to complement Pillar I capital with an additional regulatory capital requirement. Supervisor plays an indirect role here.

Pillar III: More transparent information to investors on portfolio risk profiles and capitalization. The presumption is that markets should be able to identify safe and risky banks.

The broad structure of Basel II/III is summarized in Figure 1.2.

The Basel regulatory structure has been evolved and modified over time. Pillar I requirements mainly highlight definition of capital- and risk-weighted assets. The risk weights mainly reflect the unexpected risk of losses for an asset and banks need to calculate required capital. Credit, market, and operational risks are three important parts of pillar I risk capital. Originally, Basel I accord in 1988 stipulated a minimum capital ratio of 8% of risk-weighted assets. In 1990s, the committee came out with a revised framework which culminated in the Basel II accord. It introduced three pillars in the capital adequacy framework. Under Basel II/III, Market risk has two approaches: Standardized Approach (SA) and Internal Model Approach (IMA) which are based on value at risk

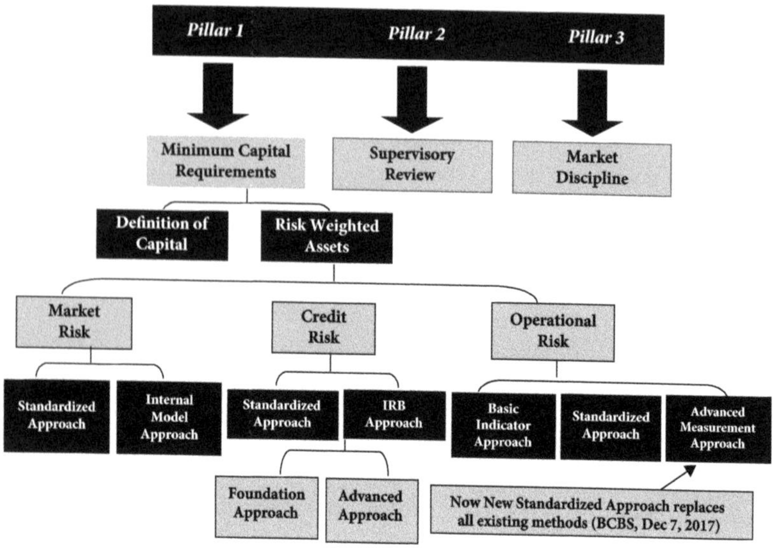

Figure 1.2 Structure of Basel Regulation
Source: Author's own illustration

(VaR) measure. Hence, market risk is to be measured either on duration approach or based on VaR. For credit risk, a bank can follow three approaches: SA, Foundation Internal Rating-Based Approach (FIRB), or Advanced Internal Rating-Based Approach (AIRB). The advanced approach is more risk sensitive and closer to the economic capital approach since it uses all internal risk inputs collected by the bank. For operational risk capital estimation, BCBS has prescribed three alternative approaches: (a) Basic Indicator Approach, (b) The Standardized Approach (TSA), and (c) Advanced Measurement Approach (AMA). However, under final Basel III approach, the new SA replaces these methods, and it is now a combination of internal loss-based and regulatory-prescribed method for capital estimation.

A few large and rare losses may wipe out its capital buffer and make it bankrupt. This is exactly what happened to the famous hedge fund Long-Term Capital Management (LTCM) in the summer of 1998. In the wake of the Russian crisis on 17 August, it was hit by large Marked to Market (MTM) losses in its trading book, which forced it into insolvency on 23 September. From this crisis, regulators as well as policy makers realized the importance of measurement and management of market risk in financial institutions. Accordingly, market risk component was incorporated in Basel II. The collapse of the famous insurance company American International Group (AIG) in 2008 was also due to similar reasons, after the bankruptcy of Lehman Brothers during global financial crisis. Thereafter, in January 2016, the Basel Committee again issued new guidelines in which market risk capital charges are based on losses beyond VaR. Subsequently, the Expected Shortfall (ES) as a measure of market risk has been introduced. The US subprime crisis has highlighted the linkages of the main types of risks, especially credit, market, and liquidity risks, and since then, the need for strengthening the capital position of commercial banks has emerged prominently.

Basel III expectation is that the bank should create capital buffer in good times so that it can be used in difficult times. It emphasizes on quality capital to absorb unexpected business losses to reduce the chance of another financial crisis. It also urges banks to maintain high credit ratings to ensure greater solvency and to avoid costs in raising additional capital under unfavourable market environment. That is why extensive risk profile investigation through statistical analysis is crucial in the new regulatory regime.

Researchers and risk management practitioners worldwide have constantly tried to improve on techniques in measuring and managing key risks: credit risk, market risk, operational risk, and liquidity risk. Massive progress have been made in the art and science of risk measurement and management for the last two decades in line with the developments in the Banking regulatory regime worldwide through Basel I, Basel II, and Basel III capital accord.

What is Risk Management?

According to Deventer, Imai, & Mesler (2005), the discipline which makes us appreciate the risks and returns from various portfolio and transaction-level strategies. At portfolio level, Chief Executive Officer, Chief Risk Officer (CRO), and Risk Management Department, Asset Liability Committee (ALCO) manages the risks in a banking institution. At transaction level, trader, Swap dealer, and loan officers manage the risk. The risks from individual transactions might be diversified away at the portfolio or institution level.

Risk management is a systematic approach to setting the best course of action under uncertainty by identifying, assessing, understanding, acting on, and communicating risk issues. A key ingredient of the risk measurement process is the accuracy and quality of master data that go into the computation of different aspects of risk. It is no surprise therefore that Master data management is a key area. Data play important role in proper assessment of risk. Without information, risk cannot be investigated. That is why the key risk drivers need to be understood and captured in banks. Regulator gives lot of importance to data aspect while supervising risk management framework and validation of risk tools. Master data management is a technology-enabled centralized process used to manage, integrate, categorize, and enrich critical business data. Banks need to develop good centralized database to improve decision-making process. It is essential for graduating to more sophisticated advanced approaches for risk management in an organization. Hence, we can say that risk management is first and foremost a 'science' and then an 'art'. Given the appetite for risk, if one uses accurate and relevant data, reliable financial models and best analytical tools, one can minimize risk and make the odds work in one's favour.

Risk management process needs to identify, measure, and manage various risks so that comparison of risks and returns is possible to set corporate strategies. Risk Management is the identification and evaluation of risks to an organization including risks to its existence, profits and reputation (solvency) and the acceptance, elimination, controlling, or mitigation of the risks and the effects of the risks.

Risk Management framework need a common metric to rank return and potential losses from different portfolios and risk categories.

Figure 1.3 explains the risk management process of a financial institution. It starts with risk identification and assessment. This step involves event identification and data collection process. The institution has to put in place a system of capturing information either through key risk drivers (KRIs) or through a rating system. Once risks are identified, risks are combined according to the following key areas impacted by the risks: people, mission, physical assets, financial assets, and customer/stakeholder trust. The next step is to Quantify and Measure risks—this means rate risks according to probability and impact. Various standard

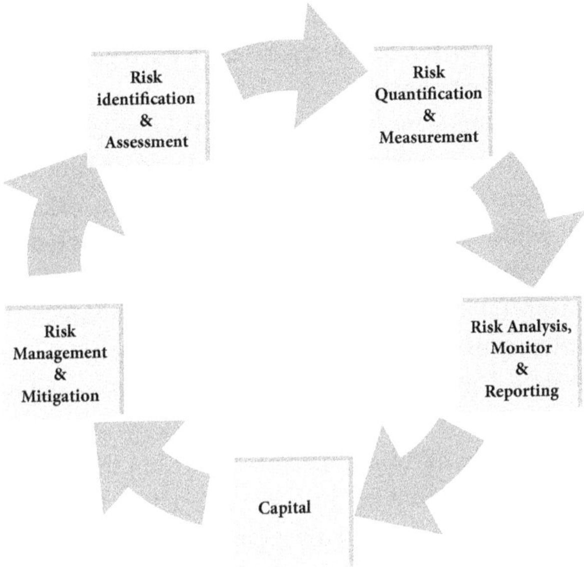

Figure 1.3 Risk Wheel-Generic Process
Source: Author's own illustration

tools are used by financial institutions to measure risk and understand their impact in terms of capital or its importance to the organization through a scoring technique. Risk analysis, monitoring and reporting send information to the top management of the organization to take strategic decisions through capital allocation, risk diversification, or adopt risk mitigation strategies (diversification, capital planning, finalize risk appetite statement, set business targets, risk transfer through a structured financial transaction, opt for insurance, or used derivative instruments for protection). This wheel sufficiently explains the entire risk management process.

Benefits of Risk Management

Risk management makes bankruptcy less likely, by making us aware of the volatility of overall cash flows. It reduces the cost of financial distress and gives a bank better access to capital markets.

A global survey by EIU-PWC (2006–07) reports that RM was viewed by banks as crucial for better reputation with regulators, customers, shareholders, and employees.

It enables the top management to adopt risk-based capital allocation based on internal measures of risk in various lines of business. By making risks and returns from different strategies comparable, risk management allows risk-adjusted performance related payments. This reduces conflict of interest between shareholders and managers. Risk-based performance measurement framework (RAPM) allows the management to compare the performance of a bond or equity trader with that of a loan officer if it uses different risk measures for bonds, shares, and loans and thereby can derive the benefit of risk integration.

Enormous strides have been made in the art and science of risk measurement and management for the last one decade in line with the developments in the banking regulatory regime worldwide through Basel III capital accord.

Types of Risks in a Financial Institution/ Organization

Risk taking is a natural part of banking transactions, and the regulatory agency is responsible for creating a sound financial environment by setting the regulatory framework where the supervisory agency monitors the financial viability of banks and checks compliance with regulations. The core risks faced by the banks are as follows:

Credit Risk: risk of changes in value, associated with unexpected changes in credit quality downgrading or outright default. Credit risk is risk resulting from uncertainty in counterparty's ability or willingness to meet its contractual obligations. In quantitative terms, credit risk is the most important risk in banking books.

The major drivers of credit risks are as follows:

- **Probability of Default (PD):** the chance that the obligor fails to service debt obligations. This may happen due to either borrower-specific or market-specific reasons. PD is the most important component of measuring credit risk since the entire exercise is primarily dependent on the incident of default. PD is the most significant driver in the risk calculations for all lending products.

- **Exposure risk (EAD)**: in the event of default, how large will be the expected outstanding obligations if the default takes place. This may be uncertain for certain line of credit (over draft, credit card, letter of credit, etc.) and off-balance sheet exposures (like derivatives). In EAD calculation, a lender will have to know how much money the customer will owe at the time they default. Banks need to estimate EAD properly for various lines of credit otherwise they will need to hold higher capital against the credit limits of all of their revolving facilities.
- **Loss Given Default (LGD):** measures the amount of the loan outstanding that would be lost if that account is defaulted. Recovery post default is uncertain as value of the collateral changes with time.
- **Correlation risk:** captures common risk factors between different borrowers, industries, or sectors which may lead to simultaneous defaults.

Market Risk: Market risk refers to the chance of losses in value of trading portfolio from market price fluctuations. It relates to risk is the risk of loss due to changes in the market price of the Bank's/FI's assets and obligations (adverse deviations in the value of the trading portfolio (bonds, equity, commodity, currency returns). It is worthwhile to mention that US subprime crisis was triggered and aggravated by a sharp and sudden decline in the market value of traded assets.

The trading portfolio consists of (i) fixed income products, (ii) commodity, (iii) currency, and (iv) equity.

Market Risk measurement and management are important because of the following reasons:

1) It provides information to senior management about risks taken by traders. The senior management can then compare the risk exposure to the available capital.
2) It allows the fixation of trading limits on the positions taken by each trader.

3) The comparison of returns to market risk, across different business lines, helps in the allocation of capital and other resources into areas with highest risk-adjusted returns.
4) The compensation structure can be based on risk-adjusted returns.
5) Internal capital estimation models can be built, in line with regulatory requirements.

Market risk is closely tied to interest rate risk as interest rate rise, prices of securities (mainly bonds) decline, and vice versa.

$$\begin{aligned} \textit{Market Risk} = & \left(\textit{Market value of current exposure in rupees}\right) \\ & \times\left(\textit{Price sensitivity}\right)\times\left(\textit{Degree of movement in risk factor}\right) \\ & \times\left(\textit{Chance of such movement}\right) \end{aligned} \quad \text{Eq. 1}$$

Irrespective of the product (i.e. bonds, equity, commodity, etc.), the goal is to find how vulnerable the current exposure is to movements in risk factors.

Market risk analysis addresses three important categories of risks:

a. Interest Rate Risk: The risk of the current value (or profit/loss) of assets and liabilities (including off-balance sheet items) being affected by changes in interest rates.
b. Foreign Exchange Risk: The risk of the current value (or P/L) of assets and liabilities (including off-balance sheet items) being affected by changes in foreign exchange rates.
c. Equity Price Risk: The risk of the current value (or P/L) of assets and liabilities (including off-balance sheet items) being affected by changes in stock prices, stock indices, etc.
d. Commodity Risk: The risk of the current value (or P/L) of assets and liabilities (including off-balance sheet items) being affected by changes in commodity prices, commodity indices, etc.

Management of market risk is crucial because it provides information to senior management about risks taken by the traders. It allows the fixation of trading limits that are aligned with risk appetite of the entity. Banks can use market price and yield data on their own portfolio positions and combine these with diverse normal and stressed scenarios to build loss forecasting models. The loss estimates would enable the bank to compute regulatory capital requirements.

Under Basel II/III, standardized duration approach (Pillar I), capital requirements for market risk generally covers interest rate risk, foreign exchange risk, and equity risk. As par Basel II guidelines released by RBI, banks are using Values at Risk (VaR) models to measure risk in trading portfolios in determining appropriate capital charges.

Operational/Business Risk: Risk of losses due to inadequate or failed internal processes, people (e.g. frauds), and systems (technology failure or downtime) or from external events (e.g. terror attack, legal risk, disaster, etc.).

These risks are the core risks faced by a banking institution. As per Basel II/III regulation, these three risks are also called Pillar I risks (BCBS, 2005, 2017).

Classification of Operational Losses as described in Basel III document:

1. **Internal Fraud**: Losses or potential losses due to acts of a type intended to defraud, misappropriate property or circumvent regulations, the law or company policy, excluding diversity/discrimination events, which involves at least one internal party. Examples:
    - Losses to the bank resulting from the instance of an employee paying illegal compensation to generate or retain business.
    - Losses to the bank resulting from unauthorized trading.
2. **External Fraud**: Losses or potential losses due to acts of a type intended to defraud, misappropriate property or circumvent the law, by a third party. Examples:
    - Losses to the bank resulting from a default of a loan where it was determined that the loan had been obtained through fraudulent documents.
    - Losses resulting from fraud by false identity or identity theft by using computer systems.
3. **Employment Practices and Workplace Safety**: Losses or potential losses arising from acts inconsistent with employment, health, or

safety laws or agreements, from payment of personal injury claims, or from diversity/discrimination events. Examples:

- Losses to the bank resulting from discrimination against employees based on age, gender, political affiliation, race, religion, or sexual orientation.
- Losses to the bank resulting from the unavailability of workforce due to strike specific to the Bank.

4. **Clients, Products, and Business Practices:** Losses or potential losses arising from an unintentional or negligent failure to meet a professional obligation to specific clients (including fiduciary and suitability requirements), or from the nature or design of a product. Examples:
   - Losses resulting from breach of corporate policies like branding, communication, corporate social responsibilities statements, email retention, external auditor independence, investigation, outsourcing, etc.
   - Losses to the bank resulting from unfounded allegations, defamation, invasion of privacy.
5. **Damage to Physical Assets**: Losses arising from loss or damage to physical assets from natural disasters or other events. Examples:
   - Losses resulting from disruption caused by civil/political actions.
   - Losses resulting to the bank from floods, landslides, etc.
6. **Business Disruption and System Failures**: Losses arising from disruption of business or system failures. It includes but not limited to
   - Losses to the bank resulting from the use of obsolete systems that cannot handle current workload, volume, or product complexity.
   - Losses caused by interruptions of communication lines, e.g. telephone lines and security access network (staff cannot enter the building).
7. **Execution, Delivery, and Process Management:** Losses from failed transactions processing or process management, from relations with trade counterparties and vendors. It includes but not limited to
   - Losses to the bank resulting from failure to deliver mandatory reports.
   - Losses to the bank resulting from the omission of valid documents in marketing materials, or from poor or non-existent documentation.

- In line with the Basel Committee guidelines, a second level of operational risk events is identified, which is having the potential to result in substantial losses. The classification will be in terms of loss causes category as follows:
    a. **People Risk:** The risk resulting from the deliberate or unintentional actions or treatment of employees and/or management—i.e. employee error, employee misdeeds—or involving employees, such as in the area of employment disputes. This risk class covers internal organizational problems and losses. Examples:
- Human resource issues (employee unavailability, hiring/firing, etc.)
- Personal injury—Physical injury (bodily injury, health and safety, etc.)
- Personal injury—Non-physical injury (libel/defamation/slander, discrimination/harassment, etc.)
- Wrongful acts emanating out of employee fraud (fraud, trading misdeeds, etc.)
    b. **Process Risk:** Risks related to the execution and maintenance of transactions, and the various aspects of running a business, including products and services. Examples:
- Business/operational process (lack of proper due diligence, inadequate/problematic account reconciliation, etc.)
- Errors and omissions (inadequate maker/checker controls, inadequate/problematic quality control, etc.)
    c. **Technology/System Risk:** The risk of loss caused by a piracy, theft, risk resulting from inadequate or failed system infrastructure including network, hardware, software, communications, and their interfaces; also includes risk of technology failing to meet business needs. Examples:
- General technology problems (operational error—technology related, unauthorized use/misuse of technology, etc.)
- Hardware (equipment failure, inadequate/unavailable hardware, etc.)
- Security (hacking, firewall failure, external disruption, etc.)
- Software (computer virus, programming bug, etc.)
- Systems (system failures, system maintenance, etc.)

d. **External Events:** The risk resulting from external events to the bank. This category also includes the risk presented by actions of external parties or in the case of regulators, the execution of change that would alter the Bank's ability to continue operating in certain markets. Examples:

- Disasters (natural disasters, non-natural disasters, etc.)
- External misdeeds (external fraud, external money laundering, etc.)
- Litigation/regulation (capital control, regulatory change, legal change, etc.)

The loss events are actually grouped into seven loss event categories (LE1–LE7). There is a need to define loss event particularly in terms of accounting. For proper measurement of risk, loss events can be recorded on the date of happening, but loss amount can be recognized only when it is debited to revenue of the bank. Banks can use loss event (LE) study for identification of risk prone products/processes and will conduct root-cause analysis to study their impact. This is why, for proper operational risk analysis, Loss Event categorization is important. This has been further explained in the subsequent section.

Measurement of Operational Risk

Step 1: Develop KRI Indexes Like

A set of key risk indicators (KRIs) attempts to detect potential operational exposures before they happen and raise signals if they are outside an established trigger level (green, amber, red zones). It actually serves as an indicator of risk and enables operational risk manager to capture necessary information for risk analysis and set-up control process.

Customer satisfaction index; employee satisfaction index; technology stability index (or system downtime); litigation exposure index, compliance risk scoring chart; loan disbursement risk score card; fraud risk indicator (e.g. no. of exceptions to lending policy, % of early default, % of applications originating from outside etc.); and IT security risk indicator

(viz. no. of vendors working with the bank, sensitive customer info., hacking, phishing attacks, access rights to application by staff etc.)

Thus, KRIs provide crucial information on the risk of potential future loss.

Step 2: Link KRIs to RCSA (Control and Audit Functions)

KRIs are factors that are capable of providing information about factors that determine risk. Such indicators enable timely action to be taken to deal with issues arising. Control assessment evaluates the effectiveness of controls that are placed to manage operational risks identified through KRIs. Risk control and self-assessment (RCSA) provide the necessary defence against operational risk. It can be done through

- Risk assessment;
- Impact evaluation;
- Meaningful aggregation of risks and reporting;
- Checking the effectiveness of controls that are in place to manage risks; and
- Risk monitoring.

Such evaluation provides greater consistency and assurance in the way that risk issues are managed across the organization. It also permits systematic adjustments to capital estimates with enhanced credibility.

Step 3: Event-Wise and Business-Wise Loss Data Capture

To serve the regulatory directives, the operational loss data are required to be mapped into eight business lines and seven event types as shown in Table 1.1.

The loss data need to be captured under each business lines and event type (called BLET matrix) over years. It helps a bank to build up operational loss matrix across business lines and event types. Such profiling enables the top management of banks to understand which business

Table 1.1 Business Lines vs. Loss Events

Business Lines (BLs)	Loss Event Types (ETs)
Corporate finance (BL1)	Internal fraud (LE1)
Trading and sales (BL2)	External fraud (LE2)
Retail banking (BL3)	Employment practices and workplace safety (LE3)
Commercial banking (BL4)	Clients, products and business practices (LE4)
Payment and settlement (BL5)	Damage to physical assets (LE5)
Agency services (BL6)	Business disruptions and system failures (LE6)
Asset management (BL7)	Execution, delivery, and process management (LE7)
Retail brokerage (BL8)	

category or event type in which branches are facing maximum risk not only in terms of number of events but also loss numbers.

Step 4: Quantification of Operational Losses

Measuring operational risk is a useful tool for risk-focused management reflecting inherent risk of business lines. It is an integral part of bank's overall optimal capital allocation process. In order to quantify the operational losses, banks may 1) divide their whole business into various business lines (e.g. corporate finance, trading and sales, retail banking, commercial banking, payment and settlement, agency services, asset management, and retail brokerage), 2) measure individual risk profiles (e.g. internal frauds, external frauds, business disruption, loss/damage of assets, etc.) in each business line, and 3) summing up these measured risks. Collection of internal loss data is a key task to internally estimate capital requirement against operational risk. The loss distribution approach (LDA) allows senior management to measure operational risks along the different lines of business (LOBs) for efficient allocation of risk capital.

Basically, there are three approaches in estimating operational risk capital: basic indicator approach (BIA), the TSA and advanced measurement approach (AMA). This path has been clearly outlined in Basel Committee documents (BCBS, 2011, 2017). Under the BIA, average positive gross income (GI) of previous three years is multiplied with α factor which is 15%. The BIA regulatory capital computation is like an ordinary least-squares technique where dependent variable is regulatory capital (RC) and independent variable is GI. The estimated regression coefficient is 0.15. TSA suggests banks to average positive GI of previous three years is multiplied with beta (β) factor which ranges from 12 to 18% for eight regulatory business lines. The beta factors are prescribed by the regulator. The multiple beta coefficients applied on estimating operational risk capital under TSA are similar to multivariate regression concept which has been discussed subsequently in Chapter 7. Under the AMA, operational risk capital is estimated through statistical methods utilizing four data elements—internal loss data, scenario data, external loss data, and business environment and internal control factors. Recently, the Basel III (December 2017) circular has introduced New SA for measurement of operational risk regulatory capital. Risk sensitivity has been introduced by incorporating the internal loss component. This approach is expected to replace all the existing approaches: BIA, TSA, as well as AMA under Basel II. Under the new SA, operational risk regulatory capital charge is estimated by multiplying the business indicator component (BIC) with the bank's internal loss multiplier (ILM). The BIC component captures the income that increases with a bank's size measured in billion euros. It has been grouped under three different buckets on the basis of size in billion euros. The regulator has suggested BI marginal coefficients in the range of 12–18% depending upon the bank size. The ILM is a risk-sensitive component which captures a bank's internal operational losses. It actually serves as a scaling factor that adjusts the baseline capital requirement depending on the operational loss of experience of the bank. The loss component (LC) is an important factor that measures risk sensitivity in capturing a bank's internal losses. In estimating LC, banks need to meet the regulatory requirements on loss data identification, collection, and treatment (BCBS, 2017). Thus, operational risk capital (ORC) = BIC × ILM. Over time, all banks will have to move to SA and they have to collect at least 10 years of loss data to estimate operational risk capital. The ILM indicator is measured by ratio of LC/BIC. The loss component (LC) corresponds to 15 times the average annual operational risk losses incurred over the previous 10 years by the bank. Thus, if a bank experiences proportionately higher operational losses in comparison to its size, it will have to keep higher regulatory capital. However, a risk-focused management can still use internal-based LDA measure for management of Pillar

II risk to ensure better capital allocation. Note that LDA approach is more in line with AMA.

However, a bank can should always analyse internal loss data and estimate operational risk capital and assess importance of KRIs in controlling those losses. The new SA approach also focuses on internal loss data. A bank must have in place a robust operational risk management framework (ORMF) to facilitate quantitative estimates of the Bank's operational risk regulatory capital.

Liquidity Risk: An entity is finding itself unable to meet its commitments on time due to unexpected cash outflow or unable to sell/settle an asset or investment loses liquidity (may arise in trading/funding). It is an important risk in a financial institution. Customer deposit run off, fall in market value of the securities, increase in funding costs and fall in borrowing capabilities are indicators of liquidity risk.

There are two types of liquidity risk. These are as follows:

1. Asset or Market Liquidity Risk: Inability to sell assets at normal market prices because the size of the trade is much larger than normal trading lots. This means that the market is unable to absorb such large volumes at quoted prices.
2. Funding or Cash-Flow Liquidity Risk: Inability to meet payment obligations. This means that the bank is unable to pay either (i) depositors on demand or (ii) off-balance sheet (OBS) loan commitments and guarantees on demand.

Need for Liquidity Risk Management

- shows the market that the bank is capable of repaying its lenders on demand;
- reduces the default premium on future borrowing;
- strengthens formal or informal loan commitments and increases bank reputation; and
- avoids needless fire-sale of assets, thereby escaping capital and interest revenue losses.

In order to assess liquidity risk, bank has to assess the liquidity gaps (examine structural liquidity statement to examine the liquidity mismatch), in different buckets (1d–14d; 15d–28d; 29d–3M; 3M–6M; 1y–3y; 3y–5y; and over 5y), across all quarters for say last five years. The shorter-term liquidity deficits might threaten the stability and NIM of any FI. Again, a jump in the share of term deposits (TD) maturing in less than 1 year may create consistent liquidity deficits in short-term buckets. The shorter-term (less than 1 year) CASA (current account and savings account) ratio[1] and share of short-term investments are also indicators of liquidity risk in a bank. The bank can check the liquidity deficit by increasing the share of short-term investment or by decreasing the share of CASA deposits. However, in a rising interest rate scenario, the rise in deposit costs may put a pressure on bank NIM from an increasing share of short term, higher cost, FDs. Further, a sharp increase in daily borrowing under stress time (like the one in India around the time of the Lehman collapse) could create liquidity problem in the bank. Naturally, if one plots the net daily lending and borrowing pattern in the call money market by the bank during such stress situation, can get a sign of stress market conditions (whether net borrowing was there throughout the year, i.e. during 1 April 2015 and 31 March 2016).

Interest Rate Risk in the Banking Book (IRRBB): Risk arises from the mismatch between the interest rate characteristics of various assets and liabilities. Interest rate risk refers to the effect of interest volatility on rate-sensitive assets and liabilities. It is also termed as asset liability management (ALM) risk. For a given change in interest rates (e.g. 1%), IRR considers the effect of shifts in the volume and composition of assets and liabilities. A bank funding a 3-year fixed-rate term loan with 6-month FD is exposed to IRR. Similarly, a bank holding a high fraction of high-cost FDs, in a falling rate environment, is also exposed them to Interest Rate Risk.

One of the key economic functions of credit institutions is to convert short-term deposits into long-term loans. Depending on the scale

[1] The CASA ratio is the ratio of deposits in the current and savings form of a bank to total deposits. Current and saving accounts are demand deposits and, therefore, pay lower interest rates compared to term deposits where the rates are higher. A higher ratio is good for a bank because interest paid on savings account is very low and no interest is paid on current account deposits. In this way, the banks get money at low cost and can maintain a good NIM.

of this maturity transformation—which essentially determines the risk arising from a bank's balance sheet structure—sharply fluctuating market interest rates can have a considerable impact on banks' earnings and on their capital base.

With a view to capturing interest rate risk appropriately, the Basel Committee on Banking Supervision breaks down interest rate risk into four main types:

Re-pricing Risk—this risk arises from mismatches in interest rate fixation periods; it mainly refers to when and how the interest payments will be reset;

Yield Curve Risk—which is caused by changes in the slope and shape of the yield curve;

Basis Risk—which arises from an imperfect correlation in the adjustment of the rates earned and paid on different products with otherwise similar repricing characteristics; and

Optionality Risk—arises primarily from options (gamma and vega effect) that are embedded in many banking book positions (e.g. early redemption rights in the case of loans).

Measurement of interest rate risk in banking book is essential for ALM.

ALM—Banks need funding liquidity to meet depositor withdrawal and customer loan demand. Since loan demand and deposit flows depend on market interest rates, liquidity positions are affected by rate fluctuations. ALM is a systematic approach to protect a bank from the mismatch risk inherent in financial intermediation. It provides a framework to define, measure, monitor, modify, and manage the impact of mismatch risk on (i) net interest income (ii) net worth, and (iii) liquidity positions. It helps a bank choose between balance sheet actions (business policy/capital plans) and off-balance sheet strategies (derivative instruments).

Reputation Risk—For financial institutions, the trust of clients is an important asset that can be significantly shaken by some types of operational loss events. These events are like negative publicity, number of customer complaints, costly litigations, brand value, etc.

The steps to assess reputational risk for the bank are as follows:

- Identification of the key drivers of the risk;
- Reputational risk scorecard; and

- Assessment of the level, adequacy, and effectiveness of reputational risk management in the bank.

Some Indicators to quantify reputation risk in a bank:

- Market/Public Perception about the Bank: e.g. its financial position, public perception, external rating, complexity and riskiness of business activities, corporate governance, stability of share price, brand promise, staff attrition, etc.
- Customer Complaints and Perception: quarterly trends of number of complaints received and pending complaints at the end of the quarter, willingness/ability, and speed in resolution.
- Negative or Adverse Publicity: any scams/adverse news and whether any mechanism in place to handle such incidents.
- Litigation Compliance with Laws and Regulations: any breach of violations involving penalties, whether the bank has adequate controls in place in respect of KYC guidelines, any instance of non-adherence to CRR/SLR, or NPA norms in last 3 years.
- Business Continuity: continuity data on system downtime and business loss, ATM downtime, data downtime in treasury, and any other warning indicators of potential higher reputation risk.

Using these indicators, one can develop statistical scorecard for measuring the extent of reputation risk, and it can be linked to bank's risk capital. High score may indicate that management anticipates and responds well to changes of a market or regulatory nature and fosters a sound culture.

Statistically, researchers have tested the following hypotheses to check the effect of reputation risk:

- Operational loss events do not significantly change the stock prices of affected companies. That is, the announcement of operational loss event is non-informative.
- Operational loss events convey no information about the firm's future cash flows and, therefore, have no effect on firm value beyond the amount of the loss itself.
- The response of a firm's stock to operational losses is independent of the firm's growth prospects.

An event-study analysis may be conducted to assess the market's reaction to operational loss events affecting banks (abnormal returns, change in market capitalization, etc.). It can be linked to market capitalization loss and Pillar II risk capital can be estimated. An exponential function may allow relating scores with risk in terms of additional capital requirements. The function can use market value of equity impact by linking the scores with its stock return (bounded between minimum and maximum return volatility).

Strategic Risk: 'Strategic risk' means negative effects on capital and earnings due to business policy decisions, deficient or insufficient implementation of decisions, or a failure to adapt to changes in economic environment. Strategic risk is the most fundamental of business risks as it is the risk associated with a bank's business model and the way a bank wants to position itself strategically. The driving force behind many banking crises appeared to be a change in the institutional or external environment coupled with a choice of unsuitable strategies by banks. Many strategic problems could also be directly related to management and staff (HR) issues within an organization due to lack of good succession plans for senior management and other key managerial positions, insufficient operational and staff support for new initiatives, inadequate in-house technical expertise to carry out highly specialized projects, or staff resistance to cultural changes. Regulator expects bank should put in place proper measures to manage strategic risk that focuses on the systems, process and controls established by the bank.

Some Strategic Risk Indicators

Demand shortfall, competitive pressure, mergers and acquisitions integration problems, pricing pressure, loss of customers, regulatory problems, R&D delays, HR and incentive problems, lack of succession plan, etc.

Regulator (RBI) expects bank should put in place proper measures to manage strategic risk that focuses on the systems, process and controls established by the bank.

Concentration Risk: Regarded as one of the most important potential causes of major losses, which can become large enough to jeopardize on-going operations. Hence, measurement and monitoring of concentration risk by banks are a necessity. It can be measured through various concentration indices like Hirschman Herfindahl Index (HHI), Theil Inequality Index, Gini coefficient, etc. Many banks follow RBI's prudential limits on big exposures (e.g. exposure to a borrower should not be more than 15% of bank's capital funds) and substantial exposure limits as a check against concentration risk. Many international best practiced banks adopt methods to work out capital requirement against concentration risk by using advanced portfolio models.

Other Risks:

Country Risk: Risks of incurring financial losses resulting from the inability and/or unwillingness of borrowers within a country to meet their obligations in foreign currency.

Residual Risk: Assessing the use of CRM policies and techniques that may lead to other risks such as legal risk, documentation risk, and liquidity risk. It requires lot of documentation to ensure that the bank has a sound process.

These risks are called Basel II and III–Pillar II risks which are examined by the supervisory review process (SREP). As part of the SREP, banks have been asked to put in place the requisite internal capital adequacy assessment process (ICAAP) with the approval of their boards.

Difference in Nature of Bank Risks

Market risk managers are more concerned with the size of losses rather than their frequency. In credit risk management, the concern is with the frequency of default increases. An operational risk model includes the frequency and severity that can be applied to find the aggregate distribution for frequency and severity. Moreover, operational risk is measured by observed losses (or historical losses) coupled with qualitative assessment (RCSA and KRIs) rather than changes in MTM value.

Measuring business risk is a useful tool for risk-focused management reflecting inherent risk of business lines. This is an integral part of bank's overall capital allocation and performance evaluation process. Collection of internal loss data is a key requirement for risk analysis. This is the basis for most capital calculations. Loss data need to be categorized according to an event-driven taxonomy: enable banks to have a risk profile for each event. Loss history represents the inherent banking risks and the state of the controls at a point in time. Thus, data and information system plays crucial role in conducting statistical risk analysis.

Integration of Risks

Sometimes risks in the enterprise are related to each other. Functional organizational structure for managing risks may be highly inadequate and ineffective in managing risks because many risks are multidimensional and interrelated, and therefore, they should not be segregated and managed by separate functions or departments on a silo basis. To predict the relationships which exist between two risks can be done through covariance matrix or through structural simulation of the model of an enterprise. As an example, using the economic scenario generation model, inflation rates and interest rates can be generated. The risk integration is also possible to analyse through structural simulation of the model. This allows a person to capture the dependencies among variable inputs in a simple, accurate, and logically consistent way of the model's cause/effect linkages of these inputs to common higher-level inputs. Banks can factor risk into their decision-making through risk-adjusted return on capital (RAROC = profit/risk capital) models as part of enterprise risk management. RAROC and economic value addition (EVA) allow a bank to take a comprehensive risk view and form the base for IRM. Through a risk-adjusted performance management framework, banks and FIs can meet the regulatory expectations regarding their conscious decision-making across business lines.

What is the Role of Statistical Approach to Manage Risk?

Understanding statistics is essential to be familiar with the methods used in the management of key risks in banks and FIs. The effectiveness of risk management depends crucially on the soundness of the techniques used to measure, monitor, and control the effect of risks. Data analysis, statistical modelling, and their applications are the fundamental requirements to achieve this objective. Those who are likely to be a successful researchers/analysts are more usually attracted by the problem-solving side of the work and the practical application of the mathematics and logic rather than the mathematics/statistical concepts per se. Modern statistical methods provide a set of quantitative approaches to equip the risk managers with sound logic and methodology for the measurement of risk and for thorough examination of the consequences of those risks on the day–to-day operations of the banking business. These data-based analyses can generate good-quality reports that can improve quality of decision-making, trace problems, assessment of risk, and opportunities in business, understand the ever changing market place and also to meet regulatory compliance. It is necessary that building blocks of the risk assessment techniques is understood widely for a smooth migration towards the more sophisticated and robust risk management system.

Summary

This chapter gives an overview of the risk management subject and its importance in financial institution. Risk taking is an essential part of business activity. Without willingness of taking risk, FIs cannot expect better return. An effective risk management process enables a bank/FI to improve business and obtain sustainable competitive advantage. The goal of risk management is not to eliminate or minimize risk but to determine the optimal level of risk. As the banks need capital to meet their growth expectations and simultaneously meeting the regulatory compliance in the Basel III era, they would have to remain responsive to the expectations of the market on a risk-adjusted basis. A well-governed bank should have the process to capture relevant data, reliable models, and statistical tools to measure and manage risk. A RAROC framework can enable the bank to build competitive advantage and enhance shareholder value.

Review Questions

1. How does core risk differ from non-core risk?
2. What are different types of risks a financial institution/bank can face in their business?
3. What is the difference between ALM and liquidity risk?
4. What is the difference between market risk and credit risk?
5. Why statistical analysis is important for risk management? or how operational risk is different from credit risk?
6. What is the difference among EAD, LGD, and PD?
7. What is yield curve risk?
8. What is BLET matrix?
9. How RCSA is different from KRI?
10. What is RAPM system? How does it work in an organization?

References

BCBS (2005). 'An Explanatory Note on the Basel II IRB Risk Weight Functions', Bank for International Settlements, July, BIS.

BCBS (2011). 'Principles for the Sound Management of Operational Risk', June. BIS.

BCBS (2017). 'Basel III: Finalising Post-Crisis Reforms', BIS Release, December. BIS.

Deventer, D. R., K. Imai, and M. Mesler (2005). 'Advanced Financial Risk Management: Tools and Techniques for Integrated Credit Risk and Interest Risk Management', John Wiley & Sons, USA.

Marrison, C. (2008). 'The Fundamentals of Risk Measurement', Tata McGraw Hill, New Delhi.

Moody's (2004). 'Risk Management Assessment, Moody's Research Methodology', July 2004.

RBI (2015). 'Guidelines on Implementation of Basel III Capital Regulations in India', May. DBOD, RBI.

Saunders, A., and M. M. Cornett (2006). 'Financial Institution Management', 5th Edition, McGrawHill, Singapore.

Stephanou, C., and J. C. Mendoza (2005). 'Credit Risk Measurement under Basel II: An Overview and Implementation Issue for Developing Countries', Policy Research Working Paper no. WPS3556, USA: Wiley-Blackwell.

Stulz, R. M. (2015). 'Risk-Taking and Risk Management by Banks', *Journal of Applied Corporate Finance*, Vol. 27, Issue 1, pp. 8–18.

2

Description of Data and Summary Statistics for Measurement of Risk

Data play important role in statistical risk analysis. Statistics and econometrics are the most widely used branch of mathematics in quantitative research. When considering the establishment of a framework for statistical testing or developing models, it is sensible to ensure the availability of a large enough set of reliable information on which to base the test. For example, if the analyst intends to find 'one-in-five-year event' the best way is to have a five-year database. Information can be obtained through primary sources either through interview or directly using the database of the bank. Data can be obtained from primary sources (bank/FI's internal data) or from secondary sources (Rating agency's published data or corporate financial data from Centre for Monitoring Indian Economy (CMIE) Prowess or through RBI published data). Data need to be properly validated, cleaned, sorted, and formatted before doing final statistical analysis.

Most of the time, analyst will have to work on a sample data drawn from the population to save time. There are many ways to draw a sample. There is always a risk that the units selected in the sample are somehow exceptional, i.e. the sample does not represent the population (sampling error tolerance level). We minimize this risk by random sampling: A sample arranged so that every element of the population has an equal chance of being selected. The aim of sampling is to produce a miniature copy of the population. Each member of the population has an equal likelihood of being selected into the sample. Hence, we can make inferences about the larger population based on the sample. There may often be factors which divide up the population into sub-populations (groups/strata), and we may expect the measurement of interest to vary among the different sub-populations. This is achieved by stratified random sampling. Alternatively, cluster sampling is done that the entire population is divided into groups, or clusters, and a random sample of these clusters is selected. Most popularly, stratified random samples are chosen to preserve the population characteristics. It is very essential to create data templates and formats for collecting data to develop statistical score cards or to develop multivariate models. Date frequencies may vary in a time series data depending on whether analyst wants to conduct daily, weekly, fortnight, monthly, quarterly, and yearly analysis. The longer the series, the better will be the predictive power of the analytical models. For cross-sectional data, template must specify key variables and cross-sectional identifiers (such as borrower or company codes, constitutions, etc.). For panel structure, it is essential to pool cross-sectional and time dimensions (stacking of the data). In panel analysis, we can obtain more observations and greater flexibility in conducting statistical analysis. The larger the sample size, more efficient and robust will be the parameter estimates.

Most research studies in risk domain result in a large volume of raw statistical information which must be reduced to more manageable dimensions if we are to see the meaningful relationships in it. This process requires tabulation (grouped frequency distribution, relative frequency, etc.), graphical presentation (histogram, bar graphs, frequency polygon, Ogive, etc.), and summary statistics (or descriptive statistics).

The objective of descriptive statistical analysis is to develop sufficient knowledge to describe a body of data. This is accomplished by understanding the data levels, their frequency (or probability) distributions, and characteristics of location, spread (or deviation), and shape (skewness).

Data Description and Presentation

Grouped frequency distribution is a tabular summary of data showing the frequency of items in each of several non-overlapping classes. Frequency distribution tabulates and presents all the occurring values arranged in order of magnitude and their respective frequencies as shown in Table 2.1.

Table 2.1 Grouped Frequency Distribution

Range	Occurrence per Bin
96–98	1
98–100	1
100–102	2
102–104	3
104–106	3

Table showing the number of result that falls in each range/bin of possible asset value

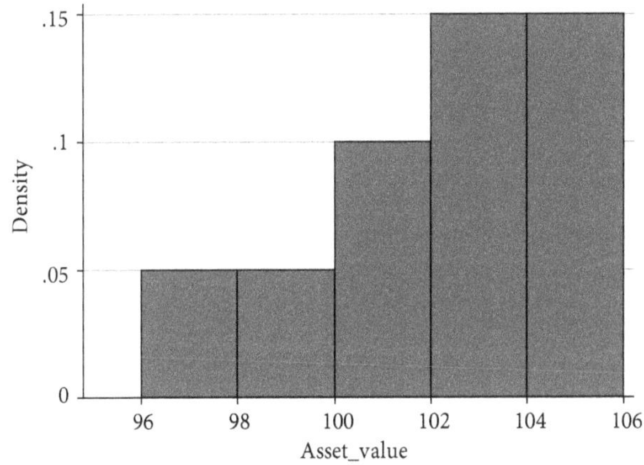

Figure 2.1 Histogram
Source: Author's own

For example, histogram can present all the occurring values (e.g. total write-off of loans in $ million) arranged in order of magnitude and their respective frequencies. An inspection of the frequency distribution gives a quick idea about the average in the series and shows how the observations vary around the average (through plotting a histogram or frequency polygon drawn from the frequency distribution).

Note that the histogram (Figure 2.1) depicts the range of asset values in a frequency (density) chart. The mean value is $102.10 and the median value is $102.75. The standard deviation (SD) is the root-mean-square deviation of values from the mean = 2.86. The utility of data presentation has been discussed in Walpole (1968) and Walpole et al. (2012).

Summary Statistics

These are the four moments about mean that describe the nature of loss distribution in risk measurement. The mean is the location of a distribution and variance or the square of SD measures the scale of a distribution. Range gives idea about the maximum spread of the values. **Range**: maximum value – minimum value

The SD is a popular measure of dispersion. It is a root-mean-square deviation from the mean. The formula for SD is as follows:

SD = Root-mean-square deviation from mean ($\overline{x}$).

$$= \sqrt{\Sigma\left(x_i - \overline{x}\right)^2/n} \qquad \text{Eq. 2.1}$$

where n = the number of observations

Exercise: The SD calculated from a set of 32 observations is 5. If the sum of the observations is 80, what is the sum of squares of these observations?

Solution: We are given $n = 32$, $\sigma = 5$, and $\Sigma x = 80$. It is required to find out $\Sigma x^2 = ?$

It can be written that

Variance or $\sigma^2 = \dfrac{\Sigma x^2}{n} - \left(\dfrac{\Sigma x}{n}\right)^2.$

Substituting the values, $25 = \dfrac{\Sigma x^2}{32} - \left(\dfrac{80}{32}\right)^2.$

Solving this, we get 1000.

If data are arranged in terms of group frequency (i.e. in terms of class intervals and corresponding frequency of observations), the SD formula will look like

$$\sigma = \sqrt{\frac{\Sigma f_i\left(x_i - \overline{x}\right)^2}{N}} \qquad \text{Eq. 2.1a}$$

SD is always considered positive and is unit free. Note that one has to make a sample adjustment that sample size is small.

SD is a common tool to measure risk of a stock or asset return $\left(R_t = \frac{S_t - S_{t-1}}{S_{t-1}}\right)$. Note that in this expression, S_t = current closing price of stock and S_{t-1} is the one period lag value of closing market price. SD is used by risk analysts to estimate within which a financial instrument or bond returns are likely to fall.

The skewness (3rd moment) is a measure of the asymmetry of the distribution. In risk measurement, it tells us whether the probability of winning is similar to the probability of losing and the nature of losses. Negative skewness means that there is a substantial probability of a big negative return. Positive skewness means that there is a greater-than-normal probability of a big positive return.

$$Skewness\ (sk) = 3(Mean - Median) / SD$$

Coefficient of variation also measures the degree of dispersion. In moment method, skewness is measured using following expression:

$$Skewness\ (SK) = \frac{\sum_{i=1}^{N} \left\{ (x_i - \bar{x})^3 / S^3 \right\}}{N} \qquad \text{Eq. 2.2}$$

where S = SD and N = the number of time periods or observations. If the SK is greater than 1 in absolute value, then the series is considered as highly skewed. If SK is between 0.5 and 1, it is moderately skewed. If SK < 0.5, the distribution is fairly symmetrical.

Note that most of the statistical packages like STATA, EVIEWS, and @RISK follow population formula-based SDs, skewness, and kurtosis. In excel, you have to adjust sample sizes if you derive sample-based estimates.

Coefficient of Variation (CV) = SD/Mean

Kurtosis is useful in describing extreme events (e.g. losses that are so bad that they only have a 1 in 1000 chance of happening).

In the extreme events, the portfolio with the higher kurtosis would suffer worser losses than the portfolio with lower kurtosis.

$$\textbf{Kurtosis} = \text{4th moment} = \beta_2 - 3 = \left(\mu_4 / \mu_2^{\,2}\right) - 3$$

This formula is based on moment functions. It is also termed as an excess kurtosis.

If $\beta_2 < 3$, distribution is platykurtic (less peakedness and greater coverage of body); if $\beta_2 > 3$, distribution is leptokurtic (fat or long tail but high peakedness). When $\beta_2 = 3$, distribution becomes normal or mesokurtic or symmetric (thin tail).

Note that one can also use following formula for estimating Kurtosis for ungrouped data.

$$Kurtosis\left(KURT\right) = \frac{1}{N}\sum_{i=1}^{N}\left(\frac{x_i - \overline{x}}{\sigma}\right)^4 \qquad \text{Eq. 2.3}$$

Note that the sign σ stands for SD.

The fourth moment Kurtosis provides idea about shape of the distribution and pertains to extremities (tail loss).

It is important to note that positive skewness with low kurtosis series promises high returns.

However, it is better to understand all the four moments of distribution of a series. Mean, SD, Skewness, and Kurtosis are the four moments about mean that describe the nature of loss distribution in risk measurement.

The mean is the location of a distribution and variance, or the square of SD measures the scale of a distribution. These are the first two moments of a series distribution. Median is mid-value and mode is most likely value.

The skew is a measure of the asymmetry of the distribution. It is also called 3rd moment around mean. In risk measurement, it tells us whether the probability of winning is similar to the probability of losing and the nature of losses. Negative skewness means that there is a substantial probability of a big negative return. Positive skewness means that there is a greater-than-normal probability of a big positive return.

Table 2.2 Computation of Summary Statistics from Bond Values

Scenario	Bond Value (x_i)	$(x-\bar{x})^2$	$(x_i-\bar{x})^3/S^3$	$(x_i-\bar{x})^4/S^4$
1	96.5	31.2481	−8.7466	18.0213
2	98.4	13.6161	−2.5158	3.4217
3	100.6	2.2201	−0.1656	0.0910
4	101.7	0.1521	−0.0030	0.0004
5	102.3	0.0441	0.0005	0.0000
6	103.2	1.2321	0.0685	0.0280
7	103.9	3.2761	0.2969	0.1981
8	104.4	5.3361	0.6172	0.5255
9	104.7	6.8121	0.8903	0.8564
10	105.2	9.6721	1.5062	1.7266
Total (Σ)		73.6090	−8.0515	24.869
Mean ($\bar{x}$)	102.09			

Source: Author's own

Kurtosis is useful in describing extreme events (e.g. losses that are so bad that they only have a 1 in 1000 chance of happening). Kurtosis is the 4th moment. In the extreme events, the portfolio with the higher kurtosis would suffer worser losses than the portfolio with lower kurtosis. Skewness and Kurtosis are called the shape parameters.

The Table 2.2 reports the market value (in $ unit) of BBB bond under 10 scenarios and computation of descriptive statistics.

From the above table, we can estimate mean value = 102.09 and median = 102.75.

$$SD = SQRT(SUM((x-\bar{x})^2)/10)$$

$$= \sqrt{\frac{73.609}{10}}$$

$$= 2.713$$

Similarly, using Equations 2.1, we obtain SD = 2.713

Using expression 2.2, we obtain skewness = −8.0515/10

= −0.80515

−0.80515

Here, the skewness of the above bond distribution is low.

In the same manner, we obtain Kurtosis as well using Equation 2.3:

$$\text{Kurtosis} = 24.869/10$$
$$= 2.4869$$

The kurtosis value is also low.

Since the series mean and median are similar and it has low skewness and kurtosis, we can consider it as a normally distributed series. There are more sophisticated tests (like JB test, chi^2 test, or Percentile–Percentile PP plot) to finally determine about the series pattern. This has been discussed in Chapters 3 and 4.

We can compute Jarque and Bera test statistic (JB) to further check normality of the series. For this, we have first plotted the data given in Table 2.2 in a histogram form and computed JB test statistic from its skewness and kurtosis values. The histogram plot has been presented in Figure 2.2. Note that the descriptive statistics are given besides the histogram chart. It gives a clear picture about the data, its range, and spread. All the four moments presented here are computed in Table 2.2. This histogram plot and the summary statistics are obtained using statistical package EVIEWS. To enter the data, you have to first create the workfile entering the data

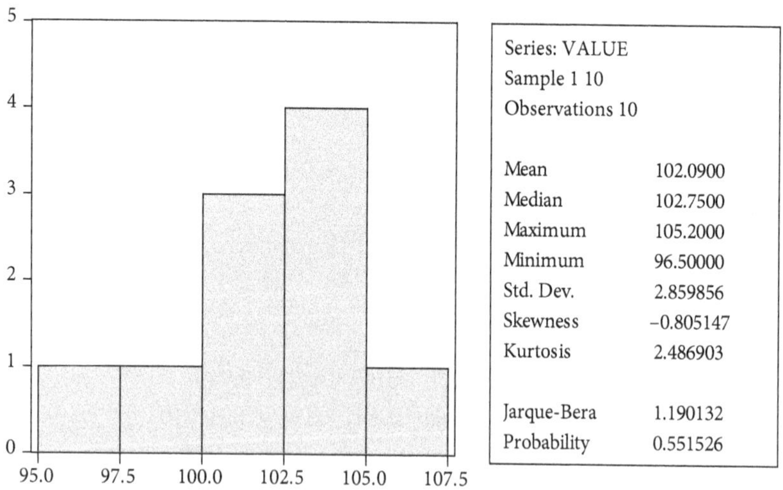

Figure 2.2 Histogram of Bond Values

frequency pattern (whether time series or undated or integer) and then enter the data from tool bar Quick & Empty group in EVIEWS software.

The Jarque-Bera value is obtained by using formula given in JB test:

$$JB = \frac{N-k}{6}\left(SK^2 + \frac{(KURT-3)^2}{4}\right) \qquad \text{Eq. 2.4}$$

Where N = sample observations, SK = skewness, and $KURT$ = kurtosis values. The value k represents the number of estimated coefficients used to create the series (here $k = 0$).

Note that the above JB value follows a chi-square distribution with two degrees of freedom. If we now plug in $N - k = 10$, $SK = -0.80515$, and $KURT = 2.4869$, we obtain $JB = 1.19013$ using the formula given in Equation 2.4.

Under the null hypothesis of a normal distribution, the JB statistic is distributed as chi square with two degrees of freedom. The reported probability is the probability that the Jarque-Bera statistic exceeds (in absolute term) the observed value under null. A small probability value ($p < 0.05$) will reject the null hypothesis of a normal distribution (null is stated here: there cannot be any distribution other than normal). In our case, since computed JB value is lower than the table value (which is 5.991465 at 5% level of significance and with two degrees of freedom), our p-value is quite higher. One can either look at chi-square table or use excel function = CHIINV(5%,2) to obtain the critical values (i.e. the thumb rule that we normally ask to decide). This indicates that we are not able to reject the null hypothesis. If we reject it, we will commit a type I error (i.e. rejecting a true hypothesis) of 55.15%. Hence, our bond value series surely follows normal distribution. A risk manager will have to fit the series this way before it is used to predict the confidence ranges. The statistical hypothesis testing procedures and interpretation of results are explained in detail in Chapter 4.

Quartiles and Percentiles

Quartiles divide an ordered list into quarters. For example, the first quartile (Q1) is a number greater (or equal) than the values of 25% of the cases and lower (or equal) than the values of the remaining 75%.

In financial risk management, quantile (indexed by sample fraction) chosen would be 90%, 95%, or 99% in most cases since the largest losses can be observed at extreme quantiles. For example, Op-risk capital from loss distribution (LDA) can be quantified by determining the 100% quintile for simulated distribution. Figure 2.3 presents ranked values of operational loss incurred by a bank.

Similarly, percentiles divide ordered lists into 100ths. One percent (p1) of the cases lies below the first percentile and 99% lie above it. For example, 1st quartile (Q1) is equal to 25th percentile (p25).

Figure 2.3 visually demonstrates the quantile or quartile concept in loss rank form. Note that the sample of operational loss (due to external frauds) values (in $ Million) is ranked in ascending order (smallest to largest). The median value is 2nd quartile value = $2090 million. The 95th percentile value, which is at higher side is $4000 million.

From simple series, the data need to be arranged in increasing order of magnitude and a rank is assigned to each observation. The smallest value is given rank 1, the next higher value gets rank 2, and so on. The largest value is given rank 3/. The ranks of partition values are estimated using following method:

$$1^{st}\text{ Quartile }(Q_1) = \frac{1}{4}(n+1) \quad \text{Eq. 2.5}$$

$$2^{nd}\text{ Quartile }(Q_2) = \frac{2}{4}(n+1) \quad \text{Eq. 2.5a}$$

It is also termed as median.

$$3^{rd}\text{ Quartile }(Q_3) = \frac{3}{4}(n+1) \quad \text{Eq. 2.5b}$$

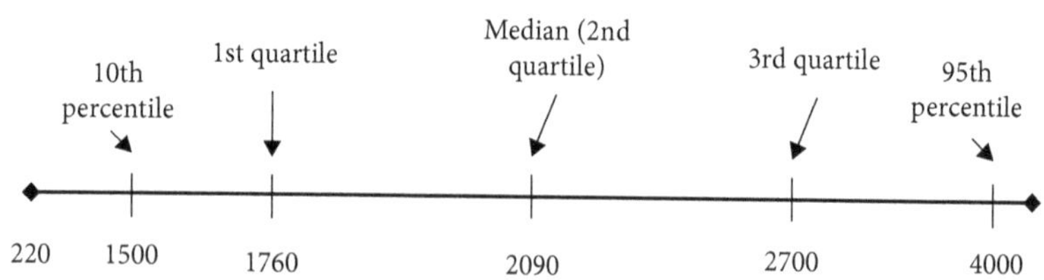

Figure 2.3 Percentiles

This way, one can also estimate Deciles and Percentiles

$$\text{Decile for } k = \frac{k}{10}(n+1) \qquad \text{Eq. 2.6}$$

Similarly, kth Percentile would be: $\frac{k}{100}(n+1)$ Eq. 2.6a

One can use Newton's interpolation method to assign value corresponding to the appropriate rank of the observations.

Note that, skewness is also measured from quartiles using the following expression:

$$Skewness = \frac{Q_3 - 2Q_2 + Q_1}{Q_3 - Q_1} \qquad \text{Eq. 2.7}$$

All these summary statistics can be done in statistical packages like STATA, SPSS, and Eviews using descriptive statistics. In STATA, one can use commands: tabstat x,stats (n mean sd sk kurt p50 p75) and can obtain table statistics.

Accordingly, using bond value data given in Table 2.2, we obtain summary statistics in STATA. For this, we create a workfile.dta and by entering the bond values in data editor.

We write the following command in STATA command box:

```
tabstat assetvalue,stats(n mean sd p50 sk kurt p75)
```

The same summary statistics presented by STATA are reported in Table 2.3.

We have obtained similar mean, median, skewness, and kurtosis values. Here, STATA reports SD based on sample assumption. We have

Table 2.3 Table Statistics in STATA

Variable |	N	Mean	SD	p50	Skewness	Kurtosis	p75
Asset value |	10	102.09	2.859856	102.75	−.8051476	2.486903	104.4

used the population formula. We can use the following conversion formula to obtain population SD:

$$\text{Sample SD} \times \sqrt{\frac{(N-1)}{N}}$$

$$= 2.859856 \times \sqrt{\frac{(10-1)}{10}}$$

$$= 2.7131$$

This value we had obtained earlier is given in Table 2.2 estimation. The detailed summary statistics and their usefulness are discussed in Gupta and Kapoor (2003), Lewis (2007).

Gini and Lorenz Curve

In risk management, Gini coefficient is used as a measure of inequality in loan distribution across borrowers, industries, regions, etc. This inequality measures loan concentration risk. Thus, higher is the Gini coefficient, greater is the inequality, and greater is the concentration risk. It is also used to measure discriminatory power of a rating model during model validation.

The Gini coefficient is a measure of inequality of a distribution. It is defined as a ratio with values between 0 and 1: the numerator is the area between the Lorenz curve of the distribution and the uniform distribution line (say area A); the denominator is the area under the uniform distribution line (A + B). Gini coefficient = A / (A + B).

The Gini coefficient is often used to measure income inequality by economists and social scientists. Here, 0 corresponds to perfect income equality (i.e. everyone has the same income) and 1 corresponds to perfect income inequality (i.e. one person has all the income, while everyone else has zero income). Thus, a low Gini coefficient indicates more equal income or distribution of loan assets with different industries/groups, sectors, etc., while a high Gini coefficient indicates more unequal distribution.

Figure 2.4 depicts the Lorenz curve and Gini coefficient. Lorenz curve is a visualization of inequality among the dataset. This parametric representation of the distribution was introduced by M. O. Lorenz.

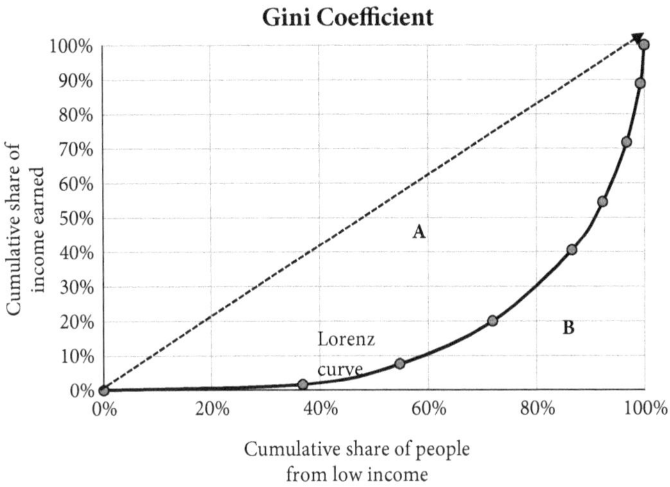

Figure 2.4 Lorenz Curve and Gini Coefficient
Source: Author's own illustration

Gini coefficient = area between the Lorenz curve and the line of equality/ area of the triangle below the diagonal.

$$\text{Thus, Gini} = A/(A+B) \qquad \text{Eq. 2.8}$$

A = Area between the Lorenz curve and the 45^0 line and B is the area remaining area below the curve.

These areas can be measured graphically. Here, we find a workable formula to estimate the Gini coefficient:

$$\text{Gini} = 1 - \sum p_i \times (z_i + z_{i-1}) \qquad \text{Eq. 2.9}$$

where p_i is the relative number of share of borrowers in a particular size class and z_i is the cumulative share of outstanding to total loan in a particular size class. Z_{i-1} is the cumulative size share in the neighbourhood class. The sign Σ represents summation. It is also termed as accuracy ratio (AR) in performing risk models' validation. The derivation of workable Gini coefficient formula has been explained in Nagar and Das (1983).

To better understand the Gini coefficient computation with reference to banking data, let us work with a data-based statistical example given in Table 2.4.

Table 2.4 Inequality in Loan Distribution

Decile Groups	% Share in Total Loan Size	Average Loan (Rs. '000)	Cumulative % Share in Total Loan Outstanding (100z)i	$100 \times (z_i + z_{i-1})$
0–10	3.01	412	3.01	3.01
10–20	4.38	599	7.39	10.40
20–30	5.39	734	12.78	20.17
30–40	6.40	872	19.18	31.96
40–50	7.42	1014	26.60	45.78
50–60	8.34	1136	34.94	61.54
60–70	9.56	1302	44.50	79.44
70–80	10.85	1479	55.35	99.85
80–90	13.75	1871	69.10	124.45
90–100	30.90	4213	100	169.10
Total	100			645.70

Table 2.4 presents the data on the distribution of personal loans by decile groups of borrowers and the average loan size for each decile group for rural zones of a commercial bank relating the financial year 2018–2019. We compute the Lorenz curve and Gini coefficients for two distributions.

Utilizing the last column, we get area = $\Sigma(z_i + z_{i-1}) = 0.10 \times 645.70100 =$ 0.6457.

Thus, Rural Gini $= 1 - \Sigma\left(z_i + z_{i-1}\right) = 1 - 0.6457 = 0.3543$.

This is the measure of inequality in the loan distribution. Similarly, if it is found that loan inequality for urban customer for the similar personal loan pool is = 0.46, therefore, we can comment that concentration risk for personal loan is relatively higher in urban region than the rural borrowers. Or conversely, rural portfolio of personal loans is more diversified than the urban portfolio.

Estimation of Gini coefficient through Lorenz curve area has popular application in measuring income inequality as well. This has been demonstrated in the following exercise. Many economic researches are guided by such analysis. Table 2.5a describes the proportion of people live and their respective income share in a state. One can estimate the Gini coefficient and measure income inequality pattern using Equation 2.9.

The steps in estimating Gini coefficient have been illustrated.

Thus, the estimated Gini coefficient = 1 − 0.29 = 0.71. If we go by area calculation, area of A = 0.355, and hence, Gini = 2 × 0.355 = 0.71.

Table 2.5a Income Inequality

Income Class	Proportion of Population	Proportion of Income
A	10%	1%
B	10%	1%
C	10%	1%
D	10%	1%
E	10%	1%
F	10%	1%
G	10%	1%
H	10%	10%
I	10%	33%
J	10%	50%

Table 2.5b Estimation of the Lorenz Curve Area and Gini Coefficient

Income Class	Proportion of Population	Proportion of Income	Cum Pop (P)	Cum Inc (I)	$Z_i + Z_{i-1}$	$p^*(Z_i + Z_{i-1})$
A	10%	1%	0%	0%		
B	10%	1%	10%	1%	1%	0%
C	10%	1%	20%	2%	3%	0%
D	10%	1%	30%	3%	5%	1%
E	10%	1%	40%	4%	7%	1%
F	10%	1%	50%	5%	9%	1%
G	10%	1%	60%	6%	11%	1%
H	10%	10%	70%	7%	13%	1%
I	10%	33%	80%	17%	24%	2%
J	10%	50%	90%	50%	67%	7%
Total	100%	100%				0.29
					Gini =	0.71

For a large dataset, the Lorenz curve will appear to be a smooth curve and not a series of straight lines. For this, one can model the Lorenz curve to find out the shape of the cumulative income share curve. To estimate the area under curve, we can use calculus and can derive the Gini coefficient. This has been shown as follows: Please refer to the Lorenz curve (Figure 2.5) that has been drawn using Table 2.5b about income inequality.

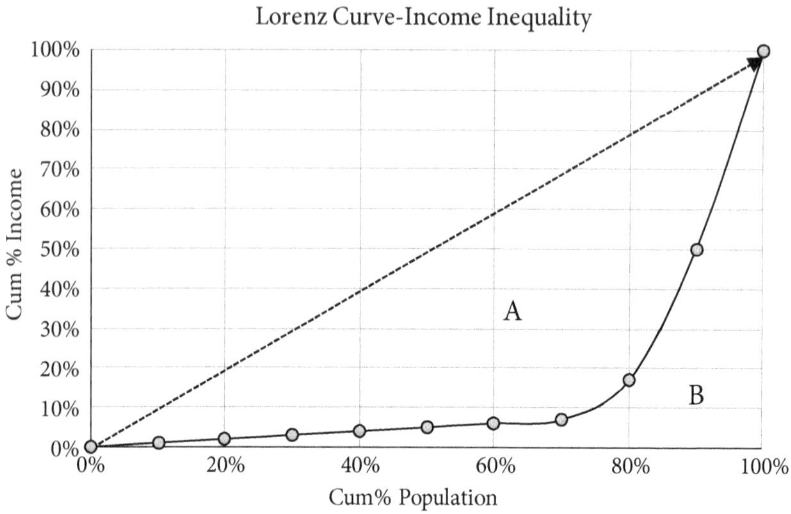

Figure 2.5 Lorenz Curve of Income Inequality

This graph has been plotted in Excel chart from scatter graph. The same graph can be generated for large set of data in STATA econometric package as well. For this, one has to use 'glcurve' command. This has been demonstrated in the later part of this discussions.

We can find area of 'A' through integral calculus as well.

Gini = 2 × Area of 'A'

It can be written as the following functional form:

$$\text{Gini} = 200 \times \int_0^1 \left(x - x^m\right) dx$$

We find $m = 5.89$ that best fits with the above curve.

$$\text{Thus, Gini} = 200 \times \int_0^1 \left(x - x^{5.89}\right) dx .$$

By solving the definite integral, we get

= 200 * (0.5 – 1/6.89)

= 71

Now dividing it by 100, we obtain the Gini coefficient = 0.71 which matches with our calculation reported in Table 2.5b.

It is quite evident that the higher the value of Gini coefficient, the greater the income inequality is.

Drawing Lorenz curve in STATA:

We have used 1978 Automobile Data that were given in the STATA website. Using 'glcurve' command, we have generated the Lorenz curve for price inequality.

The following steps were followed:

```
glcurve mpg, pvar(p1) glvar(l1) lorenz nograph
new variable l1 created
new variable p1 created
graph two way (line l1 p1, sort yaxis(1 2)) (function y = x, range(0 1)
    yaxis(1 2))
```

This gives us the following Lorenz curve (Figure 2.6) of mileage inequality. Y line is the line of equality (45 degree line).

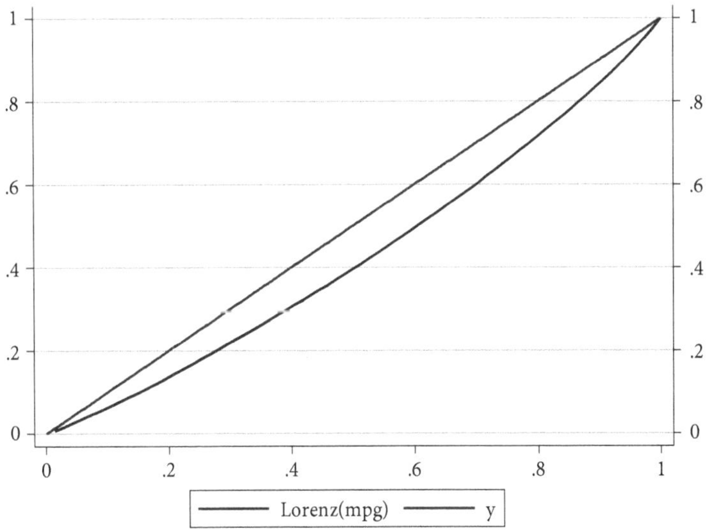

Figure 2.6 Mileage Inequality Lorenz Curve in Stata

Same way, pricing inequality is also assessed.

Stata Commands:

```
glcurve price, pvar(p2) glvar(l2) lorenz nograph
new variable l2 created
new variable p2 created
. graph twoway (line l2 p2, sort yaxis(1 2)) (function y = x, range(0 1)
    yaxis(1 2))
```

It produces Figure 2.7 reported as follows:

The graph (Figure 2.8) was drawn using command:

```
graph twoway (line l1 p1, sort yaxis(1 2)) (line l2 p2, sort yaxis(1 2))
  (function y = x, range(0 1) yaxis(1 2))
```

It is important to note that, the greater the price inequality, the higher the market power of an automobile firm is.

Like price and income inequality, these metrics can be used to measure loan inequality and loan concentration in a bank. The higher the value of the Gini coefficient and the greater the deviation of the Lorenz curve

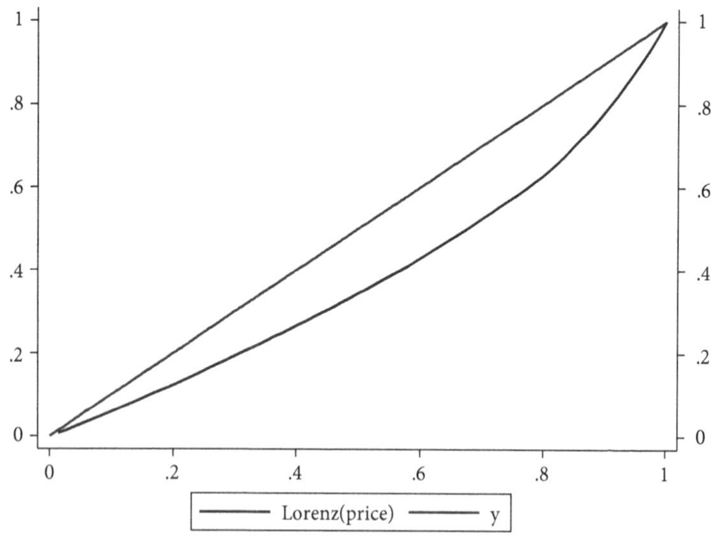

Figure 2.7 Price Inequality Lorenz Curve in Stata

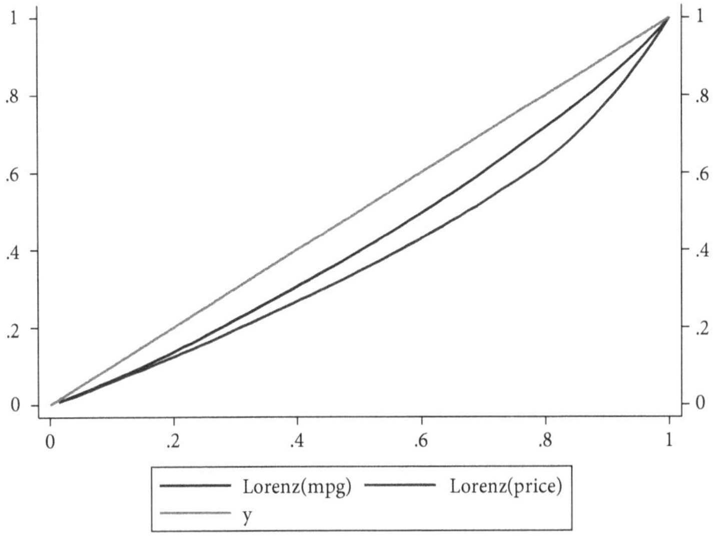

Figure 2.8 Price Inequality vs. Mileage Inequality-Comparing Lorenz curve

from the line of equality (defined by the diagonal 45 degree line), then the greater the inequality in loan disbursement across zones or sectors is and the higher the concentration risk will be. These commands are given in STATA manual (2005).

Other Statistical Indices of Loan Inequality/Concentration

The degree of inequality can be compared over time. The other popular measures of concentrations are mean deviation, coefficient of variation (SD/mean), the Hirschman and Herfindahl index (HHI), and Theil inequality.

The HHI is calculated by summing the squares of the exposure share of each individual contributor (a borrower/sector/region etc.) to the total portfolio outstanding. For example, an equal allocation of loans in each of 100 borrowers would lead to a diversified HHI of 0.01. In contrast, if the firms are divided amongst five sectors in the ratio 5:2:1:1:1, then the implied HHI by sector is 0.32, indicating a significant concentration. On the other hand, a lower value of HHI (<0.18 or 1,800 in 100×100 unit point) indicates greater diversification in the loan portfolio.

It uses the following formula:

$$\text{HHI} = \sum_{i=1}^{n} s_i^2 \qquad \text{Eq. 2.10}$$

where exposure share $s_i = E_i/E_T$

Note that E_i = Exposure of any borrower in the pool; E_T = Total exposure in the pool.

The inverse of HHI is also termed as coefficient of concentration. If it is perfectly diversified, inverse of HHI (i.e. 1/HHI) would exactly give us the actual number of loans in the pool. However, if the HHI is higher, we will observe that the effective number of loans will be sharply reduced. For example, if in a pool, we have 200 assets and HHI detects loan concentration, one can find that inverse of HHI is only 20. That means effectively, the pool is utilized by only 20 borrowers. However, if the loan pool is highly concentrated, this effective number can be further reduced to below 10. This signifies high level of loan concentration in the pool.

The Theil index is a popular entropy measure to capture loan concentration. It is measured by index:

$$T = \sum_{j=1}^{n} s_i \ln\left(\frac{s_i}{p_i}\right) \qquad \text{Eq. 2.11}$$

where s_i is the relative share of loan outstanding in the whole pool.

The symbol p_i is each sub-group's number share in total population (i.e. number of borrowers) in the pool. For perfect equality, $T = 0$. Accordingly, the higher the value of T, the greater the inequality in loan distribution (or loan concentration) is.

Summary

Various descriptive statistics are useful in risk analysis. The application of summary statistics, central tendency (mean, median mode), dispersions (such as SD, skewness, and kurtosis), and data distribution (percentile, Lorenz curve) in risk measurement has been demonstrated with examples in this chapter. The analysis of these metrics will enable a risk manager to get idea about the nature of risk inherent in the business. Information about mean, SD, skewness, and kurtosis is essential in estimating frequency and severity of losses. The Gini coefficient, HHI, and Theil Index assist risk manager to get idea about nature of concentration risk in investment or loan portfolio.

Review Questions

1. What is the role of descriptive statistics in research? Suppose you have data on the price, weight, mileage rating, and repair record of 22 foreign and 52 domestic automobiles. You want to summarize these variables for the different origins of the automobiles. How will you describe the data using STATA in tabular form? How the table will look like?
2. Do you think that quantitative and qualitative data have similar applications in risk-related empirical research?
3. Why data cleaning and sorting are important in risk analysis?
4. What is the difference between primary data and secondary data?
5. What the key differences are between cross-sectional and time series data?
6. Why panel data have more observations?
7. Do you think lower degrees of freedom in data analysis would lead to biased opinion about the results?
8. Is it true that the width of the confidence interval measures how uncertain we are about the unknown population parameters?
9. Is it true that when the Gini Coefficient for distribution of exposure in a loan portfolio approaches 1, then the concentration risk is very high?
10. A researcher has taken up a project to compare property price return series between two cities in India, which are presented in Table 2.6. The range of changes is summarized in the form of descriptive statistics:

Now answer the following questions:

a) Which city house price return is more stable? And why? What statistical measures will you use for this?

Table 2.6 Summary Statistics for Pune and Bangalore Property Price Returns (Based on Quarterly Data from March 2006–December 2010)

	Pune	Bangalore
Mean	24.13	12.02
Median	21.54	10.01
Maximum	75.59	47.12
Minimum	−4.24	−18.3
SD	23.5	16.4
Skewness	0.63	0.48
Kurtosis	2.23	5.78
Observations	20	20

b) Using the Jarque-Bera test, check whether property returns series follow normal distribution? Find out their p-value range (or level of significance) using chi-square approximation of JB test statistics.

c) In which city property return distribution is more asymmetric? And why?

d) Where you will obtain these data? Either from primary or secondary sources?

11. What is the main difference between 'Cluster Sampling' and 'Stratified Random Sampling'? Which one is advantageous? How will you conduct stratified random sampling from a data file?
12. If loan exposures are divided in five sectors in the ratio of 3:3:2:1:1, find the HHI of the portfolio of the sector:
    a) <1000
    b) 1000–1999
    c) 2000–3000
    d) >3000
13. If the Rs. 15,000 crores is distributed amongst a pool of 15 borrowers in the following manner:

Find out the HHI and comment on the loan pool's degree of concentration? Also find out the effective number of accounts in the pool.

Table 2.7 Loan Exposure Distribution

SL#	1	2	3	4	5	6	7	8	9	10
Exposure	50	120	400	7,000	70	240	900	800	100	820
SL#	11	12	13	14	15	Total				
Exposure	500	400	100	3,400	100	15,000				

14. A researcher has obtained following Lorenz curve by plotting income and population distribution in a country XYZ ((Refer Figure 2.9 given in the next page):

The area 'A' has been estimated as 0.20 and area B as 0.30. Now calculate the Gini coefficient and comment on income inequality of country XYZ.

If the area A for another country LMN rises to 0.26 and area B is reduced to 0.24, then re-estimates the Gini coefficient. Which country has greater income inequality? How will you compare them in one graph?

15. Write the difference between CV and Percentile.
16. What is the difference between the Theil inequality and Lorenz Curve?
17. What is the difference between population and sample? How sampling error can be minimized?
18. Which option is correct? For ungrouped data, *k*th decile would be
    a) $k(n + 1) / 10$
    b) $k(n + 1) / 100$
    c) $k(n + 1) / 4$
    d) $k(n + 1) / 50$
19. Tick the right option. The coefficient of variation is measured by which formula:
    a) Mean / SD
    b) SD / Mean
    c) SD × Mean
    d) SD + Mean
20. Is it true that in a fit test, the higher the value of Chi^2, the lower the probability would be that the actual distribution of the data series would be deviated from the hypothesized one?

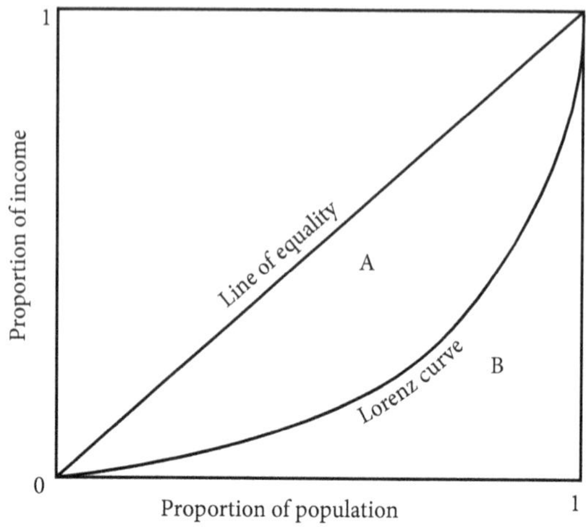

Figure 2.9 Lorenz Curve for Income Inequality

21. If the price of a traded bond has 20 observations, mean value = Rs. 40 and SD = 10, Skewness = 2, and Kurtosis = 6. Whether the estimated Jarque-Bera value (JB) would be greater than the table value of 14 (which is significant at 1% level)?
22. On a test of rating various borrowers, the average borrower score was 74 and the SD was 7. If 12% of the classes are given a rating of 'A's, and the grades are curved to follow a normal distribution, what is the lowest possible 'A' and the highest possible 'B'?

References

Nagar, A. L., and R. K. Das (1983). 'Basic Statistics', 2nd Edition, Oxford University Press, New Delhi.

Lewis, N. D. C. (2007). 'Operational Risk with Excel VBA-Applied Statistical Methods for Risk Management', Wiley & Sons, USA.

Gupta, S., and V. K. Kapoor (2003). 'Fundamentals of Mathematical Statistics', Sultan Chand & Sons, New Delhi.

STATA (2005). Manual, Stata Press, USA.

Walpole, R. E. (1968). 'Introduction to Statistics', Macmillan, USA.

Walpole, R. E., R. H. Myers, S. L. Myers, and K. Ye (2012). 'Probability and Statistics for Engineers and Scientists', Ninth Edition, Pearson, USA.

3
Probability and Distribution Theorems and Their Applications in Risk Management

The theory of probability provides a basis for the scientific analysis of uncertainty. Its applications enable a risk manager or analyst to derive a degree of probability from uncertain states of nature. A risk is a random event that may possibly occur and may erode organization's value (profit, capital etc.). Random experiments are those experiments in which results depend on chance. The word 'random' may be taken as equivalent to 'depend on chance'. The chance of making profit or loss from loan disbursement or from investment in equity is integral part business. Banks are in the business of incurring, transforming, and managing risk. In risk assessment, the primary concern is to identify the scenario and its probability of occurrence. The word probability literally denotes the chance, and the theory of probability deals with laws governing the chances of occurrence of phenomena that are unpredictable in business. In technical sense, probability is a mathematical measure of uncertainty. Risk is the volatility of unexpected outcomes. Probability theorem has very useful applications in measurement and management of risks in banking business. Researchers and risk management practitioners worldwide have extensively applied probability theorems to improve on techniques in measuring and managing key risks: credit risk, market risk, and operational risk. In this chapter, we explain the basic probability and distribution concepts and demonstrate how they can be useful in measurement and management of various risks.

Probability Theorems

Probability is a numerical measure of the likelihood that an event will occur out of all possible outcomes in the experiment. Sample space is the set of all experimental outcomes. The probability of an entire sample space is 1. The outcomes of a random experiment are said to be 'equally likely'.

In any random experiment, if a trial results in total 'n' exhaustive, mutually exhaustive and equally likely cases and 'r' is the number of equally likely cases favourable to an event 'E', the probability of occurrence of E:

$$P(E) = \frac{\textit{No. of ways in which event E can occur}}{\textit{No. of all possible outcomes in the experiment}} \qquad \text{Eq. 3.1}$$

Therefore,

$P(E) = r/n$.

This is as per the classical definition of probability.

In a simplest experiment of tossing an unbiased coin, what is the probability of getting head (H)?

The prob (H) = 1 / (1 + 1) = ½ = 0.5; similarly, probability of obtaining tail is

P(T) = ½ = 0.5.t

Here, the events, head and tail, are called mutually exclusive events since both cannot occur at the same time.

Similarly, in an experiment of tossing two unbiased coins, the following total possible mutually exclusive events can occur as follows:

TT, TH, HT, HH

All possible outcome of the above trial is called sample space or probability space.

Therefore, P(A = one H & one T) = 2/4

Prob (both heads) = P(A) = 1/4

Prob (at least one head) = ¾

The above probabilities are also termed as cases favourable to an event.

Note that several events are said to form an exhaustive set if at least one of them must necessarily occur. For example, in tossing a coin, H and T form an exhaustive set because one of these two must necessarily occur.

The complete group of all possible elementary events of a random experiment gives us an exhaustive set of events.

Similarly, when a dice is thrown, there are six possible outcomes: 1, 2, 3, 4, 5, and 6. Find the probability that the dice is giving even number? The answer should be 3/6 = 0.50, since the dice has 3 even numbers (2, 4, and 6) and 3 odd numbers (1, 3, and 5).

In the same way, there are 36 possible outcomes in the random experiment of a single throw of 2 dices (or two throws of one dice). They are (1,1), (2,1), . . . , (6,1), (1,2), (2,2), . . . , (6,2), . . . , (1,6), (2,6), . . . , (6,6).

If we would like to estimate the sum of the points on the two dice, the possible outcomes may again be listed as follows: 2, 3, 4, 5, 6, 7, 8, 9, 10, 11, and 12.

Exercise: Consider an experiment in which a coin is tossed and a six-sided die is tossed simultaneously. How many possible elementary outcomes are generated? What is the probability of obtaining heads and an even number? What probability should be assigned to the event 'Heads and Number greater than Four'?

Solution: Using the multiplication rule, there are 6 × 2 = 12 possible outcomes for the joint experiment. They are

H,1 H,2 H,3 H,4 H,5 H,6
T,1 T,2 T,3 T,4 T,5 T,6

If E denotes the compound event of obtaining 'heads and an even number', then

E = (H2, H4, H6).

Therefore, P(E) = 3/12 = ¼.

Similarly, the event 'heads and a number greater than 4' can occur in 2 possible ways H5 and H6

Hence, the required probability is = 2/12 = 1/6.

Probability Properties

Probability satisfies two important properties

Convexity Property: In probability theory, a convex function applied to the expected value of a random variable is always less than or equal to the expected value of the convex function of the random variable. This result is known as Jensen's inequality. It has important implications in building expectation functions and curve fitting.

Complement Property: An event and its complement are mutually exclusive and exhaustive. This means that in any given experiment, either the event or its complement will happen but not both. For example, either a borrower can default or not default in a loan pool.

Probability Rules

- Probability always ranges between 0 and 1. It neither can be negative nor exceeding unity.
- If two events A and B are mutually exclusive (that is only one of them can occur at a time) and p_A and p_B are the probabilities of occurrence of A and B, respectively; then $p_A + p_B$ is the probability that one of them will occur. This is called addition rule of probability. It can be extended to three events, four events, and so on: $p_A + p_B + p_C + \dots$
- If A and B are the only two possible outcomes of an experiment, then $p_A + p_B = 1$.
- If two events A and B are independent and p_A and p_B are their probabilities of occurrence, respectively, then their product is $p_A p_B$. This is the multiplication rule.
- $P(A \cap B) = P(A) \times P(B/A)$; where P(A) is unconditional and P(B/A) is conditional probability. Note that the $P(B/A) = P(A \cap B) / P(A)$.
- The probability of complimentary event is $P(A^c) = 1 - P(A)$. Since A and A^c are mutually exclusive events.
- For any two events A and B which may or may not be mutually exclusive, $P(A \cup B) = P(A) + P(B) - P(A \cap B)$. This follows from Boole's inequality.

It is important to note that many of these events described above are derived by set theorem. The Venn diagrams are used to understand the set operations. More detailed discussions on probability rules are given in Balakrishnan et al. (2019).

Conditional Probability

In many situations, once more information becomes available, we are able to revise our estimates for the probability of further outcomes or events happening.

The probability of an event occurring given that another event has already occurred is called a conditional probability.

Since we are given that event A has occurred, we have a reduced sample space. Instead of the entire sample space S, we now have a sample space of A since we know A has occurred. So, the old rule about being the number in the event divided by the number in the sample space still applies. It is the number in A and B (must be in A since A has occurred) divided by the number in A. If you then divided numerator and denominator of the right-hand side by the number in the sample space S, then you have the probability of A and B divided by the probability of A.

The usual notation for 'event A occurs given that event B has occurred' is 'A | B' (A given B). The symbol | is a vertical line and does not imply division. P(A | B) denotes the probability that event A will occur given that event B has occurred already.

A rule that can be used to determine a conditional probability from unconditional probabilities is

$$P(A|B) = \frac{P(A \cap B)}{P(B)} \qquad \text{Eq. 3.2}$$

where

P(A | B) = the (conditional) probability that event A will occur given that event B has occurred already.

P(A∩B) = the probability that event A and event B both occur. The symbol '∩' denotes intersection or overlap.

P(B) = the (unconditional) probability that event B occurs.

The above relationship is derived from the theorem of compound probability.

Let A and B be any two events associated with a random experiment. The probability of occurrence of event A when the event B has already occurred is called the conditional probability of A when B is given and is denoted as P(A/B).

Exercise: A box contains five yellow balls and two green balls. What is the probability that three balls randomly taken from the box (WOR) will all be yellow?

Solution: Let us define the events this way:

A = first ball is yellow; B = second ball is yellow; C = third ball is yellow
Therefore, as per conditional probability,
$P(A \cap B \cap C = P(A)\ P(B/A)\ P(C/A \cap B)$
The symbol $\cap$ denotes intersection or overlap.
$P(A) = 5/7$, i.e. 5 yellow balls in a box of 7
$P(B/A) = 4/6$, i.e. 4 yellow balls left in a box of 6
$P(C/A \cap B) = 3/5$, i.e. 3 yellow balls left in a box of 5
Therefore, the required conditional probability would be
$P(A \cap B \cap C) = (5 \times 4 \times 3) / (7 \times 6 \times 5) = 2/7$
Probability rules are explained in Nagar and Das (1983); Stoyanov (2014).

Risk Example: Suppose the probability of transaction error = 0.53 and probability of system fail = 0.50. The probability of both fail = 0.27. This can be obtained from their joint counts.

What is the probability that there will be transaction error when there is system fail?

$\text{Prob}(\text{Trans\_error} | \text{System Fail}) = 0.27/0.50 = 0.54.$

Similarly, for example, in mitigating risks in software development, Mr. X uses the number of software modules (e.g. risk weights calculator under Basel III) developed by two different types of programmers (types A and B). The statistical data obtained from the department in terms of counts are shown in Table 3.1.

Table 3.1 Model Error Test Data

Programmer A		Programmer B		Total	Developed
Models developed	<industry average	Models developed	<industry average	All	<Average
2000	850	3000	920	5000	1700

In order to achieve this, Mr X uses the following notation:

P_A denotes the event that the model is developed by a type A programmer.

P_B denotes the event that the model is developed by type B programmer.

Z denotes the event that the model has fewer serious calculation errors than the industry average.

Now, using the law of condition probability, Mr X can get the answers of

$\text{Prob}(Z|P_A) = \text{Prob}(P_A \cap Z)/\text{Prob}(P_A)$

And $\text{Prob}(Z|P_B) = \text{Prob}(P_B \cap Z)/\text{Prob}(P_B)$.

Now, using the above frequency table, he can estimate

$\text{Prob}(P_A) = 2000/5000 = 40\%$ and $\text{Prob}(P_B) = 3000/5000 = 60\%$; these are also called prior probabilities.

The probabilities where below average models developed by Programmer A and Programmer B:

$\text{Prob}(P_A \cap Z) = 850/5000 = 17\%$

$\text{Prob}(P_B \cap Z) = 920/5000 = 18.40\%$

Thus, the conditional probability that the below industry average model was prepared by a type A programmer:

$\text{Prob}(Z|P_A) = 17\% / 40\% = 42.50\%$

Similarly, it was developed by a type B programmer would be

$\text{Prob}(Z|P_B) = 18.40\% / 60\% = 31\%$.

Thus, Mr X can now decide that the job may be given to Programmer B to prepare the next capital calculator to have fewer serious defects than the industry average.

Joint Dependence

If events are not independent,

For example, Probability of A and B to default is 0.25% and1.5% and probability of both to default is 0.35%, respectively. What is the probability that A or B might be default?

P(A∪B) = 0.25% + 1.5% – (0.35%) = 1.40% when events have overlap due to some common factors.

P(A∪B) denotes probability of the union of any two events A and B. We have utilized Boole's inequality to solve the above problem.

Exercise: A bag contains 8 white and 6 black balls. If 5 balls are drawn at random without replacement (WOR), what is the probability that 3 are white and 2 are black?

Solution: 5 balls can be drawn out of 14 in $14C_5$ ways, and these cases are mutually exclusive, exhaustive, and equally likely. However, in a group, 3 white balls can be drawn out of 8 in $8C_3$ ways, and 2 black balls out of 6 in $6C_2$ ways. So, the number of favourable cases is $8C_3 \times 6C_2$.

By the classical definition of probability,

$$p = \frac{8C_3 \times 6C_2}{14C_5}$$

$$8C_3 = \frac{8\times7\times6}{1\times2\times3} = 56;\ 6C_2 = \frac{6\times5}{1\times2} = 15;\text{ and } 14C_5$$
$$= \frac{14\times13\times12\times11\times10}{1\times2\times3\times4\times5} = 14\times13\times11.$$

Therefore, $p = \frac{56\times15}{14\times13\times11} = 60/143.$

In risk management, many correlation analyses about joint dependence between assets and borrowers are based on this concept.

Let us consider an example. A loan portfolio contains 8 solvent accounts and 5 defaulted accounts. Two successive draws of 3 accounts are made WOR. Find the probability that the first drawing will give 3 defaulted and the second 3 solvent facilities.

Solution: Let A denote the event of first drawing gives 3 defaulted loans and B denotes the event second drawing gives 3 solvent loans. We have to find out Prob (A∩ B).

We know by conditional probability theorem P(A∩B) = P(A) × P(B/A).

Hence, P(A) = $[{}^8C_0 \times {}^5C_3]/{}^{13}C_3$ = [1 × 10]/286 = 5/143 = 3.45% (approx.).

Next, we have to find: P(B/A) = $[{}^8C_3 \times {}^2C_0]/{}^{10}C_3$
= [56 × 1]/120 = 7/15 = 46.68% (approx.)

Hence, required probability is P(AB) = (5/143) × (7/15) = 7/429 = 1.63%

This concept has major applications in operational risk as well as credit risk portfolio modelling exercises.

Similarly, you can now answer this question. A loan portfolio contains 8 IG (AAA rating to BBB rating) and 6 NIG (below BBB) category of assets. If 5 accounts are drawn at random, what is the probability that 3 are IG and 2 are NIG?

Solution: the estimated probability would be

$$P = \left[{}^{8}C_{3} \times {}^{6}C_{2}\right] / {}^{14}C_{5} = 60/143 = 42\% \text{ (approx.)}$$

Various probability applications are illustrated in Balakrishna, Koutras and Politis (2019) and Walpole et al. (2006).

Mutually Exclusive vs. Non-Exclusive Events

Mutually exclusive events cannot occur together. However, two events A and B are said to be mutually non-exclusive events if both A and B have at least one common outcome between them. The probability of two mutually exclusive events happening is zero. If we take out a card from a deck of 52 playing cards and find out whether event A: the card is a spade or B: the card is an ace is happening. The two events are not mutually exclusive since there exists on ace of spades. P(A) = 4/52 and P(S) = 1/4, and P(A∩S) = (4/52) × (1/4) = 1/52. This is the overlap event probability.

Similarly, the good and bad events recognition in credit risk should not have any overlap.

The difference between the two events has been further elaborated with practical examples.

What is the probability of picking up an ace and a king from a well-shuffled pack of 52 cards?

Here, P(A or B) = P(A) + P(B)

It is also written as P(A∪B) = P(A) + P(B)

Hence, the answer would be 4/52 + 4/52 − (0) = 2/13; since kings and aces are mutually exclusive events.

Thus, we can say that independence and mutual exclusivity are defined by

$$P(AB) = P(A) \times P(B) \text{ and } P(A + B) = P(A) + P(B).$$

Note that '∩' is the intersection symbol (e.g. A and B) and '∪' represents the Union symbol (e.g. A or B).

Similarly, in cards game, king and queen cannot come at the same time and they are mutually exclusive events.

Thus, in a deck of 52 cards, the probability of a king is 1/13, so P(King) = 1/13.

The probability of a queen is also 1/13; since P(Queen) = 1/13.

When we combine the two events, we get

The probability of a king or queen is

$$P(\text{K or Q}) = (1/13) + (1/13) = 2/13.$$

It is also written as follows:

$$P(K \cup Q) = 2/13.$$

This is happening because $P(K \cap Q) = 0$.

However, the question is: What is the probability of getting a diamond or a queen from a well-shuffled deck of 52 cards?

In this case, there will be an intersection since events are non-mutually exclusive one and the answer would be 13/52 + 4/52 – (1/52) = 4/13 (due to overlap of diamond queen).

Similarly, probability of getting hearts (H) and kings (K) are also mutually non-exclusive events. Hearts and kings together are only the king of hearts. Here, the estimated probability would be

$$P(\text{H or K}) = P(H) + P(K) - P(\text{H and K})$$

Here, the number of favourable cases = 13 hearts + 4 kings – 1 king of hearts = 16 cards in total.

Total number of cards in a pack = 52.

Hence, estimated probability: P(H or K) = 16/52 = 0.3077.

In another example, consider 15 people in a graduation course to study German, 30 to study Spanish, and there are total 50 students all together. There are 5 students learning both German and Spanish. Find out the total probabilities.

This is definitely mutually non-exclusive case since a student can opt for both German and Spanish. The required probabilities are

P(German) = 15/50; P(Spanish) = 30/50; P(German and Spanish) = 5/50.

Thus, P(G or S) = P(G) + P(S) – P(G and S).

$\Rightarrow 50/50 = (15 + 30 - 5)/50$

$= 40/50$

$= 80\%.$

Concisely, if we ask what is the probability of picking up an ace and a king from a well-shuffled pack of 52 cards? Since the events are mutually exclusive, the estimated probability would be

$4/52 + 4/52 - (0) = 2/13.$

However, if we ask what is the probability of getting a diamond or a queen from a well-shuffled deck of 52 cards? Here, the events are mutually non-exclusive. The estimated probability would be $13/52 + 4/52 - (1/52) = 4/13$.

In the management of credit risk; for example, probability of default (PD) and probability of repayment (PS) are mutually exclusive events. However, default events from 'A'-graded corporates and default from 'BBB'-graded companies can be mutually non-exclusive. This is because there may be positive joint probability of default from both the grade since both borrowers may belong to same industry or region or in related sectors.

Mutually Exclusive Events vs. Independent Events—Mutually exclusive events cannot happen at the same time. For example, when flipping a coin, the result can either be heads or tails but cannot be both. Similarly, if event 'A' is the roll of die is odd and event 'B' is the roll of die is even; the roll of die must result in a number which is either even or odd. It cannot happen simultaneously. Therefore, we can say that event A and B are mutually exclusive events. For example, if an account status in NPA (days past due 90 days), it cannot be considered as a standard asset category at the same time. A loan is an asset in the account books of the banks. Generally, a loan is defined as a non-performing asset (NPA) when it becomes bad and ceases to generate income for the bank.

Events are called independent if the happening of one event does not influence (and is not influenced by) the occurrence of the other(s).It is important to note that even if events A and B are not mutually exclusive, they can be independent. For example, in a coin flipping experiment, event A is defined as the event that has first toss is a head and event B is defined as the event that has the second flip is a head. We write the event experiment as follows:

A = {HH, HT}
B = {HH, TH}

Since the outcome of the first flip has no influence over the outcome of the second flip, events A and B can be termed as independent events. However, they are non-mutually exclusive in this case.

For example, the event of default and non-default is mutually exclusives if banks correctly recognize their bad assets. A loan becomes non-performing or bad asset when the interest and or instalment of principal remain overdue for a period of more than 90 days. In that case, PD + PS = 1; i.e. probability of default plus probability of solvency is equal to unity. This relationship is crucial for building powerful default prediction models. However, PD in one sector may be independent of default in another sector. This happens when joint default probability between the two sectors is equal to the product of their individual default probabilities.

Independent Events

If events are independent, the occurrence of one event does not affect the occurrence of the other event.

What is probability that either of the first or second coin gives heads?

When two coins flip, one way to get the correct probability is to double count and then subtract the outcome that are double counted. This is the addition rule: P(A or B) = P(A) + P(B) – P(A&B).

Hence, the estimated probability would be P(A or B) = 1/2 + 1/2 – (1/2*1/2) = 3/4 or 0.75.

Here, events are independent but not mutually exclusive.

In this case, HH and HT give heads on the 1st coin. HH and TH give heads on the 2nd coin. If we count all 4, HH is counted twice. The correct probability is counting HH only once, and it is = 3/4.

If events A and B are mutually exclusive, P(A or B) = P(A) + P(B) and $P(A \cap B) = 0$. For example, if a standard six-faced dice is rolled and A is the number 1 and B is the number 2, then A and B are mutually exclusive since the dice cannot be both a 1 and a 2. In this case, the probability that a dice will be either 1 or 2 is 1/6 + 1/6 = 1/3.

Exercise: A card is drawn from each of two well-shuffled packs of cards. Find the probability that at least one of them is an ace.

Solution: Let us denote by A = event that the card from Pack 1 is an ace and B = event that the card from Pack 2 is an ace.

It is required to find P(A + B)

We will use additional theorem of probability:

$$P(A + B) = P(A) + P(B) - P(AB)$$

Since there are 4 aces in a pack of 52 cards, P(A) = 4/52 = 1/13.

Similarly, P(B) = 1/13.

The events A and B are independent, because the drawing of an ace or otherwise from one pack does not any way affect the probability of drawing an ace from another pack. So,

$$P(AB) = P(A) \times P(B) = 1/13 \times 1/13 = 1/169$$

Substituting the values, we get

$$P(A + B) = 1/13 + 1/13 - 1/169 = 25/169.$$

Similarly, in probability theorem, if events A and B are independent, then their complement events A^c and B^c are also independent.

Exercise: The odds in favour of an event A are 3:4. The odd against another event B are 7:4. What is the probability that at least one of the events will happen?

Solution: Odds in favour of A are a:b signifies P(A) = a/(a + b) and Odds against A are b:a signifies P(A) = b/(a + b)

Here, P(A) = 3/7 and P(B) = 4/11. Also, since A and B are independent, we have P(AB) = P(A) × P(B) = 3/7 × 4/11 = 12/77.

The probability of occurrence of at least one of the events A and B is given by

$$\begin{aligned} P(A + B) &= P(A) + P(B) - P(AB) \\ &= 3/7 + 4/11 - 12/77 = 7/11. \end{aligned}$$

However, if events are dependent, P(AB) = 0.

The above probability concept is widely used in portfolio risk management, estimation of joint default risk, and calculation of portfolio unexpected loss.

Exercise: Three retail loans X, Y, and Z having odds in favour of non-default are 2:5, 3:7, and 6:11. Find the probability that all will remain solvent at the end of the year?

Solution: $P(X^c)$ = Probability that A will default = 1 – 2/7 = 5/7

Similarly, $P(Y^c)$ = Probability of B will default = 1 – 3/10 = 7/10

& $P(Z^c)$ = Probability of C will default = 1 – 6/17 = 11/17.

Note that default and solvent are complimentary sets.

Since they are independent,

$\text{Prob}(X^c Y^c Z^c) = 5/7 \times 7/10 \times 11/17 = 0.714 \times 0.70 \times 0.647 = 0.323$

Thus, the probability that all three will remain solvent = $1 - \text{Prob}(X^c Y^c Z^c)$

= 1 – 0.323

= 67.7% (approximately)

Let us take another example to understand the concept. The probability of Indian Cricket Team wins a test match against Australia in Australia is 1/15. If India and Australia play 5 test matches there, what is the probability that India will lose all the test match? Also estimate the probability of winning at least one match by India?

The probability of losing a match by India is 1 – (1/15) = 14/15. As the outcome of all the matches is mutually independent, the estimated probability of losing all the 5 matches is

$$\frac{14}{15} \times \frac{14}{15} \times \frac{14}{15} \times \frac{14}{15} \times \frac{14}{15} = \left(\frac{14}{15}\right)^5 = 0.708.$$

Hence, the probability of winning at least one test match $= 1 - \left(\frac{14}{15}\right)^5 = 0.2917.$

In another exercise, it has been found that Mr. Benjamin can solve a problem in risk statistics is 4/5, that Mr. Sugata can solve with 2/3, and that Mr. Benjamin can solve it is 3/7. If all of them try independently, they find the probability that the problem will be solved.

Bayes' Probability Theorem

The conditional probability $P(E_i/M)$ of a specified event E_i, when M is stated to have actually occurred, is given by

$$P(E_i / M) = \frac{P(E_i) \times P(M / E_i)}{\sum_{i=1}^{n} P(E_i) \times P(M / E_i)} \qquad \text{Eq. 3.3}$$

It describes probability of an event based on prior conditions.

In a SME loan factory, models A, B, and C sanctions, respectively, 25%, 35%, and 40% of the total loans in a region (say Mumbai region). Of their output 5%, 4%, and 2% are defaulted loans. A borrower file is drawn at random from the product and is found to be defaulted one. What are the probabilities that it was sanctioned by rating models A, B, and C?

In order to solve this problem, we have to take help of Bayes' theorem. Here is the solution:

Let E_1, E_2, and E_3 denote the events that a borrower selected at random is sanctioned by the rating models 1, 2, and 3, respectively and let M denote the event of its being defective.

Then we have $P(E_1) = 0.25$; $P(E_2) = 0.35$; and $P(E_3) = 0.40$.

The probability of drawing a defaulted borrower sanctioned by model A is $P(M/E_1) = 0.05$; similarly, we have $P(M/E_2) = 0.04$ and $P(M/E_3) = 0.02$.

Hence, the probability that a defaulted loan selected at random is generated by model M is computed based on the Bayes probability theorem given in Equation 3.3.

Table 3.2 Bayes' Probabilities

Event: E_i	$P(E_i)$: Prior Probabilities	$P(M/E_i)$	$P(E_i) \times P(M/E_i)$
E_1	0.25	0.05	0.0125
E_2	0.35	0.04	0.0140
E_3	0.40	0.02	0.0080
Total	1.00		0.0345

Therefore, $P(E_1/M) = (0.0125/0.0345) = 36.23\%$

$$\text{Similarly, } P(E2/M) = \frac{P(E_2)\times P(M/E_2)}{\sum_{i=1}^{3} P(E_i)\times P(M/E_i)} = \frac{0.0140}{0.0345} = 40.580\%$$

Finally, we get $P(E_3/M) = (0.0080/0.0345) = 23.188\%$.

Clearly, the second model has the highest probability of defaults.

Bayes' theorem has lot of applications in development as well as validation of credit-scoring models. Like in Altman's *z* score, once we obtain *z* score value of a borrower from its financial ratios, the said theorem helps us to assign which group the borrower will now fall and with what probability? That means it helps us to predict based on this score (say $z = 4$) whether the company will be in defaulted or solvent category? This is possible if we know the prior proportions (if whether 50% bad and 50% good in the sample). A detailed discussion on Altman *Z* score based on multivariate analysis has been discussed in Chapter 7.

Repeated Trials—Draws with Replacement

In certain experiment, the probability of occurrence of an event is p, and consequently, the probability of non-occurrence is $1 - p = q$. Suppose in n repeated trials of the experiment, if p remains a constant in each trial, then the probability that the event occurs in t times follows the Bernoulli or discrete binomial distribution. It is also termed as simple random sampling with replacement. Here, we need a probability distribution function. This has been explained subsequently in discrete probability distribution section.

Probability and Expectations

Let us consider a discrete random variable x that assumes the values x_1, x_2, ... x_n with probabilities p_1, p_2, ..., p_n, respectively. Then the expected value of x is defined as the sum of the product of probabilities of the different values of x with the corresponding probabilities.

Thus,

$$E(x) = \sum p_i x_i \quad \text{Eq. 3.4}$$

This is also termed as the mean (μ) of a random variable. Thus, the mean of a probability distribution is the expected value of x.

Similarly, the expected value of x^2 is defined as

$$E(x^2) = \sum p_i x_i^2 \quad \text{Eq. 3.5}$$

Variance is the expected value of $(x - E(x))^2$.

$$\text{Thus, } Variance(\sigma^2) = E(x - E(x))^2 \quad \text{Eq. 3.6}$$

$$= E(x - \mu)^2$$

$$= E(x^2) - \mu^2$$

The expected value of a constant C is also a constant.

$$E(C) = C \quad \text{Eq. 3.7}$$

$$E(X + Y) = E(X) + E(Y) \quad \text{Eq. 3.8}$$

$$E(XC) = CE(X) \quad \text{Eq. 3.9}$$

These are the common rules applied in estimating expected values of random variables. Expectation theorems and properties are elaborated in Nagar and Das (1983).

Probability Distribution

In reality, there are an infinite number of possible outcomes for the asset value. We represent the distribution of these possible outcomes with a probability density function (which is linked to the histogram).

Probability distributions are of two types: discrete distribution and continuous distribution.

Discrete Distributions

The binomial, Poisson, and negative binomial are the most three popular examples of discrete distributions that predicts the likelihood of number of events of occurrence.

A useful rule of thumb for choosing between these popular distributions is

Binomial:	variance < mean
Poisson:	variance = mean
Negative Binomial:	variance > mean

Thus, if we observe that our sample variance is much larger than the sample mean, the negative binomial distribution may be an appropriate choice. There are standard Chi-square fitness tests popularly used by statisticians or risk analysts to find out the best fitting distributions. This fitting method has been explained later.

Binomial Distribution

If k (lies between 0 and total number of trials N) is the number of success over N trials, then the binomial probability function is given by

$$P(X=k)=nC_k p^k q^{n\text{-}k}, \text{ where } p+q=1 \qquad \text{Eq. 3.10}$$

Thus, $f(r)=\dfrac{N!}{r!(N-r)!}p^r(1-p)^r$

This expression is known as the **binomial coefficient** stated as n choose r (or n C r) or the number of possible ways to choose r 'success' from n observations. The function $f(r)$ is known as probability mass function.

The mean of the above distribution function is given by

$$\bar{X} = Np \text{ and standard deviation by } \sigma = \sqrt{Np(1-p)}.$$

In a certain repeated experiment, the possibility of occurrence of an event is p and consequently the probability of non-occurrence is $1 - p = q$.

In n repeated trials of the experiment, the probability of occurrence of an event of r times is

$$P(r) = nC_r p^r q^{n-r}$$

The above expression follows Bernoulli or Binomial distribution as defined in Equation 3.10.

For example, the number of ways to achieve two heads in a set of four tosses is 4 choose 2 or $4!/(2!2!) = (4 \times 3) / (2 \times 1) = 6$. This gives us the first component of the above expression or the expression $f(r)$. Or, we can say the value of 6 is the derived estimate of binomial coefficient.

The possibilities are {*HHTT, HTHT, HTTH, TTHH, THHT, THTH*}

Where '*H*' represents head and '*T*' represents a tail.

Finally, we have to multiply the derived value of binomial coefficient by the possibilities p and q.

Therefore, the probability of obtaining 2 heads from a set of 4 tosses is

$P(r = 2) = (1/2)^2 \times (1/2)^2 \times 6$
$= 6/16$
$= 37.5\%$

Let us consider another example. If 4% of defaulted accounts are present in a loan pool, determine the probability that out of 4 borrowers chosen at random at most 2 will be defaulting?

Answer: using the above binomial expression, we try to find

$P(r =< 2) = P(r = 0) + P(r = 1) + P(r = 2)$,
where $n = 4$, $p = 4\%$, and $q = 96\%$

One can solve the above problem by the binomial distribution function.

For example, $P(r = 0) = nC_0 \times (0.04)^0 \times (0.96)^{4-0}$.

By combination theorem, $nC_0 = 1$.

Therefore, $P(r = 0) = 1 \times 1 \times 0.849 = 0.849$.

Similarly, $P(r = 1)$ and $P(r = 2)$ can be estimated and they can be finally added to derive the desired probability.

Here, we have used permutation and combination mathematical theorems to derive desired probabilities.

This sort of probability calculation is popularly applied in predicting default risk in financial institutions.

Normal, beta (credit risk, market risk) *t*, chi square, exponential, and Weibull (extreme distribution—thick tail) are the popular candidates of continuous distributions that are widely used in estimating losses by risk professionals.

Poisson Distribution

Another popular candidate of discrete distribution is Poisson distribution.

The probability density function of the passion distribution is given by

$$f(x) = \sum_{k=0}^{x} \frac{e^{-\lambda} \lambda^k}{k!} \qquad \text{Eq. 3.11}$$

where $x >= 0$ (k = number of trails = 0, 1, 2, . . . , ∞) and the parameter $\lambda > 0$ can be interpreted as arithmetic mean. The 'e' function is exponential in which value is 2.718 approximately.

Note that the passion mean is equal to its variance. This makes Poisson a popular candidate of distribution to predict the probability of occurrence of risk events. Thus, if mean (λ) is known, one can easily draw the passion distribution.

Poisson is considered the most preferred choice by analysts in predicting number of frauds per quarter or year in a bank. It is widely used in generating frequency distribution for operational losses.

Table 3.3 summarizes the number of Internal Frauds recorded by a bank on a monthly basis. The numbers are arranged in group frequency distribution in Table 3.3.

Table 3.3 Number of Frauds (per month) in LMN Bank in Grouped Frequency Form

Number of Frauds (x_i)	Observed Number (O) or Frequency (f_i)	Weight ($f_i \times x_i$)	Fitted Probability using Poisson Fit	Expected Number (E)	$(O_i - E_i)^2/E_i$
0	0	0	1.16%	2	2.000
1	8	8	5.17%	7	0.143
2	18	36	11.53%	16	0.250
3	20	60	17.12%	23	0.391
4	29	116	19.07%	26	0.346
5	21	105	17.00%	23	0.174
6	18	108	12.62%	17	0.059
7	10	70	8.03%	11	0.091
8	8	64	4.47%	6	0.667
9	2	18	2.22%	3	0.333
10	1	10	0.99%	1	0.000
11+	1	11	0.40%	1	0.000
Total	136	606			
Mean (λ)		= 606/136 = 4.46			4.454

Source: Author's own illustration

From Table 3.3, we can estimate the mean value = 606/136 = 4.46. Once the mean value is known, we can fit the frequency pattern in the shape of a Poisson distribution. Using the excel function POISSON(A2,4.46,FALSE), we have got the fitted probability estimates reported in the fourth column of Table 3.3. Note that the A2 values are reported in column 1 (i.e. x_i) values. This function is repeated for values 1, 2, ... , 11 to obtain the fitted probabilities. Next, the fitted probabilities are multiplied by total frequency ($N = 136$) to obtain expected frequency that has been reported in the fifth column of the Table 3.3.

The frequency distribution is then fitted in Poisson distribution function as shown in Figure 3.1:

Clearly, the fit is quite good. This further gets confirmed by the chi-square test. In the hypothesis section (Chapter 4), we have clearly explained how to find out the statistical significance of a test and when to reject or accept the null hypothesis.

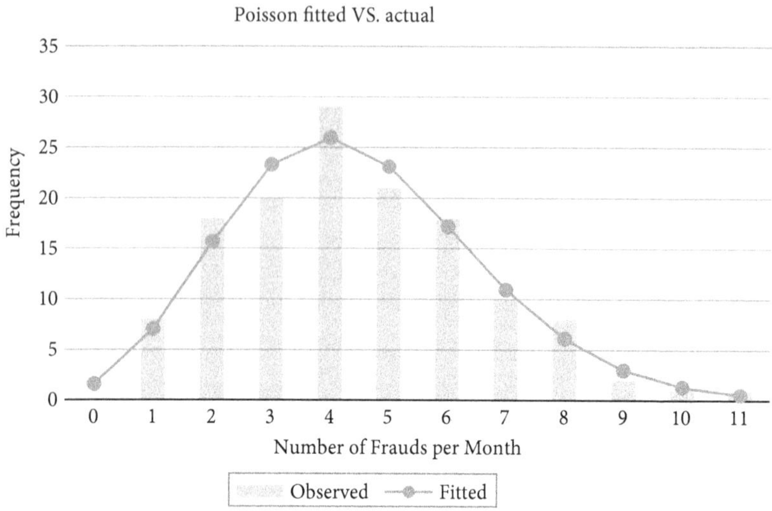

Figure 3.1 Poisson Fit
Source: Author's own computation

The risk manager needs to run a chi^2 fit test to further confirm the right selection of distribution. In our chi^2 goodness-of-fit test, we use the following test statistic.

$$\tilde{T} = \sum_{i=1}^{n} \frac{(O_i - E_i)^2}{E_i} \qquad \text{Eq. 3.12}$$

The null hypothesis (H_0): The fraud frequency series cannot be other than the Poisson distribution.

Accordingly, the alternate hypothesis (H_a): The data do not follow the Poisson distribution.

Here, the Chi^2 test statistic reported in the above equation is calculated by dividing the data into n number of bins (or ranges). Note that O_i is the observed number of events obtained from the data. The expression E_i is the expected or fitted number of events using the Poisson fit. There are n numbers of bins. The degrees of freedom in the test statistic = $n - k$. Here, $n = 12$, $k = 1$. Thus, d.f. = 11.

The chi-square value ($\tilde{T}$) is estimated in column and value is = 4.454. At 5% level of significance and degrees of freedom of 11, the table value of

chi^2 is = 19.675. Since the obtained chi-square value ($\tilde{T}$) < table value of chi^2; we cannot reject the null hypothesis (i.e. p-value > 0.10). Hence, the fraud frequency data fit well with the Poisson distribution. The concept about hypothesis testing and statistical significance (meaning of p-value) has been explained in the next chapter.

Once the Poisson distribution as best fit has been identified, we can then use Excel function to generate the Poisson distribution functions by plugging the lambda value and predict the range of values in terms of probability through random number generator. This method is called Monte Carlo simulation technique. Later, in Chapter 8, we have explained the technique and its application in great detail.

The above probability concepts are very useful in estimating monthly probability of occurrences of frauds. For further details about its applications, refer Lewis (2004).

Continuous Distribution

Normal Distribution

Normal probability distribution is the most popular candidate of continuous probability distribution. We use continuous distribution when we deal with nominal values (in Rupee or Dollar) rather than the number of events. It is called continuous since there can by any values in between two particular range of values (say between 100$ and 150$). Its probability density function is bell shaped and determined by its mean 'μ' and standard deviation 'σ'.

μ = meu; σ = sigma

Normal probability distribution is a good model for a continuous random variable in which values depend on a number of factors, each exerting a comparatively small influence.

It is a bell-shaped symmetric distribution of values around the mean (μ), median, and mode. Probability of obtaining a value far away from mean becomes progressively smaller.

In normal distribution, mean = median = mode; skewness = 0; and kurtosis = 0 (mesokurtic).

Statisticians have estimated that 68.26%, 95%, 95.44%, 99%, and 99.73% of area are covered by 1, 1.96, 2, 2.58, and 2.99 SD, respectively. Statistically, these areas are given in the normal table (see Appendix).

If X is a normal random variable with mean μ and SD σ, the equation of the normal curve is

$$f(x) = n(x;\mu,\sigma) = \frac{1}{\sqrt{2\pi\sigma}} e^{-\frac{1}{2}\left(\frac{x-\mu}{\sigma}\right)^2}; \quad \text{Eq. 3.13}$$

where x value ranges from minus infinity to plus infinity and the value of pi (π) = 3.14159 and exponential (e) = 2.71828

μ = meu = Mean; σ = sigma = SD.

Normal probability distribution is a good model for a continuous random variable in which the values depend on a number of factors, each exerting a comparatively small influence. It is a bell-shaped symmetric distribution of values around the mean (μ), median, and mode. Probability of obtaining a value far away from mean becomes progressively smaller.

In normal distribution, mean = median = mode; skewness = 0; and kurtosis = 0 (mesokurtic).

Statisticians have estimated that 68.27%, 95%, 95.45%, 99%, and 99.73% of area is covered by 1, 1.96, 2, 2.58, and 2.99 SD, respectively. Statistically, these areas are given in the normal table (see Figure 3.2 and statistical table given in Appendix).

The above representation in Figure 3.2 implies that if a random variable x is normally distributed with mean μ and standard deviation σ, then almost all the values of x will lie between the limits $\mu - 3\sigma$ and $\mu + 3\sigma$.

One can use 'normsdist(X, Mean, SD, False)' function in Excel and using sample mean and standard deviation, normal distribution graph can be generated on the X data variables.

Suppose a credit officer is analysing the risk assessment model (RAM) score of 65 borrowers in a data pool. Note that RAM score combines a corporate credit score after assessing its industry risk, financial risk, business risk, management risk, and project risk. The average RAM score obtained from corporate rating model is 7 with a SD of 1.3. The scoring distribution for all 65 borrowers is fitted into a normal distribution using excels function. We have used a SD increment of 0.10 to generate a

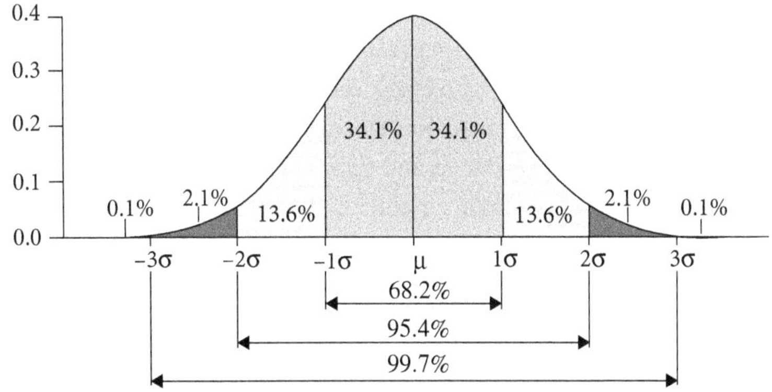

Figure 3.2 Area under the Normal Curve
Source: Author's own illustration

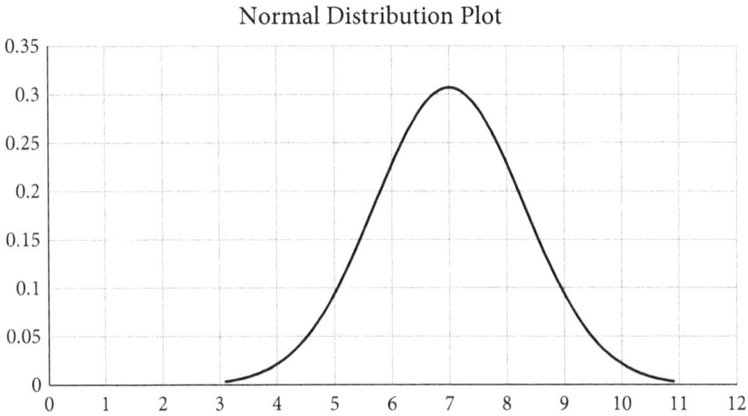

Figure 3.3 Normal Curve for RAM Score
Source: Author's computation

smooth graph. For this, X data have been re-generated using Mean-3SD at the first observation, and subsequently SD increment of SD/10 scalar has been used for SD of −2.9, −2.8, and so on. The normal probability distribution graph is plotted below Figure 3.3.

Note that the mean value of the credit score = 7 which comes at the midpoint of the score distribution.

Normal distribution has many useful algebraic properties for which it is used widely in risk analysis. The normal approximation simplifies the work of testing statistical hypothesis and is also very useful to find the confidence limits of various risk parameters.

A risk manager this way can check the pattern of a loss series and can estimate normalized loss ranges or percentiles. It gives him/her idea about score ranges: mean, lower range, and upper range. The detailed specificity of a normal distribution has been explained in Walpole et al. (2006).

Standard Normal Distribution

Normal distribution with 0 mean and 1 standard deviation is called a standard normal distribution. This is obtained by putting 0 as mean and 1 as standard deviation in the above normal function. This can be done by means of transformation: $Z = (X - \mu) / \sigma$.

The standard normal function is expressed as follows:

$$p(z) = \frac{1}{\sqrt{2\pi}} e^{-\frac{1}{2}z^2}; \qquad \text{Eq. 3.14}$$

where $-\infty < z < \infty$

This is a special case of normal distribution with mean 0 and standard deviation 1. Further details about nature of standard normal distribution are described in Nagar and Das (1983).

Exercise: Given that the daily change in price of a security follows the normal distribution with a mean of 70 bps and a variance of 9. What is the probability that on any given day, the change in price is greater than 75 bps?

Solution:

$Z = (75 - 70)/3 = 1.67$

$P(X > 75) = P(Z > 1.67)$

$= 1 - P(Z < 1.67) = 1 - 0.9525 = 0.0475$

The area has been estimated using the area of the normal curve given in the statistical table that contains range of *z* values and respective level of confidence (in terms of probability). These areas are already measured by the statisticians. To read the statistical table, please go through the *z* values say 1.6 and then in the table go rightward to add 0.07 to obtain the

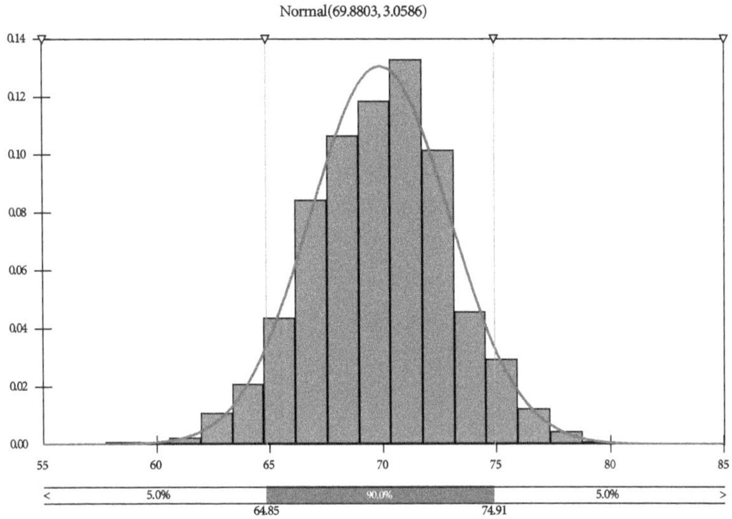

Figure 3.4 Simulated Normal Distribution of Security Price Change

corresponding probability for the z threshold 1.67. These observations are plotted in Figure 3.4.

The above normal chart was plotted using the Palisade best-fit software.

Note that the area of the entire normal curve is = 1. One can also simulate these probabilities using excel standard normal function (= normsdist(z)). Next, using random function and then linking the probability with mean (= 70) and standard deviation (= 3), one can run simulations to generate 1000 probable values of change in stock prices. For simulation, one has to link the random probabilities with properties of fitted distribution (mean and standard deviation) and using excel 'norminv' function. One has to write function: norminv((rand),70,3) and 1000 simulated probable values would be generated. The normal plotting of these predicted values is presented in Figure 3.4.

As a next step, these values can be fitted into a normal probability curve to predict the probability values aligned with range of stock price changes. We can perform goodness-of-fit check (GOF) using chi-square fit test for normal distribution as well. A chi-square estimate lower than the table value would indicate fit is good (that is p-value > 0.10). One can also perform percentile–percentile (P–P) plot or Jarque-Berra test (JB) for normality test. This way, risk managers use Monte Carlo simulation method to predict stock prices. This concept is also applied in estimating VaR. We have discussed various simulation methods in VaR section. This has also been elaborated in Vose (1996).

It is important to note that the RiskMetrics™ methodology for calculating VaR was evolved by J. P. Morgan in 1994 assumes that a portfolio of bond returns follows a normal distribution. The return volatility, bond spread, and variance covariance method were used to calculate the VaR which became an industry benchmark twenty-five years back. Suppose the risk manager chooses a look back period of 252 days or one trading year as his investment horizon. If investment yields good return, the bank will do well. However, the risk manager will choose a confidence level of 99% and corresponding z value must be multiplied by the standard deviation of the portfolio returns to measure risk. The z values can be obtained from the areas under the normal curve from a statistical table. The actual daily standard deviation of the portfolio over one trading year is estimated as 4%. The z score for the 99% is 2.326. Therefore, the VaR of the portfolio, under the 99% confidence level is −9.304% (= −2.326×4%). Negative sign arises because risk translates into large adverse returns at the tail side of the return distribution. Therefore, there is a 1% probability that the portfolio loss would exceed 9.304% over the given time horizon. However, actually, portfolio returns may follow non-normal distribution (e.g. log normal). Hence, it is essential to fit non-normal distributions to estimate risk capital threshold. Note that recently, Jalan committee report released by RBI (2019) has utilized VaR method to estimate reserve requirements for the Central Bank. Nagar and Das (1983) explains the detailed properties of normal distribution.

Non-Normal Distributions

Distributions with a kurtosis greater than the normal distribution are said to be leptokurtic (or fat tail distribution). Weibull, Pareto, and inverse Gaussian distributions are the popular candidates of extreme distributions. These distributions are used in operational risk capital calculations. In credit risk loss estimation, beta distribution and log normal distributions are commonly used by the best practiced banks. Beta and log normal are non-normal distributions and have positive skewedness.

Note that, to better understand the shape of the distributions, we have known its mean (location) and standard deviation (scale) parameters.

For non-normal cases, we will also have to measure its skewness and kurtosis since they define the shape of the distributions.

It is important to know that, in practice, loss distributions may be non-normal in nature. In those cases, risk managers will have to fit loss data with most obvious candidates of distributions. This can be done using Palisade @Risk software or any other distribution fitting software. Many analysts use chi^2 test for checking the distribution fit.

The most popular candidates of non-normal distributions for loss simulation are log normal distribution and beta distribution. In market risk assessment, normal distribution is commonly used. However, Laplace distribution is also used to take care abnormality in the return distribution. In operational risk, nature of loss distributions may have fat tail (Leptokurtic) due to low frequency and high severity (e.g. big frauds or legal loss events etc.). In those cases, the Weibull and Pareto distributions are used to better fit the loss series. In such cases of abnormal distributions, instead of only chi-square fit test, Anderson Darling test (AD statistic) and Kolmogorov–Smirnov (KS) tests are conducted to identify most suitable candidates of distribution. The details about their shapes are given in Lewis (2004) and Vose (1996).

Concept of Confidence Interval

A confidence interval is an interval constructed from a sample, which includes the parameter being estimated with a specified probability known as the confidence level.

If a risk indicator for example was sampled on many occasions, and the confidence interval calculated each time, then $(1 - \alpha)\%$ of such intervals would cover the true population parameter being estimated.

A very narrow interval indicates less uncertainty (or less error rate) about the value of the population parameter than a very wide interval.

In risk management, confidence levels are often more useful than confidence intervals because we are usually concerned with the downside risk or worst-case level (tail risk).

It is a single number and level (α) that will not be exceeded, with a given probability (%).

For example, there is only a 5% chance that a variable drawn from a standard normal distribution will have a value greater than 1.64.

We can, therefore, say that the 95% confidence level for this variable is 1.64 (α). The inverse of the confidence level (α) is the percentile.

Suppose the mean credit loss = \$434,045 and set confidence multiplier $\alpha = 5\%$ so that we have a $(1 - \alpha) = 95\%$ confidence interval around the estimate of mean. Such an interval can be calculated using

$$\bar{X} \pm z_{\alpha} \times \text{Stdev}(X)$$

Stdev(X), the SD of X = \$73,812, and z is the standard normal variable for $\alpha = 5\%$. Using the Normsinv() function, we see that Normsinv(0.95) = 1.64 (Or see the standard normal table). Therefore, we can set $z = 1.64$ and calculate 95% confidence interval as \$312,635 to \$555,455.

In this case, the credit risk manager may feel comfortable stating that the average credit risk loss as \$434,045, although we have 95% confidence that the actual (population) value will lie somewhere close to this value, say, between \$312,635 and \$555,455.

Summary

Probability concepts and distribution theorems provide the risk managers with effective tools to gain insights into the nature of uncertainty. Various probability measures and their application rules have been demonstrated using numerous examples. Understanding of probability rules would enable the risk manager to predict uncertain outcomes and related it with management of loss. In this chapter, we have illustrated how to interpret and use discrete as well as continuous distributions to predict loss ranges. The most common candidates of discrete distributions are binomial distribution and Poisson distribution. Binomial distribution is popularly used to fit default probabilities for the assessment of credit risk. Poisson distribution has lot of applications in predicting frauds for operation risk analysis. Understanding of nature and pattern of loss distributions is essential to estimate risk capital. The idea of distributions is also helpful to perform various statistical significance tests which have been addressed in the subsequent section.

Review Questions

1. What is the difference between mutually exclusive events and independent events?
2. If the probability of scoring no goals in a tournament (event A) is 20% and scoring exactly 1 (event B) is 15%, then find out the probability of scoring non-goals and 1 goal. Also find out the probability of scoring no goals and 1.
3. Is there any difference between mutually exhaustive events and mutually exclusive events?
4. A card is drawn from each of two well-shuffled packs of cards. Find the probability of at least one of them is an ace.
5. The probability that a math teacher will take a surprise test during any class session is 1/5. If a student is absent twice, what is the probability that they will miss at least one test?
6. A loan portfolio contains 8 AA and 6 BB categories of assets. If 5 accounts are drawn by the auditor at random, what is the probability that 3 are AA and 2 are BB?
7. If the probability of back office staff leaving the treasury job is 0.40, probability of transaction error = 0.60; and probability of both happening = 0.30. Then, estimate the probability of occurrence of transaction error conditional upon back office people leaving the job?
8. If the probability of transaction error = 0.20 and the probability of system failure = 0.50, what is the probability that a transaction failure will happen when there is system failure?
9. The probability that Ashok can solve a problem in business statistics is 4/5, that Johny can solve it is 2/3, and that Abdul can solve it is 3/7. If all of them try independently, find the probability that the problem will be solved?
10. How to estimate probability for repeated drawings with replacement? How it is useful for the risk managers?
11. The probability that a corporate project loan will be approved by a bank is 0.4. Determine the probability that out of 5 entering loan proposals, (a) none, (b) one, and (c) at least one will be pass the approval process?

12. What is Bayes' theorem? How it can be used to predict default risk of a loan?
13. What are the major differences between continuous distribution and discrete distribution?
14. How will you identify a discrete distribution?
15. How to fit a normal distribution in Excel?
16. How to predict security prices using Standard Normal Z statistic?
17. Try to perform fit tests using Palisade @RISK
18. What are the popular candidates of non-normal distributions for operational risk?
19. What distribution is popularly used in market risk assessment? Why?
20. If the life of a personal loan in days is assumed normally distributed with mean life = 155 days and SD = 19 days, what is the probability that life of a borrower less than 117 days, more than 193 days, and between 117 days and 193 days?
21. A security analyst finds monthly price of a bond follows normal distribution with a mean of Rs. 110 and a variance of 16. What is the probability that on a given month, the bond price would be less than 100? Also estimate the probability that the price would be between 100 and 120?
22. A frequency data that report monthly incidents of fraud has mean = 10 and SD = 3, check whether it would follow binomial distribution?

References

Balakrishnan, N., M. V. Koutras, and K. G. Politis (2019). 'Introduction to Probability: Models and Applications', Wiley, USA.

Lewis, N. D. (2004). 'Operational Risk with Excel and VBA', Wiley Finance, 2004, USA.

Nagar, A. L., and R. K. Das (1983). 'Basic Statistics', 2nd Edition, Oxford University Press, New Delhi.

Stoyanov, J. M. (2014). *Counterexamples in Probability*, 3rd Edition, Dover Publications.

Vose, D. (1996). 'A Guide to Monte Carlo Simulation Modeling', 1st edition, John Wiley & Sons, USA.

Walpole, R. E., S. L. Myers, K. Ye, and H. Myers (2006). 'Probability and Statistics', Raymond, USA.

4

Hypotheses Testing in Banking Risk Analysis

Testing of hypothesis is one of the main objectives of sampling theory. Hypothesis tests address the uncertainty of the sample estimate. Any statement or assertion about a statistical population or the values of its parameters is called a statistical hypothesis. A risk manager requires to take a decision to select a single alternative from a number of possible alternatives. In this context, hypothesis testing provides a formal procedure for making rational decision based on the information available to the researcher.

When we have to make a decision about the entire population based on the sample data, hypothesis tests help us in arriving at a decision.

It attempts to refute a specific claim about a population parameter based on the sample data.

The process which enables us to decide on the basis of the sample results whether a hypothesis is true or not, is called test of hypothesis or test of significance. In test of significance, we start with a null hypothesis (H_0) about the population characteristic. The null hypothesis generally starts with negative (e.g. does not happen or does not different from etc.). The null hypothesis is tested against an alternative hypothesis. It differs from the null hypothesis. The alternative hypothesis is not tested, but it acceptance (or rejection) depends on the rejection (acceptance) of the null hypothesis. The choice of an appropriate critical region depends on the type of alternative hypothesis. It can be both sided or one sided (right or left) or specified alternative.

To determine the accuracy of your hypotheses on which decision needs to be made, a risk manager needs to collect a sizeable sample of data on which basis he or she wants to make inference. This is called statistical significance. In this chapter, we explain the statistical approach to hypothesis testing and relate its relevance to management of risk.

Hypothesis Testing Procedure

All hypothesis tests are conducted in the same way. The researcher states a hypothesis to be tested, formulates an analysis plan, analyses sample data according to the plan, and accepts or rejects the null hypothesis, based on results of the analysis.

Step 1—State the hypotheses. Every hypothesis test requires the analyst to state a null hypothesis and an alternative hypothesis. The hypotheses are stated in such a way that they are mutually exclusive. That is, if one is true, the other must be false and vice versa.

Step 2—Formulate an analysis plan. The analysis plan describes how to use sample data to accept or reject the null hypothesis. It should specify the following elements.

Step 3—Set the appropriate significance level. Often, researchers choose significance levels that are equal to 0.01, 0.05, or 0.10, but any value between 0 and 1 can be used.

Statistical Concept behind Hypothesis Testing

First, fix two numerical values or critical values of t say t_0 and t_1 on the t-axis (It is also termed as z-statistic). Next, reject the H_0 if the sample value of $t < t_0$ and $t > t_1$. The statistical hypothesis rule states that does not reject the null hypothesis H_0 if $t_0 < t < t_1$. The critical region is defined as the region of the rejection of H_0. This is highlighted in Figure 4.1.

Let the sampling distribution of t (or z, measured in the horizontal axis) be as shown in Figure 4.1. When $\Theta = \Theta_0$ (or say mean $z = 0$), i.e. H_0 is true and when $\Theta = \Theta_1$ (or mean $z = 1$), i.e. when the alternate hypothesis H_1 is true (and H_0 is false).

If H_0 is true, i.e. $\Theta = \Theta_0$, the shaded area under the curve as indicated in the diagram with continuous line beyond t_0 and t_1 gives us the probability of rejecting the H_0 hypothesis. Let the probability $= \alpha$, then we can write

$$\Pr\left[\text{Reject } H_0 \mid_{H0}\right] = \Pr\left[\, t <= t_0 \text{ or } t >= t_1 \mid H_0 \right] = \alpha$$

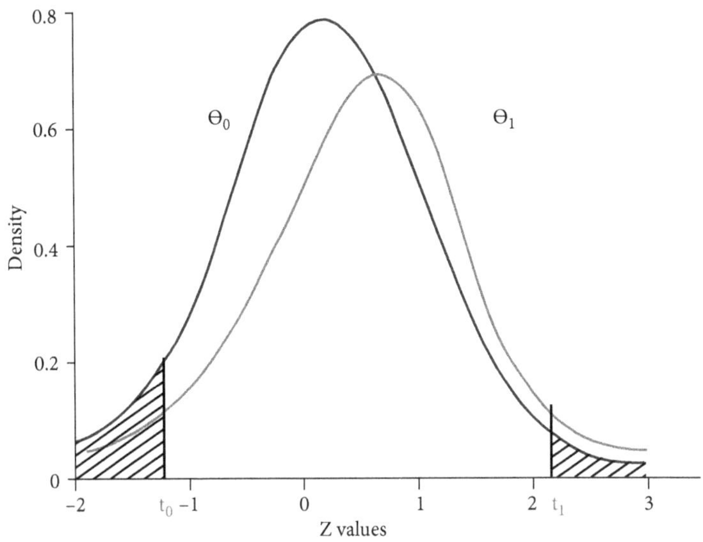

Figure 4.1 Type 1 Error, Type 2 Error, and Power of a Test

Here, alpha (α) represents type 1 error rate which has to be set at least at 5% level. Lower the type I%, greater is the statistical significance and the researcher (or risk analyst) would have enough evidence to reject the null hypothesis (H_0).

Power of Test

Power of a test is measured in the following way:

$$\Pr\left[\text{Reject } H_0 \mid H_1\right] = \Pr\left[t <= t_0 \text{or } t >= t_1 \mid H_1\right] = 1 - \beta$$

where t is the test statistic.

It can also be interpreted in terms of standard normal distribution as shown above.

Thus, $1 - \beta$ = Reject null (H_0) when it is false or when alternate hypothesis (H_1) is true.

$$\text{Or, } 1-\beta = \Pr\left[t <= t_0 \text{ or } t >= t_1 \mid H_1\right]$$

It should be noted that rejecting null H_0 when it is false is a good thing. We should maximize the probability of β which is called power of the test.

Thus, type II error can be written as follows: β. Type II error is committed when we fail to reject a null hypothesis (H_0) by the test when it is actually false. Note that the probability of Type II error depends on the specified value of the alternate hypothesis. This is used in evaluating the efficiency of a test.

Thus, power of a test = 1 − Probability of type II error (Nagar and Das, 1983)

There should be a right balance between type I and type II error rates since both are important, which is gathered as statistical evidence.

Few practical illustrations are given to better understand the applications of these two errors in risk management.

Risk analyst while testing a model performance generates a confusion matrix to check the type I and type II errors.

This is summarized in Table 4.1:

You have committed a type I error if you have rejected the null hypothesis tested when it was true. Similarly, you have committed a type II error if you failed to reject the null hypothesis tested when a given alternative hypothesis was true. It has major application in hypothesis testing as well as in model validation tests.

Popularly, t-statistic (from t-distribution) or z-statistic (from standard normal distribution) is commonly used to perform statistical significance tests.

Table 4.1 Confusion Matrix: Type I Error and Type II Error Check

Statistical Decision	True State of the Null Hypothesis	
	H_0 True	H_0 False
Reject H_0	Type I error	Correct
Do not Reject H_0	Correct	Type II error

One-Tailed vs. Two-Tailed Test

- One-tailed Test
  A test of a statistical hypothesis, where the region of rejection is on only one side of the sampling distribution, is called a one-tailed test. In such tests, we are only interested in values greater (or less) than the null. The following figure shows the acceptance and rejection zones.

A one-sided hypothesis test is interpreted as follows:

- Test $H_0: \mu = 0$ against $H_A: \mu > 0$ or $\mu < 0$ & we reject the null if $|T_{comp}| > T_{critical}$
  Note that the symbol T is the test statistic. Critical or table value of T can be obtained from statistical tables (either using t-distribution or standard normal z-distribution).
- Two-tailed Test
  A test of a statistical hypothesis, where the region of rejection is on both sides of the sampling distribution, is called a two-tailed test. In such tests, we are interested in values greater and smaller than the null hypothesis.

Two-tail test result is interpreted as follows:

- Test $H_0: k = 0$ against $H_A: k \neq 0$ & we reject the null if $|T_{comp}| > T_{critical}$
- In the two-sided hypothesis, we calculate critical value using $\alpha/2$. For example, $\alpha = 5\%$, the critical value of the test statistic is $T_{0.025}$.

Illustration of the Concept with Examples

Consider the null hypothesis (H_0) that the average Home Loan Borrowers in India is 30 inches against the alternative hypothesis that it is unequal to 30. Therefore, we can frame the hypothesis as follows:

$H_0: \mu = 30$,
$H_1: \mu \neq 30$

The alternative hypothesis allows for the possibility that $\mu < 30$ or $\mu > 30$. Assume that the standard deviation of the population of home loan borrowers to be $\sigma = 4$.The sample size $n = 45$ and the sampling distribution of $\bar{X}$ is approximately normally distributed with standard deviation $\sigma_{\bar{X}} = \frac{\sigma}{\sqrt{n}} = 4/\sqrt{45} = 0.596$.

Assume that the x values follow normal distribution.

A sample mean that falls close to the hypothesized value of 30 would be considered evidence in favour of the null hypothesis H_0. On the other hand, a sample mean that is considerably less than or more than 30 would be evidence inconsistent with H_0, and therefore, we then reject the H_1 and accept in favour of alternate hypothesis H_1. A critical region, indicated by the shaded area in figure below, is arbitrarily chosen to be $\bar{X} < 29$ and $\bar{X} > 31$.

The acceptance region will, therefore, be $29 < \bar{X} < 31$. Hence, if our sample mean $\bar{x}$ falls outside the critical region, H_0 is rejected; otherwise, we accept H_0.

Note that the null hypothesis will be rejected if the sample mean is too big or if it is too small.

Here, we can use z value to statistically test the hypothesis; $= \frac{\bar{x} - \mu}{\sigma / \sqrt{n}}$.

The significance can be confirmed through a two-tailed test. We have used standard normal table to obtain critical values.

The level of significance of our test (or probability of committing type I error) is equal to the sum of the areas that have been shaded in each tail of the distribution in the above figure.

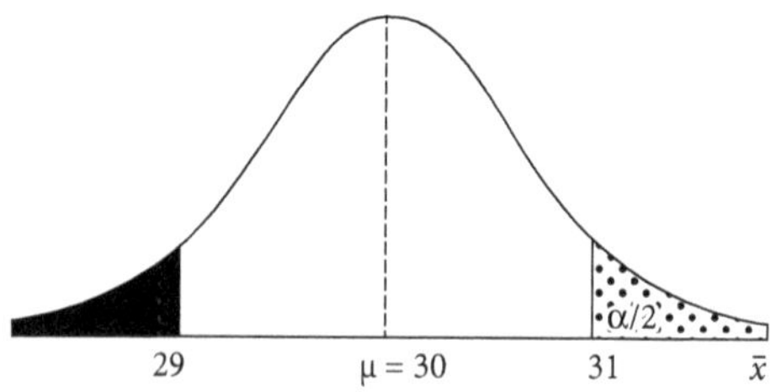

Figure 4.2 Standard Normal Distribution

Thus, level of significance = probability of type I error = α = Prob ($\bar{X} < 29$ when H_0 is true) + Prob ($\bar{X} > 31$ when H_0 is true)

The z values corresponding to threshold = 29 and = 31 when H_0 is true are

$$z_1 = \frac{29-30}{0.596} = -1.68 \quad \text{and} \quad z_2 = \frac{31-30}{0.596} = 1.68$$

Note that standard error (S.E.) $=\sigma/\sqrt{n} = 4/(\sqrt{45}) = 0.596$.

Therefore, from the area of above standard normal distribution,

$\alpha = \Pr(Z < -1.68) + \Pr(Z > 1.68)$

$= 2\Pr(Z < -1.68)$; since it is a bell-shaped distribution

$= 2 \times 0.0465$

$= 0.093.$

It is estimated from the normal table given in Appendix.

Thus, 9.93% of all samples of size 45 would lead us to reject mean age = 30 years when it is true.

Note that the type I error rate is the probability that the null hypothesis is rejected when it is true (here assume that the true average age of the borrower was 30). Thus, in this exercise, type I error rate is high.

To further reduce the type I error rate, statisticians prefer either increase the sample size n or widen the acceptance region.

Suppose we increase the sample size to 70 and then SE = $4/\sqrt{81}$ = $4/9 = 0.44$.

Now,

$$z_1 = \frac{29-30}{0.44} = -2.25 \quad \text{and} \quad z_2 = \frac{31-30}{0.44} = 2.25.$$

Hence,

$\alpha = \Pr(Z < -2.25) + \Pr(Z > 2.25)$

$= 2\Pr(Z < -2.25)$, since it is a bell-shaped distribution.

$= 2 \times 0.0122$

$= 0.0244.$

The reduction is α indicates rejection of H_0. However, this reduction in α is not sufficient by itself to ensure a good testing procedure. For this, we must also evaluate the type II error 'β'. This has to be done for various alternate hypotheses that we feel should be accepted if true. Therefore, if it is important to reject H_0 when the true mean is some value $\mu >= 35$ or $\mu <= 25$, then the probability of committing a type II error should be computed and examined for the alternatives (H_1) $\mu = 25$ and $\mu = 35$.

Figure 4.3 depicts the critical region for the alternate hypothesis. Numerous statistical examples are given in Walpole et al. (2012).

The age distribution with normal fit is presented as follows:

If the z value $\dfrac{\bar{x}-\mu_0}{\sigma/\sqrt{n}}$ falls in the region $-z_{\alpha/2} < Z < z_{\alpha/2}$, we conclude that mean of a population $= \mu_0$; otherwise, we reject the null H_0 and accept the alternate hypothesis that$_t$.

It is statistically desirable result when there is a little chance of accepting H_0 when it is false.

If the power is graphically plotted against all specified alternatives (like in testing the quality of a rating model across various rating grades), the curve obtained is known as 'Power Curve'. It determines the extent to which a test can discriminate between true and false null hypothesis.

The application of hypothesis testing in risk management has been further elaborated with the following numerical example.

Exercise: A bank has developed a new scoring model for evaluating the default risk of manufacturing firms. The model developer claims that the mean score for a safe borrower is 150 with a standard deviation of 5. Test

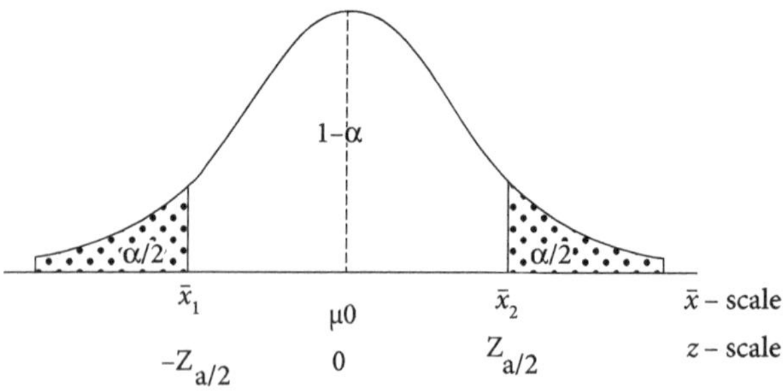

Figure 4.3 Level Significance and Critical Range

the hypothesis that mean (meu = μ) = 150 against the alternative hypothesis that $\mu \neq 150$ if a random sample of 50 safe borrowers is tested and found to have a mean score of 148. Use a 0.01 level of significance to perform the statistical test.

Solution: A stepwise solution is as follows:

$H_0: \mu = 150$
$H_1: \mu \neq 150$
$\alpha = 0.01.$

The critical region: $Z < -2.58$ and $Z > 2.58$ (since it is a two-tail test).

Note that z values are obtained from the standard normal table given at the end. One can also derive the z values using standard normal assumption using excel functions.

Since the obtained mean score = 148 and $n = 50$

The computed $z = \dfrac{148 - 150}{5/\sqrt{50}} = -2.828.$

Conclusion: Reject the H_0 and conclude that the average score for safe borrower is not equal to 150.

It is important to mention that the statisticians also perform one-tail test to be sure whether average credit score for safe borrowers (i.e. borrowers with high/highest credit worthiness) is greater than a threshold (say 150). In such cases, we have to look at one side of the tail of the standard normal distribution.

Statistical Significance through *t*-Statistic

The probability curve for t-distribution is symmetric about the line $t = 0$. As t increases, $f(t)$ decreases rapidly and trends to zero as t tends to infinity. However, the variance of t-distribution is greater than that of standard normal distribution and t-distribution is more flat on the top than the normal curve. Thus, the tails of the t-distribution have greater probability area than the tails of standard normal distribution. T statistic is used popularly used in statistical significance test. For large n (degrees of freedom), t-distribution tends to standard normal distribution.

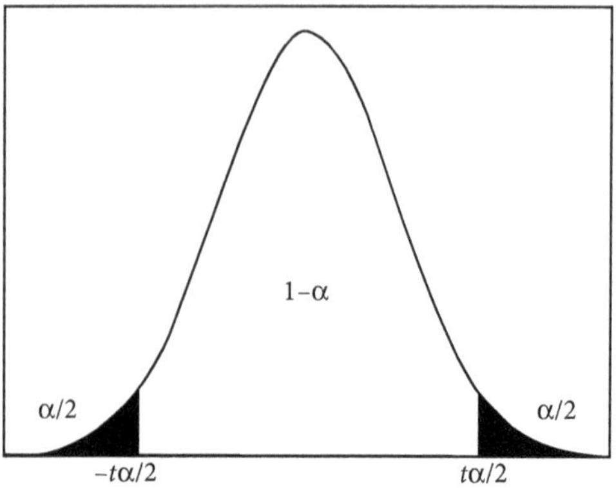

Figure 4.4 The *t*-Distribution (Two Tail)

The critical values of *t* can be interpreted from Figure 4.4. The critical values of *t* at level of significance α and d.f. v for two-tailed test are given by the equation:

$P[|t|>t_v(\alpha)] = \alpha$ is the rejection region
$P[|t|\leq t_v(\alpha)] = 1 - \alpha$ is the acceptance region.

The lower the rejection region, the greater the power of statistical test. The values of $t_v(\alpha)$ have been tabulated in Fisher and Yates' Tables for different values of α and v and are given in Table 2 in Appendix at the end of the book.

Since *t*-distribution is symmetric about $t = 0$, it can be shown that

$$P[(t > t_v(\alpha)] + P[t < -t_v(\alpha)] = \alpha$$

$$=> P[t > t_v(\alpha)] = \alpha / 2$$

Therefore, $P[t > t_v(2\alpha)] = \alpha$.

Alpha is the type I error rate. The lower the alpha, the greater the evidence in favour of statistical significance is. Figure 4.5 shows the acceptance zone and critical region for a two-tail test. The type I error zone (α) for one-tail test has been highlighted in Figure 4.6.

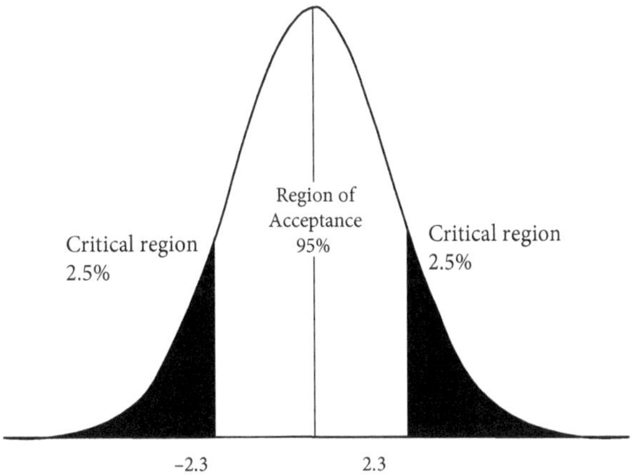

Figure 4.5 Two-Tailed Test at the 5% Level of Significance
Decision Rule: Reject null hypothesis if $|t| > t_{\alpha/2, df}$

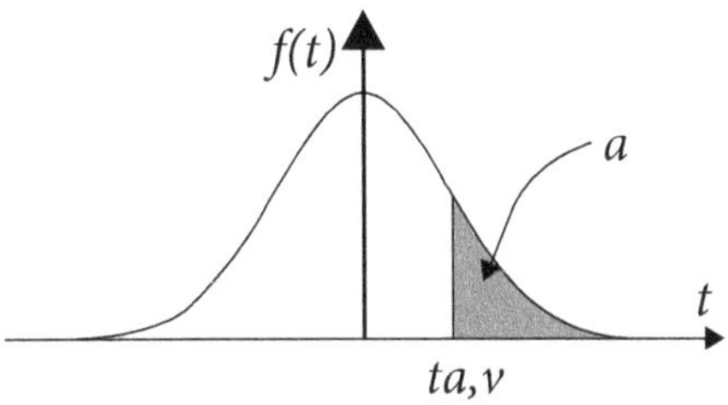

Figure 4.6 Hypothesis Testing *t*-Distribution (One Ttail)

$t_v(2\,\alpha)$ gives the significant value of t for a single-tail test (right tail or left tail since the distribution is symmetrical) at level of significance α and v degrees of freedom.

Example of One-Tailed Test

ABM bank has 300 zonal heads. The Human Resource Management head of the bank thinks that the average IQ on Risk Management Awareness is at least 110. To prove her point, she administers an IQ test to 20 randomly selected heads. Among the sampled zonal officers, the average IQ is 108 with a standard deviation of 10. Based on these results, should the HR principal accept or reject her original hypothesis? Assume a significance level of 0.01.

Solution

Null hypothesis: $\mu = 110$
Alternative hypothesis: $\mu < 110$
Note that these hypotheses constitute a one-tailed test. The null hypothesis will be rejected if the sample mean is too small.

Analyse the Sample Data

Using sample data, we compute the standard error (SE), degrees of freedom (DF), and the *t*-score test statistic (*t*).

SE = SD/sqrt(n)
= 10/sqrt(20)
= 10/4.472
= 2.236

Here, degrees of freedom (v)
= $n - 1 = 20 - 1 = 19$

The computed test statistic $t = (x - \mu)/\text{SE} = (108 - 110)/2.236 = -0.894$

Where SD is the standard deviation of the sample, SE is the standard error, x is the sample mean, μ is the hypothesized population mean, and n is the sample size.

Since we have a one-tailed test, the *p*-value is the probability that the *t*-score having 19 degrees of freedom is less than −0.894.

We use the *t*-distribution calculator to find $P(t < -0.894) = 0.19$. Thus, the *p*-value is 0.19. To confirm the table value of t at degrees of freedom 19, check the t-table given in the Appendix.

Statistical Test Results Interpretation

Since the *p*-value (0.19) is greater than the critical significance level (which is set at 0.01), we cannot reject the null hypothesis. This way, statistical test results are interpreted.

Mean Comparison Test (*t*-Test)

Many problems arise where we wish to test hypotheses about the means of two different populations (e.g. comparing ratios of defaulted and solvent firms or comparing performance of public sector bank vis-à-vis private banks etc.).

In order statistically check the differences, statisticians normally perform un-paired *t*-test.

The *t*-test is a popular statistical test to compare means between two groups (say defaulted vs. solvent).

Un-paired test:

$$H_0 : \bar{x}_1 - \bar{x}_2$$
$$H_A : \bar{x}_1 \neq \bar{x}_2$$

Start by assuming H_0 is true and use the following test statistic to arrive at a decision:

$$t = \frac{(observed\ difference) - (null\ difference)}{Standard\ Error\ of\ observed\ difference} \qquad \text{Eq. 4.1}$$

$$t = \frac{\bar{x}_1 - \bar{x}_2}{SE(\bar{x}_1 - \bar{x}_2)}$$

$$= \frac{\bar{x}_1 - \bar{x}_2}{\sqrt{\frac{s_1^2}{n_1} + \frac{s_2^2}{n_2}}} \qquad \text{Eq. 4.1a}$$

where SE: standard error; $\bar{x}_1 = mean\ of\ group\ 1$; $\bar{x}_2 = mean\ of\ group\ 2$; s_1^2 : variance of group 1; s_2^2 = variance of group 2; n_1 = number of observations in group 1 and n_2 = number of observations in group 2.

For pair-wise test, we commonly use pooled variance (s_p^2). It is estimated using the following equation:

$$s_p^2 = \frac{(n_1 - 1)s_1^2 + (n_2 - 1)s_2^2}{(n_1 - 1) + ((n_2 - 1)} \qquad \text{Eq. 4.2}$$

For pooled variance, the t-statistic value would be

$$t = \frac{\bar{x}_1 - \bar{x}_2}{s_p \sqrt{\frac{1}{n_1} + \frac{1}{n_2}}} \qquad \text{Eq. 4.3}$$

This is the test statistic for paired t-test.

A low p-value (< 0.05) will reject the null and a high p-value (> 0.10) will fail to reject the null.

It is important to note that the p-values are the probability values that confirm whether the evidence obtained is statistically significant or not. Statisticians have encoded evidence on a 0 to 1 scale, where smaller values establish greater evidence of statistical significance and p-value less than 0.05 is generally accepted benchmark.

Similarly, there is a paired t-test where equal pooled variance is considered in the t-test.

The above test can be used to compare and examine which variables or risk factors can significantly differentiate the solvent set of customers from their defaulted counterparts. Or, before building a regression model, an analysis can quickly check whether regression factors are meaningful or not.

These tests can be run in standard statistical packages like STATA, EVIEWS, SPSS, and also in R studio.

The pair-wise t-test has been further illustrated with an example. Suppose a marketing research firm tests the effectiveness of a new flavouring for a leading beverage company using a random sample survey of 20 people. Half of the total 20 people under study taste the beverage with old flavouring and the other half check their taste buds with new flavouring. The people under study are given a score chart which evaluates how enjoyable the beverage was. The higher the score, the better it tastes. The scores are given in Table 4.2.

In Table 4.2, we arranged the data systematically and performed pair-wise t-test with equal variance. The pooled variance is estimated using Equation 4.2, and the obtained value is 16.05. Next, we plug in the mean values of treatment group (BevgD = 1) and control group (BevgD = 0) and pooled variance into Equation 4.3 to obtain the t-value. Note that the obtained t-value is 2.1768 and it is higher than the critical t value (= 2.1009) obtained from statistical table at 5% level of significance and

Table 4.2 Example of Pair-Wise Mean Equality t-Test Testing the Effectiveness of New Flavour Given in the Beverage

Sample Code	BevgD=1 (Treatment Group)	Score of New Beverage	Sample Code	BevgD=0 (Control Group)	Score of Old Beverage
1	1	13	11	0	12
2	1	17	12	0	8
3	1	19	13	0	6
4	1	11	14	0	16
5	1	20	15	0	12
6	1	15	16	0	14
7	1	18	17	0	10
8	1	9	18	0	18
9	1	12	19	0	4
10	1	16	20	0	11
Obs.	10		10		
Mean		15	11.1		
Std. Dev.		3.65	4.33		
Poole Var.			16.05		
d.f.			18		
t with equal var.			2.1768		
p-value			0.0431		

Source: Author's own illustration

degrees of freedom of 18. Alternatively, we have estimated the type I error rate which is the p-value, and it is 0.0431. Hence, we can state that if we reject the null hypothesis of equal mean and accept that the mean differs, then we will commit a type I error of less than 5%. Thus, the mean difference is statistically significant.

The data reported in the above table is pooled in an excel template and exported to create work file in statistical package STATA. The data arrangement has been shown later. The same t-test was run in the package to cross check the test results. In stata, the following command was given:

```
ttest score,by(BevgD)
```

Where score is the pooled score given by all 20 people participated in the survey and 'BevgD' is the dummy variable that segregates the new

Table 4.3 Two-Sample t-Test with Equal Variances

Group |	Obs	Mean	Std. Err.	Std. Dev.	[95% Conf. Interval]	
0 |	10	11.1	1.369915	4.332051	8.001037	14.19896
1 |	10	15	1.154701	3.651484	12.38789	17.61211
Combined |	20	13.05	.9799973	4.382681	10.99884	15.10116
diff |		-3.9	1.791647		−7.664111	−.1358887
diff = mean(0) − mean(1)						t = −2.1768
Ho: diff = 0						Degrees of freedom = 18
Ha: diff < 0			Ha: diff!= 0			Ha: diff > 0
Pr($T < t$) = 0.0215			Pr(|T| > |t|) = 0.0431			Pr(T > t) = 0.9785

beverage (=1) from its older counterparts (=0). Statistical results are summarized below:

Now let us try to interpret the above reported t-test result (Table 4.3). Please note the mean and standard deviations of scores amongst two groups are summarized in the upper panel. The mean score for old group (=11.1) is reported first, followed by the score of new beverage (group 1, mean = 15). The null hypothesis states that H_0: diff = 0; i.e. mean (0) − mean(1) = 0. To arrive at a decision, we have to check the t-statistic and then look at the alternative hypothesis p-value. The obtained t-value = −2.1768 which is the same we have derived without the help of the package. To read the above table results, one should first check the alternate Ha: diff! = 0. Here, the p-value Pr($|T| > |t|$) = 0.0431. It means, if we reject the H_0 and accept the H_a, the type I error will be less than 5%. This is called two-tail test. Thus, we can conclude that there is a statistically significant difference in mean of perception. If we want to check whether first beverage (new type) tastes significantly better than the second one (old beverage). For this, we have to check the one-tail alternative hypotheses. If we check the right tail results, Ha: diff > 0 and Pr($T > t$) = 0.9785.

This states that if we reject null and accept the alternative hypothesis, then we will commit an error of 97.85%. Since it is higher than 5% threshold level, we should not accept the H_a. Now, look at the left-hand-side result. Here, Ha: diff < 0 and $\Pr(T < t) = 0.0215$. It means, if we reject H_0 and accept H_a, we will commit an error less than 5%. Thus, we conclude that means are unequal and mean score of new beverage (group 1) is significantly higher than the mean score of old beverage (group 2).

For unequal variance-based *t*-test, one has to write STATA command:

```
ttest score,by(BevgD) unequal
```

Non-Parametric Wilcoxon Rank-Sum Test

The Wilcoxon rank-sum test is a non-parametric alternative method to the two-sample *t*-test. The test statistic is computed based solely on the rank of values in which the observations are obtained from the two samples. Basically, it checks if there is a difference in distribution of values. It is also termed as median difference test.

The hypothesis statements function the same way as the two-sample *t*-test—but we are focused on the medians rather than on the means:

$$H_0: \eta_1 - \eta_2 = 0$$
$$H_1: \eta_1 - \eta_2 \neq 0$$

The Wilcoxon test is based upon ranking of the combined observations $(n_A + n_B)$. Each observation has a rank. The smallest has rank 1, the second smallest has rank 2, and so on. The Wilcoxon rank-sum test statistic is the sum of the ranks of the observations arranged in ascending order. These could also be expressed as one-tailed tests. The details about rank sum test have been discussed in Wild (1997) and also in Ronald et al. (2012).

Test Procedure

Step 1: List the data values from both samples in a single list arranged from the smallest to largest.

Step 2: In the next column, assign the numbers 1 to N (where $N = n_1 + n_2$). These are the ranks of the observations. As before, if there are ties, assign the average of the ranks that the values would receive to each of the tied values.

Step 3: Estimate the sum of the ranks $\left(\sum_{i=1}^{n} R_{1i}\right)$ for the obs. from population 1 and standard deviation of combined ranks.

To test the difference between rank-sum, the following statistics are used:

$$T = \sum_{i=1}^{n} R_{1i}; \qquad \text{Eq. 4.4}$$

$$E(T) = \frac{n_1(n_1 + n_2 + 1)}{2}; \qquad \text{Eq. 4.5}$$

$$\text{and } Var(T) = \frac{n_1 n_2 s^2}{(n_1 + n_2)}; \qquad \text{Eq. 4.6}$$

where $E(T)$ is expected rank and s is the standard deviation of combined ranks. This is standard deviation approach is used in STATA. However, theoretically, the following variance formula is also used:

$$Var(T) = \frac{n_1 n_2 (n_1 + n_2 + 1)}{12}; \qquad \text{Eq. 4.6a}$$

The test statistic is

$$z = \frac{T - E(T)}{\sqrt{Var(T)}}; \ \&\, z \sim N(0,1) \qquad \text{Eq. 4.7}$$

In Wilcoxon (1945) and Mann and Whitney (1947) rank-sum test, we are checking whether z is significant at 5% (i.e. $p < 0.05$); and then we can conclude that medians are statistically different.

If there is no difference between the two medians (and the null is true), the value of z will be around half the sum of the ranks—$\{(n_1(1 + N))/2\}$ and z will be insignificant.

Table 4.4a Wilcoxon Rank-Sum Test on Beverage Test Sample

Sample Code	BevgD = 1 (Treatment Group)	Perception Ranks New (R_1)	Sample Code	BevgD = 0 (Control Group)	Perception Ranks Old (R_2)
1	1	11	1	0	9
2	1	16	2	0	3
3	1	19	3	0	2
4	1	6.5	4	0	14.5
5	1	20	5	0	9
6	1	13	6	0	12
7	1	17.5	7	0	5
8	1	4	8	0	17.5
9	1	9	9	0	1
10	1	14.5	10	0	6.5
Total		130.5			79.5

Table 4.4b Wilcoxon Rank-Sum Test Statistics

Parameters	Values
n_1	10
n_2	10
R_1	130.5
R_2	79.5
$E(R_1)$	105
$StdDev.(T)=\sqrt{Var(T)}$	13.2
Z	1.93
p-value	0.053

We now have performed Wilcoxon rank-sum test on the same beverage data that we have recorded in Table 4.2. Since it is a non-parametric test, instead of observations, we have taken the ranked values. The ranked observations are documented in Table 4.4.

It is important to note that the rank values are tie adjusted.

Based on the above table figures, we summarize the Wilcoxon test results below:

The non-parametric test result confirms that we can reject the null hypothesis of equal distribution (or equal median) at a 5% significance (or error) level. Note that rank-sum test can accommodate outliers and large variation in values since the test statistic is based on rank of the observations. Hence, it is a better test than the *t*-test.

We now run the same test in STATA. For this, data have been arranged in the following order:

Table 4.5 tabulates the beverage data in orderly manner. The first column represents the person code. The second column records the perception score based on the questionnaire data. Beverage type and beverage dummy (D_Bevg) are presented in column third and fourth. The dummy has been created so that we can run the test in the statistical package that requires such codification. For statistical testing, it is

Table 4.5 Beverage Data in Template Form

Code	Percep_Score	Bevg_Type	D_Bevg	Rank	Revised Rank
1	13	New	1	11	11
2	17	New	1	16	16
3	19	New	1	19	19
4	11	New	1	6	6.5
5	20	New	1	20	20
6	15	New	1	13	13
7	18	New	1	17	17.5
8	9	New	1	4	4
9	12	New	1	8	9
10	16	New	1	14	14.5
11	12	Old	0	9	9
12	8	Old	0	3	3
13	6	Old	0	2	2
14	16	Old	0	15	14.5
15	12	Old	0	10	9
16	14	Old	0	12	12
17	10	Old	0	5	5
18	18	Old	0	18	17.5
19	4	Old	0	1	1
20	11	Old	0	7	6.5

necessary to specify control group (D_Bevg = 0) and treatment group (D_Bevg = 1). The rank values and revised ranks (tie adjusted) are presented in the last two columns. From Table 4.4, we can get back to figures reported in Table 4.3 results summary produced in STATA.

As a next step, we export the Table 4.5 data to STATA data editor and create the work file. After the creation of the work file (.dta), we run Wilcoxon rank-sum test using the following command in the STATA command box:

```
ranksum score,by(BevgD)
```

The test results are reproduced in Table 4.6:

We are getting the similar result in the package as well. The expected rank and sum of ranks and *z* values are similar like what we have obtained manually. We can conclude that there is a significant difference in scoring distribution between new beverage and old one. Hence, new beverage is significantly tastes better than the old one at around 5% level of significance.

Both mean comparison *t*-test and non-parametric Wilcoxon rank-sum test have important usage in developing statistical scorecard. These tests should be run before selecting ratios or factors in a multivariate

Table 4.6 Two-Sample Wilcoxon Rank-Sum (Mann-Whitney) Test

BevgD |	Obs	Rank Sum	Expected
0 |	10	79.5	105
1 |	10	130.5	105
Combined |	20	210	210

Unadjusted variance 175.00
Adjustment for ties −0.92

Adjusted variance 174.08
Ho: score(BevgD== 0) = score(BevgD== 1)
$z = -1.933$
Prob > $|z| = 0.0533$

model. When comparing ratios for solvent set of customers with their defaulted customers, these tests are conducted to check which variables/ ratios better differentiate 'good' firms from 'bad'. For details about STATA commands, refer STATA (2005) reference book.

Analysis of Variance (ANOVA)

An ANOVA hypothesis tests the difference in means between more than two groups. Examples: Studying the effectiveness of various training programmes on learning/skill development tests if occupational stress varies according to age, whether credit officers have different opinion about certain loan proposals, whether there is any difference between default rates across retail pools or job categories.

In this context, the following hypothesis is formed.

- H_0: All the age groups have equal stress on the average or $\mu_1 = \mu_2 = \mu_3$
- H_a: The mean stress of at least one age group is significantly different.

The one-way ANOVA is an extension of the independent two-sample *t*-test.

ANOVA basically tests how much of the variance of dependent variable (say occupational stress or default rates) is explained by the treatment group (job categories). Table 4.7 provides detail about crucial ANOVA test procedures and relevant test statistics to read and understand the results.

To run ANOVA in STATA (2005), we use following command:

oneway *y x*

where *y* is the dependent variable (DV) and *x* is the category (e.g. income class or programme types etc.).

Stata produces ANOVA table and read the F-statistic and *p*-value to test the hypothesis.

By default, it also reports Bartlett's test of equal variance across samples. It is also called homogeneity of variances. ANOVA (Fisher's test statistic) assumes that variances are equal across groups or samples. The Bartlett test can be used to verify the assumption.

Table 4.7 ANOVA Table

Source of Variation	d.f.	Sum of Squares	Mean Sum of Squares	F-Statistic	P-Value
Between (m groups)	$df_1 = m - 1$	SSB (sum of squared deviations of group means from grand mean)	SSB/$m - 1$	$\frac{SSB/m-1}{SSW/mn-m}$	Go to $F_{m-1,mn-m}$ chart to check the p-value
Within (n individual per group)	$df_2 = m \times (n - 1)$	SSW (sum of squared deviations of observations from their group mean)	SSW/$mn - m$		
Total variation	$m \times n - 1$	TSS (sum of squared deviations of observations from grand mean)	TSS = SSB + SSW		

The Levene test (in SPSS package) is an alternative to the Bartlett test that is less sensitive to departure from normality.

The Bartlett test statistic is designed to test for equality of variances across groups against the alternative that variances are unequal for at least two groups. It uses chi^2 test statistic to check the difference between pooled variance and group variance. If it is insignificant, then group variances are equal.

To perform ANOVA test in SPSS, go to Analyse=>Compare Means=>Oneway ANOVA. This is the most common way to run ANOVA.

ANOVA helps us to statistically check many hypotheses (e.g. whether stress level varies across job categories). It examines variability amongst the means and compares that against the variability within each mean in terms of individuals within each group.

Let us take an exercise to better understand the test results and interpret the crucial tests statistics.

Problem Statement: The Risk Management Department (RMD) in a bank wishes to compare four programmes for training workers to perform a certain risk calculation task. Twenty new MBAs are randomly assigned to the risk management training programmes, with five in each programme. At the end of the training period, a test is conducted to see how quickly trainees can perform the task. The number of times the task is performed per minute is recorded for each trainee, with the following results:

The data are sorted in a template form:

The records arranged in Table 4.8 can be used to perform ANOVA in statistical packages like SPSS and STATA. It can also be run in R studio.

To better understand the computation process, we present the following workout method for ANOVA test.

The above data are arranged in the following manner to compute the relevant test statistics (such as WSS, BSS, and TSS and F).

In Table 4.9, means of mean is the grand mean = average (11.8, 8.8, 12.2, 8.6) = 11.8.

SSB = 5 × (11.8 – 10.35)^2 + 5 × (8.8 – 10.35)^2 + 5 × (12.2 – 10.35)^2 + 5 × (8.6 – 10.35)^2 = 54.95

SSW = 14.8 + 10.8 + 6.8 + 9.2 = 41.6

The value 14.8 is the sum of the weights for programme 1. It is obtained by adding the sum squares deviations from the subgroup mean: (9 – 11.8)^2 + (12 – 11.8)^2 + (14 – 11.8)^2 + (11 – 11.8)^2 + (13 – 11.8)^2

Table 4.8 Data Template for ANOVA Analysis

Staff Code	Test Scores	Prog_Cat
1	9	1
2	12	1
3	14	1
4	11	1
5	13	1
6	10	2
7	6	2
8	9	2
9	9	2
10	10	2
11	12	3
12	14	3
13	11	3
14	13	3
15	11	3
16	9	4
17	8	4
18	11	4
19	7	4
20	8	4

From the above table, we can now compute Fisher's F-statistic = 7.0449.

Note that $F = (54.95/3) / (41.6/16) = 7.0449$.

The p-value corresponding $F = 7.0449$ is obtained excel by plugging in:

= FDIST(x,df1,df2)

= FDIST(7.0449,3,16)

= 0.0031

Hence the computed F-statistic is statistically significant since p-value is less than 1% (Prob > F = 0.0031). Therefore, we can reject the null hypothesis of equal mean across groups. One can compare these results with the detailed test statistics provided in Table 4.7 for interpretation purpose. Thus, there is statistically significant difference in performance due to training across groups. ANOVA examines variability amongst the means and compares that against the variability within each mean

Table 4.9 ANOVA Procedure

Observations	Prog 1	Weights	Prog 2	Weights	Prog 3	Weights	Prog 4	Weights
1	9	7.84	10	1.44	12	0.04	9	0.16
2	12	0.04	6	7.84	14	3.24	8	0.36
3	14	4.84	9	0.04	11	1.44	11	5.76
4	11	0.64	9	0.04	13	0.64	7	2.56
5	13	1.44	10	1.44	11	1.44	8	0.36
Total = Σyij	59	14.8	44	10.8	61	6.8	43	9.2
Mean of Groups (μj) = $\Sigma yij/Nj$	11.8		8.8		12.2		8.6	
Means of Mean	10.35							
SST	96.55	d.f.=	mn − 1		19			
SSW	41.6	d.f.=	$m(n-1)$	$mn-m$	16			
SSB	54.95	d.f.=	$m-1$		3			

Table 4.10 ANOVA Result Output in STATA

Source	Analysis of Variance				
	SS	df	MS	F	Prob > F
Between groups	54.95	3	18.3166667	7.04	0.0031
Within groups	41.6	16	2.6		
Total	96.55	19	5.08157895		

Bartlett's test for equal variances: $chi^2(3) = 0.5685$ Prob > $chi^2 = 0.904$

Table 4.11 Levene Test Results in SPSS

Test of Homogeneity of Variances			
Levene Statistic	Test scores		
	df1	df2	Sig.
.190	3	16	.902

in terms of individuals within each group. Hence, we have found enough empirical evidence that training from particular institutions has significant influence on risk computation performance skills.

When we run the same test using data arranged in 4.8 after creating work file in STATA, we obtain following results:

```
oneway testscores prog_cat
```

The ANOVA result STATA output has been documented in Table 4.10.

The same test performed in SPSS statistical package has been presented in Table 4.11.

STATA by default reports Bartlet's test of equal variance. The chi-square value is low and Prob > chi^2 > 10%. This means that the result does not suffer from heterogeneous variance. Note that, SPSS also reports the Levene test of homogeneity of variance which is similar to Bartlet's test. So, we run the same test in SPSS package as well and obtain the Levene test results.

We arrive at the similar conclusion that there no heterogeneity problem.

If there is a presence of heterogeneity of variance, we will have to check Brown-Forsythe test statistic that gives more protection non-normality

Table 4.12 ANOVA Result Output in SPSS

Part A:
ANOVA
Test Scores

	Sum of Squares	df	Mean Square	F	Sig.
Between Groups	54.950	3	18.317	7.045	.003
Within Groups	41.600	16	2.600		
Total	96.550	19			

Part B:
Robust Tests of Equality of Means
Test scores

	Statistic	df1	df2	Sig.
Welch	6.934	3	8.813	.011
Brown-Forsythe	7.045	3	14.837	.004

a. Asymptotically F distributed.

of the data. Similarly, if variance is heterogeneous, then look at whether Welch is statistically significant ($p < 0.01$) as it is a more robust estimate.

Table 4.12 reports same ANOVA test results and also robust tests of equality of means conducted in SPSS software. Welch is closest to what ANOVA is doing, but it accommodates heterogeneous variances. In both Welch and Brown-Forsythe test, one can notice that the degrees of freedom are different than the original F test.

Summary

Statistical hypothesis testing empowers the risk manager to gather statistical evidence in order to take conscious decision. It equips him/her to select a single alternative from a number of possible alternatives to take management decisions. We have explained steps to conduct statistical hypothesis using real-life business cases. Various parametric as well as non-parametric test procedures and their applications in banking have been discussed in this chapter with numerical examples. This chapter also elaborates statistical concepts pertaining to one-tail vs. two-tail hypothesis. It also explains the meaning of type I error and type II error and power of a statistical test. All these concepts will enable the reader to understand the meaning of statistical significance in data analysis. Two group difference mean *t*-test and rank-sum tests (treatment group vs. control group) and ANOVA test for multiple groups mean comparison tests have been explained with examples.

Review Questions

1. A market risk analyst is examining the loss rate from a bond return series. The bond rating is BBB. The return series has been analysed and statistical hypothesis is conducted (mean comparison test) in STATA. The result is summarized in Table 4.13:

Hint: Here, the reported probability value is the *p*-value, or marginal significance level, against a two-sided alternative. Since this probability value is greater than the size of the test which is 0.05, we cannot reject the null hypothesis. Thus, the mean returns 128 basis points.

Table 4.13 Hypothesis Testing and Significance Level

Hypothesis Testing for LOSS_RATE_BSP

Sample: 1 19
Included observations: 19

Test of hypothesis: Mean = 128
Assuming Std. Dev. = 72.45

Sample Mean = 127.68
Sample Std. Dev. = 72.45

Method	Value	Probability
Z-statistic	−0.019	0.985
t-statistic	−0.019	0.985

Table 4.14 Hypothesis Testing Part B

Hypothesis Testing for LOSS_RATE_BSP		
Sample: 1 19		
Included observations: 19		
Test of hypothesis: Mean = 80		
Assuming Std. Dev. = 72.45		
Sample mean = 127.68		
Sample Std. Dev. = 72.45		
Method	**Value**	**Probability**
t-statistic	2.869	0.0102

2. Now the same analyst examines bond loss rate where she hypothesizes that the mean loss rate would be 80 basis points. The test results are summarized in Table 4.14:

What would be the decision of the analyst? Whether null hypothesis will be rejected? Or it cannot rejected? Give your arguments.

3. Which statement is correct?

The higher the value *z*-statistic, the greater the chance that the null hypothesis of equal mean between two groups will be

   a) Accepted
   b) Rejected
   c) Uncertain
   d) Undefined

4. A researcher wants to empirically test if a sample of retail borrowers' debt to income ratio (DEBTINC) significantly differs by their default status (defaulted vs. non-defaulted; coded by 1 and 0). The researcher has performed a paired *t*-test in STATA. The test result is shown in Table 4.15.
   a) How will you interpret the tabulated result? Identify the one-tail and two-tail test results.

Table 4.15 Reading t-Test Result in STATA

Two-sample t-test with equal variances

Group |	Obs	Mean	Std. Err.	Std. Dev.	[95% Conf. Interval]	
0 |	952	8.076891	.1747247	5.391044	7.734	8.419781
1 |	548	13.14745	.3171213	7.42362	12.52452	13.77037
Combined |	1500	9.929333	.1722673	6.671884	9.591423	10.26724
diff |	−5.070554	.3330325	−5.723814	−4.417295		
	diff = mean(0) - mean(1)					$t = -15.2254$
	Ho: diff = 0					Degrees of freedom = 1498
		Ha: diff < 0		Ha: diff!= 0		Ha: diff > 0
	$Pr(T < t) = 0.0000$	$Pr(\|T\| > \|t\|) = 0.0000$	$Pr(T > t) = 1.0000$			

b) Read the two-tail test, what will be your conclusion? Whether the difference is statistically significant?
c) Which group has relatively higher debt to income ratio? Is this statistically significant?
d) What are control group and the treatment group? What is the STATA command for running this test?

5. Suppose you test the effectiveness of a new fuel additive. You run an experiment with 24 cars: 12 cars with the fuel treatment and 12 cars without. You input the dataset with 24 observations. The variable 'mpg' records the mileage rating and treats records 0 if the mileage corresponds to untreated fuel and 1 if it corresponds to treated fuel. Using rank-sum test in STATA, we get the results in Table 4.16:
   a) What this result indicates?
   b) How will you compute the Z value? (Mention the formula and the estimate)
   c) Write the STATA command?
   d) Is it a better test than the t-test? And why?
6. Which option is the correct statement? In a hypothesis test, type I error refers to when
   a) A null hypothesis is accepted when it is true
   b) A null hypothesis is rejected when it is true

Table 4.16 Two-Sample Wilcoxon Rank-Sum (Mann-Whitney) Test

Treat	Obs	Rank sum	Expected
0	12	128	150
1	12	172	150
Combined	24	300	300

Unadjusted variance 300.00
Adjusted for ties −4.04

Adjusted variance 295.96
H_0: mpg(treat == 0) = mpg(treat == 1)
$Z = -1.279$
Prob > $|z| = 0.2010$

c) A null hypothesis is accepted when it is false
d) A null hypothesis is rejected when it is false

7. Select the write option. Jarque-Berra (JB) statistics follow
   a) Normal distribution
   b) T-distribution
   c) F-distribution
   d) Chi^2 distribution
8. In ANOVA test, if between-sum squared is 100 and within-sum squared is 200 and there are four groups and 20 observations per group, the estimated Fisher's F-statistic would be
   a) < 5
   b) 5–10
   c) 10–15
   d) >15
9. Based on the above results, now comment whether ANOVA F-test is statistically significant?
   a) p-value < 1%
   b) 1% < p-value < 5%
   c) 5% < p-value < 10%
   d) p-value > 10%

References

Mann, H. B. and Whitney, D. R. (1947). On a Test of Whether One of Two Random Variables is Stochastically Larger than the other. *Annals of Mathematical Statistics*, Vol. 18, pp. 50–60.

Nagar, A. L. and R. K. Das (1983). 'Basic Statistics', 2nd Edition, Oxford, New Delhi.

STATA (2005). Manual-ranksum. URL: https://www.stata.com/manuals13/rranksum.pdf

Walpole, R. E., R. H. Myers, S. L. Myers, and K. Ye (2012). 'Probability and Statistics for Engineers and Scientists', 9th Edition, Prentice Hall, USA.

Wilcoxon, F. (1945). Individual Comparisons by Ranking Methods. *Biometrics*, Vol. 1, pp. 80–83.

Wild, C. (1997). The Wilcoxon Rank-Sum Test, mimeo, University of Auckland. URL: https://www.stat.auckland.ac.nz/~wild/ChanceEnc/Ch10.wilcoxon.pdf

5

Matrix Algebra and their Application in Risk Prediction and Risk Monitoring

Matrix algebra has numerous application in the measurement of credit risk as well as market risk. A matrix is a rectangular array of elements. The order of a matrix is given by the number of rows and the number of columns. The transition matrix is derived from the concept of matrix algebra. It provides us the profile of credit quality changes or migrations that have taken place for the selected credit portfolio between any two years that are selected. Transition matrix is a promising tool for credit portfolio capital allocation, loan monitoring, and performance evaluation. It is popularly used in monitoring performance bond portfolios as well. It uses Markov chain process to estimate the probabilities of migration.

Transition Matrix Analysis—Computation of Probability of Default

To better understand the methodology for computing rating transition matrix, let us take a numerical example. Suppose Delta Bank Ltd. is a lending institution, and its IRMD has studied the historical rating migration pattern of IG- and NIG-rated corporates over past five years. The following yearly cohorts capture their rating movements including default.

These cohorts can be created using PIVOT table in excel.

Using the migration count, one can estimate one-year average probability (for period 2015–2019) that IG-rated borrower will be downgraded to NIG (refer to Table 5.1). The year-wise rating migration probabilities (e.g. P_{11}, P_{12}, . . . , $P_{1,D}$, . . . $P_{21,}$ . . . .P_{nD}) for different rating grades can be estimated by counting the number of companies migrating from grade in the

Table 5.1 Computation of Rating Transition Matrix from Yearly Rating Migration

		2016						2017			
		IG	NIG	D	Total			IG	NIG	D	Total
2015	IG	600	40	10	650	2016	IG	570	45	15	630
	NIG	60	350	40	450		NIG	65	370	45	480
		2018						2019			
		IG	NIG	D	Total			IG	NIG	D	Total
2017	IG	546	45	21	612	2018	IG	565	40	15	620
	NIG	50	410	60	520		NIG	70	400	45	515

Source: Author's own analysis of data

Table 5.2 Estimation of One-Year Average Rating Transition Probabilities

	IG	NIG	D
IG	P_{11}= (600+570+546+565)/ (650+630+612+620)	P_{12}= (40+45+45+40)/ (650+630+612+620)	P_{1D}= (10+15+21+15)/ (650+630+612+620)
NIG	P_{21}=(60+65+50+70)/ (60+65+50+70)	P_{22}=(350+370+410+400)/ (60+65+50+70)	P_{2D}=(40+45+60+45)/ (60+65+50+70)
D	P_{1D}=(0+0+0+0)/ (60+65+50+70)	P_{2D}=(0+0+0+0)/ (60+65+50+70)	P_{nD}=(0/(60+65+50+70)

beginning year to end grade over the one year. This has to be counted and added for each migration and for grade and dividing by the total number of firms in that grade at the beginning of the year. This has been explained in the following formula:

$$P_{ij} = \frac{T_{ij}^{2015-16} + T_{ij}^{2016-17} + T_{ij}^{2017-18} + T_{ij}^{2018-19}}{N_{ij}^{2015} + N_{ij}^{2016} + N_{ij}^{2017} + N_{ij}^{2018}} \qquad \text{Eq. 5.1}$$

where P_{ij} is the probability that borrower in the beginning year at ith rating grade at tth time period moves to jth grade at the end of the year. Note that i rating may be different from j rating. This is for different grades movement. For within grades retention, $i = j$.

The probability calculations using Equation 5.1 are reported in Table 5.2 transition matrix.

Table 5.3 Estimated Migration Probabilities Including PD

	IG	NIG	D
IG	90.804%	6.768%	2.428%
NIG	12.468%	77.863%	9.669%
D	0.000%	0.000%	100.000%

The estimated probabilities for different cells of the rating migration matrix are reported in Table 5.3.

Note that the sum of probabilities for IG as well as NIG grade = 100% which is the total space of the matrix. The above matrix is termed as square matrix since number of rows = number of columns.

Similarly, one-year average probability that a company is moving from *ith* to *jth* rating is given by formula:

$$\frac{T_{i,j}}{N_i} \qquad \text{Eq. 5.2}$$

In the same logic, the default probability of default (PD) of obligors from the rating grade (say *i*) or industry is given by

$$\frac{T_{i,D}}{N_i} \qquad \text{Eq. 5.3}$$

The average historical one-year default probability (also known as the expected default probability or expected default frequency) for *i*th rating grade or industry (PD*i*) is obtained by weighted average:

$$PD_i = \sum_{i=1}^{n} w_i^t \frac{T_{i,D}^t}{N_i^t} \qquad \text{Eq. 5.4}$$

where weight

$$w_i^t = \frac{N_i^t}{\sum_{s=1}^{n} N_i^s} \qquad \text{Eq. 5.5}$$

Using Equation 5.5, we obtain that the rating-wise marginal PD (MPD) as well as average annual PD is estimated. These formulations are given in Servigny and Renault (2004). Schuermann and Hanson (2004) explains the transition matrix-based probability of default measures.

Note that MPDs are computed using Equation 5.3. The weights are estimated using Equation 5.5.

Finally, we obtain annual average PD for both IG and NIG categories of borrowers using Equation 5.4.

The estimated average PD for IG (i.e. PD_{IG}) is the weighted sum of MPDs. It is estimated like this:

$$1.538\% \times 0.259 + 2.381\% \times 0.251 + 3.431\% \times 0.244 + 2.419\% \times 0.247 = 2.428\%.$$

This value is same as if we divide sum of counts of D by sum of counts of N (61/2512 = 2.428%) for IG-graded borrowers. Thus, our weighted PD method specified in Equations 5.1 and 5.4 produces same result.

In the same manner, we can compute annual average PD for NIG borrower and this estimate is (PD_{NIG}) 9.669%.

Using Table 5.4 figures, one can estimate the cumulative probability of default (CPD) based on mortality analysis. Many globally established rating agencies use the following formula to compute CPD from annual MPDs.

Table 5.4 Computation of Yearly Marginal PDs and Annual Average PD

Year	IG				NIG			
	N	D	MPD	Weight	N	D	MPD	Weight
2015–2016	650	10	1.538%	0.259	450	40	8.889%	0.229
2016–2017	630	15	2.381%	0.251	480	45	9.375%	0.244
2017–2018	612	21	3.431%	0.244	520	60	11.538%	0.265
2018–2019	620	15	2.419%	0.247	515	45	8.738%	0.262
Total	2512	61		1	1965	190		1
Annual PD			2.428%					

Source: Author's own

$$CPD(n) = d(1) + d(2) \times (1 - d(1)) + d(3) \times \left(1 - d(1)\right) \times (1 - d(2)) + \ldots + d(n)\prod^{n-1}\left(1 - d(n)\right), \quad \text{Eq. 5.6}$$

where $d(n)$ is marginal probability of defaults or year default rates and n represents year. The cumulative PD formulation method has been referred in Hamilton (2002, 2006) and Bandyopadhyay (2019).

This method is further illustrated with an example. If we focus on NIG borrowers, using expression 5.6, we can obtain four-year CPD. It is also termed as CPD(4).

Here, CPD(4) = MPD(1) + MPD(2) × (1 – MPD(1)) + MPD(3) × (1–MPD(1)) × (1–MPD(2)) + MPD(4) × (1 – MPD(1)) × (1 – MPD(2)) × (1 – MPD(3)).

Thus, the estimate value for NIG CPD(4) =

8.889% + 9.375% × (1 – 8.889%) + 11.538% × (1 – 8.889%) × (1 – 9.375%) + 8.738% × (1 – 8.889%) × (1 – 9.375%) × (1 – 11.538%)
= 33.34%.

CPD depicts the probability of a borrower over a horizon of four years from now.

Using the same approach, we can obtain NIG CPD(3) = 26.96%. Similarly, CPD(3) provides us cumulative probability of default of NIG borrower over a horizon of three years onwards from now. In the same manner, one can also estimate CPDs for IG borrowers as well for different time horizons. CPDs are important for calculating credit spread for long-term loans. It is also used for estimation of expected credit loss (ECL) for life time of the loan or assets.

Next, we have studied the global corporate rating migration pattern that has been studied using yearly data published by Standard and Poor (S&P). We have gone through rating migration statistics given by S&P (2018). The average migration pattern across investment grade (AAA to BBB) and non-investment grade (BB to CCC) has been documented below:

Table 5.5 One-Year Average Global Corporate Rating Transition, 1981–2018

	IG	NIG	Default
IG	93.06%	1.87%	0.09%
NIG	2.26%	82.64%	3.66%
Default	0.00%	0.00%	100%

Source: S&P published data.

As can be observed from the probability figures reported in Table 5.5, 93.06% is the probability that a corporate begins the year as IG category remains in the same category at the end of the year as well. Similarly, 1.87% is the estimated probability that IG corporates will be downgraded to NIG category within a year. In the same logic, 2.26% is the probability that a NIG corporate will be upgraded to IG category within one year. In the same manner, the PD for IG category corporate is estimated as 0.09%. In comparison, the NIG rate corporate's one-year PD is significantly higher, and it is estimated as 3.66%.

The S&P annual average rating transition matrix is reported in Table 5.6. This depicts the overall corporate risk position globally. S&P matrix can be used as a good benchmark for comparing credit risk. The Study of Rating Transition Matrix and Estimation of PD are useful for management of credit risk. It is popularly used in credit allocation decisions, the follow-up of credit commitments, monitoring, and reporting processes.

Measurement of the PD over a given investment horizon is often the first step in credit risk modelling, management, and pricing. The PD estimate enables investor or risk analyst to estimate the credit risk inherent in their investment portfolio. The migration statistics as reported in Table 5.6 can be used for bond valuation as well. The correlation between ratings and yields is well established in the finance literature.

Using CRISIL's published rating data, following one-year average rating transition matrix has been constructed:

Table 5.7 reports the seven-year average transition matrix is constructed based on loan-rating movements of 300 large corporates. These yearly loan ratings are published by CRISIL over the time period 2008–2015. It is a square matrix. The diagonal probabilities give us estimates of rating retention. The off-diagonal probabilities are capturing the rating

Table 5.6 S&P Global Transition Matrix, 1981–2016, All Global Corporate Obligors

	AAA	AA	A	BBB	BB	B	CCC/C	Default	NR
AAA	87.05%	9.03%	0.53%	0.05%	0.08%	0.03%	0.05%	0.00%	3.17%
AA	0.52%	86.82%	8.00%	0.51%	0.05%	0.07%	0.02%	0.02%	3.99%
A	0.03%	1.77%	87.79%	5.33%	0.32%	0.13%	0.02%	0.06%	4.55%
BBB	0.01%	0.10%	3.51%	85.56%	3.79%	0.51%	0.12%	0.18%	6.23%
BB	0.01%	0.03%	0.12%	4.97%	76.98%	6.92%	0.61%	0.72%	9.63%
B	0.00%	0.03%	0.09%	0.19%	5.15%	74.26%	4.46%	3.76%	12.06%
CCC/C	0.00%	0.00%	0.13%	0.19%	0.63%	12.91%	43.97%	26.78%	15.39%

Source: S&P Annual Global Corporate Default Study

Table 5.7 Corporate Rating Transition in India

		T+1							
		AAA	**AA**	**A**	**BBB**	**BB**	**B**	**CCC**	**D**
	AAA	**98.39%**	1.61%	0.00%	0.00%	0.00%	0.00%	0.00%	0.00%
	AA	0.44%	**92.94%**	4.42%	1.99%	0.00%	0.22%	0.00%	0.00%
T	A	0.00%	4.60%	**89.08%**	5.36%	0.38%	0.00%	0.00%	0.57%
	BBB	0.00%	0.00%	4.83%	**82.82%**	9.85%	0.77%	0.19%	1.54%
	BB	0.00%	0.00%	0.45%	9.55%	**74.09%**	5.91%	0.91%	9.09%
	B	0.00%	1.69%	0.00%	3.39%	6.78%	**64.41%**	3.39%	20.34%
	CCC	0.00%	0.00%	0.00%	0.00%	0.00%	7.14%	**71.43%**	21.43%
	D	0.00%	0.00%	0.00%	0.00%	0.00%	0.00%	0.00%	100%

Source: CRISIL Rating Scan

slippage. For example, the estimate 98.39% is measuring the probability that an AAA-rated borrower in the current year will remain as AAA in the next year as well. The probability figure 1.61% gives us what proportion of AAA-rated borrower at the beginning of the year will downgrade one notch to AA at the end of the year. Note that there is no other migration of AAA. If we add all these probabilities, we get total probability = 100% which is the total probability space in the matrix. The probability that a AAA will move to end rating D is 0%. Thus, we can say that PD of a AAA-rated corporate loan is equal to 0%. Similarly, PD of a BBB-rated borrower asked for bank loan is 1.54%. The CCC-rated borrower is the riskiest since it not only carries the highest PD = 21.43% but also has comparatively very low rating stability (only 71.43% retention rate).

Note that the banks and Fis can use the transition matrix for valuation of assets as well as loan portfolio monitoring. The industry level, geography-wise matrices would enable the bank to compare slippage movements and proactively monitor their loan portfolio.

Further, to better understand the portfolio movement, the risk management department (RMD) should monitor how the loan exposures are shifting from low-risk segment (AAA-A) to moderate risk (BBB and BB), to high risk (B and CCC) and even default (default) through a cohort analysis as described in Table 5.8.

RMD can also monitor the pattern across geographies (East, West, Central, North, etc.) and across regions and industries. This will enable them to better understand the portfolio movement and control future non-performing assets (NPAs) by restricting further slippage.

As shown in Table 5.9, the transition matrix has been generated using rating history of 5,315 corporates in India. In order to predict

Table 5.8 Grade-Wise Portfolio Risk Monitoring Matrix

	LR >50%	MR <40%	HR <5%	Default <5%
LR(AAA-A) & ceiling >50%				
MR (BBB & BB) & ceiling<40%				
HR(B & CCC) &<5%				
Default (ceiling<5%)				

Table 5.9 A TTC Transition Matrix Analysis for Indian Corporates

		T+1							
		AAA	*AA*	*A*	*BBB*	*BB*	*B*	*C*	*D*
	AAA	***98.210%***	1.535%	0.000%	0.000%	0.000%	0.256%	0.000%	*0.000%*
	AA	1.174%	***95.054%***	3.437%	0.168%	0.080%	0.000%	0.000%	*0.084%*
	A	0.000%	3.072%	***91.126%***	4.778%	0.853%	0.000%	0.043%	*0.085%*
T	*BBB*	0.000%	0.063%	3.880%	***86.841%***	7.845%	0.380%	0.148%	*0.844%*
	BB	0.000%	0.000%	0.130%	8.071%	***81.264%***	5.284%	0.259%	*4.992%*
	B	0.057%	0.000%	0.057%	0.631%	13.876%	***73.108%***	1.261%	*11.009%*
	C	0.000%	0.000%	0.000%	0.000%	6.250%	17.969%	***49.219%***	*26.563%*
	D	0.000%	0.000%	0.000%	0.000%	0.000%	0.000%	0.000%	*100.000%*

the migration probabilities reported in the above matrix, we have studied the yearly cohort-wise their migration pattern for the period 2000–2019. Since it is based on a longer time history, the above estimates give us through the cycle (TTC) probability predictions. It is TTC because it provides long-term and stable estimates. The above migration matrix can be used by banks as well as Fis who are engaged in corporate lending to predict future rating migration (up-gradation as well as down-gradation) including migration to default. The last column of the matrix gives us the estimates of long run average PD (annual PD).

Matrix Multiplication and Estimation of PD for Different Time Horizons

Matrix multiplication is achieved by repeated applications of vector multiplication. This has been shown as follows:

$$\underset{(2\times3)}{\begin{bmatrix} a_1\vec{b}_1c_1 \\ a_2b_2c_2 \end{bmatrix}} \times \underset{(3\times2)}{\begin{bmatrix} p_1p_2 \\ q_1q_2 \\ r_1r \end{bmatrix}} \downarrow \qquad \text{Eq. 5.7}$$

First matrix has order 2 × 3 and second one has order 3 × 2.

Arrows show the multiplication direction in respect of row with column.

After multiplication, we obtain following square matrix of order 2 × 2.

$$\begin{bmatrix} a_1p_1 + b_1q_1 + c_1r_1 & a_1p_2 + b_1q_2 + c_1r_2 \\ a_2p_1 + b_2q_1 + c_2r & a_2p_2 + b_2q_2 + c_2r_2 \end{bmatrix} \qquad \text{Eq. 5.8}$$

This way, matrix multiplication works. Matrix properties and multiplication rules are elaborated in great details in Chakravorty and Ghosh (1972).

Matrix multiplication algebraic method can be used to estimate forward looking CPD as well as conditional probability of default. This exercise has been demonstrated here with an example.

We first estimate two-year point-in-time (PIT) transition matrix based on a bank's rating data. This has been estimated using migration history from 2016 to 2017 and 2017 to 2018. The average migration behaviour has been estimated using the Markov method. Since it reflects the risk behaviour of recent years, we can consider it as PIT estimates of rating movements including movement to default.

The average 5-year transition matrix (2013–2018) has been reported in Table 5.10:

Next, we apply matrix multiplication to derive CPDs (Chris Marrison, 2002). CPDs are important to find out default probabilities over future horizon years for different rating buckets. This is crucial for derivation of ECL for stage 2 accounts as stipulated in IFRS 9 global accounting standard.

It is important to note that International Financing Reporting Standards 9 (IFRS 9) has introduced fundamental changes in credit impairment standards and assessment of loss allowances which are expected to have a significant impact on the financial statements of banks and financial institutions. India has adopted Indian Accounting Standards (Ind AS) that is line with IFRS 9. The Reserve Bank of India (RBI) has extended the implementation deadline for commercial banks beyond the original date of implementation of 1 April 2018. However, many non-bank financial institutions (NBFCs) have already migrated to IFRS financial statements. In line with IFRS 9, Ind AS 109 has introduced a forward-looking approach for identification of credit impairment and estimation of ECL that will enable banks to make timely and adequate accounting treatment of loss provisions.

The International Financial Reporting Standards 9 (IFRS9) rule has introduced important changes in credit impairment standards since it suggests accounting practice should recognize expected loss-based provision in the balance sheet instead of incurred loss-based provisioning. The risk drivers of ECL are PD (probability of default), LGD (loss-given default), and EAD (exposure at default). Three stages have been specified under the new accounting standard to determine the amount of impairment to be recognized as ECL at each reporting date.

Table 5.10 Recent 2-Year Average PIT Transition Matrix (2013–2018)

	BR1	BR2	BR3	BR4	BR5	BR6	BR7	BR8	Default
BR1	66.67%	33.33%	0.00%	0.00%	0.00%	0.00%	0.00%	0.00%	0.00%
BR2	1.15%	65.38%	26.92%	6.15%	0.38%	0.00%	0.00%	0.00%	0.00%
BR3	0.00%	5.18%	66.28%	21.11%	4.59%	0.20%	0.10%	0.00%	2.54%
BR4	0.00%	1.05%	14.53%	60.99%	13.93%	2.79%	0.53%	0.15%	6.02%
BR5	0.00%	0.00%	2.62%	22.13%	49.64%	11.50%	1.89%	0.15%	12.08%
BR6	0.00%	0.00%	0.44%	5.75%	15.93%	38.50%	12.39%	2.21%	24.78%
BR7	0.00%	0.00%	0.00%	0.00%	5.88%	16.18%	27.94%	5.88%	44.12%
BR8	0.00%	0.00%	0.00%	0.00%	0.00%	0.00%	6.67%	33.33%	60.00%
Default	0.00%	0.00%	0.00%	0.00%	0.00%	0.00%	0.00%	0.00%	100.00%

IFRS9 introduces a three-stage approach to impairment as follows:

- Stage 1—the recognition of 12-month ECLs that is the portion of lifetime ECLs from default events that are expected within 12 months of the reporting date, if credit risk has not increased significantly since initial recognition. For this, banks need to estimate 12-month PD which has been reported in the last column of the matrix presented in Table 5.10. In stage 1, 12-month ECL = EAD × LGD × $PD_{1year.}$
- Stage 2—lifetime ECLs for financial instruments for which credit risk has increased significantly since initial recognition. For stage 2, due to significant increase in credit risk, banks need to estimate lifetime PD for the remaining maturity of the loan. Here comes the concept of CPD which can be estimated through matrix multiplication that we are discussing now. Here, Lifetime ECL = EAD × LGD × Lifetime CPD (or Conditional PD).
- Stage 3—lifetime ECLs for financial instruments which are credit impaired. Here, PD is considered as 100% since the loan has already defaulted. Hence, Lifetime ECL = (Outstanding + Overdues) × LGD.

12-month ECLs are the portion of the lifetime ECLs that result from default events that are possible within the next 12 months weighted by the probability of that default occurring. At initial recognition, a 12-month ECL is provided for. At the next reporting date, ECL will become lifetime, i.e. the losses that might occur in the whole life of the asset are that there is a significant increase in the credit risk of the account. Finally, if the account becomes impaired of non-performing, it is categorized as stage 3 and lifetime ECL is calculated for it.

Let us now comeback to the original computation part. In this approach, we have used most recent PIT transition matrix of the bank and then using matrix multiplication (row×column) to derive CPDs. Matrix multiplication can be done in Excel using function 'MMULT (array1, array2)', where array 1 (say BR3 row probabilities as highlighted in Table 5.10) is the first array to multiply and array 2 (Default column as highlighted in Table 5.10) is the second array to multiply.

The estimated CPD figures across various rating grades are reported in Table 5.11.

Table 5.11 CPDs Derived from Rating Migration History

Horizon (Years)	BR1	BR2	BR3	BR4	BR5	BR6	BR7	BR8
0	0.00%	0.00%	0.00%	0.00%	0.00%	0.00%	0.00%	0.00%
1	0.00%	0.00%	2.54%	6.02%	12.08%	24.78%	44.12%	60.00%
2	0.00%	1.10%	6.14%	12.76%	23.25%	43.39%	64.69%	82.94%
3	0.37%	3.25%	10.58%	19.63%	32.94%	55.80%	75.46%	91.96%
4	1.33%	6.31%	15.56%	26.25%	41.03%	64.06%	81.57%	95.68%
5	2.99%	10.11%	20.82%	32.44%	47.71%	69.78%	85.32%	97.33%

It may be noticed that the figures in Table 5.11 are CPDs, which gives the probability of having fallen into the default grade. It shows the PD over five years.

Few globally best practiced banks extract z index from normally plotted smooth transition matrix and then compare with good time as well as bad time-rating transition matrix. After extracting the z index that represents the common macroeconomic effects, they project the forward-looking z index and apply on those transition matrices and generate forward-looking CPDs through matrix multiplication. This z index adjustment has been explained in J. P. Morgan (1998) technical paper and also in Perederiy(2015).

We can estimate the conditional PDs from the CPDs. The conditional probability is the probability that the borrower will default in the given year, given that it did not default in any of the previous years. The conditional probability for a given year is estimated using the following formula:

$$PD - conditional\ at\ T = \frac{PDcum,\ T - PDcum,\ T-1}{1 - PDcum,\ T-1} \qquad \text{Eq. 5.9}$$

These conditional PDs can be used to derive ECL estimates for stage 2 accounts (under IFRS 9) that are having data on amortizing EAD for each of the future years up to contractual maturity as shown in Table 5.12.

Table 5.12 Conditional PDs Derived from CPDs

Horizon (Years)	BR1	BR2	BR3	BR4	BR5	BR6	BR7	BR8
0	0.00%	0.00%	0.00%	0.00%	0.00%	0.00%	0.00%	0.00%
1	0.00%	0.00%	2.54%	6.02%	12.08%	24.78%	44.12%	60.00%
2	0.00%	1.10%	3.70%	7.17%	12.70%	24.75%	36.82%	57.35%
3	0.37%	2.17%	4.73%	7.87%	12.63%	21.91%	30.49%	52.87%
4	0.964%	3.17%	5.57%	8.24%	12.06%	18.70%	24.92%	46.32%
5	1.68%	4.05%	6.22%	8.39%	11.33%	15.90%	20.30%	38.21%

These PDs can be used as forward-looking PDs for estimation of ECL for stage 2 accounts for which amortizing EAD data are available. However, for stage 1,estimation of ECLs, bank will have to used 1 year PDs (or 12 months) given in the 2nd rows of the above two tables. It is important to mention that these forward-looking PDs are derived based on purely historical pattern and trends. This has been proposed in the new accounting standard popularly known as IFRS9. Under the proposed new norms, banks as well as Fis are supposed to make loan loss provisions based on their exposure to exposure internal estimation of expected loss. Accordingly, the provision amount will have impact on their cost of credit and profitability.

It is interesting to note that using conditional PD formula given in Equation 5.9, we can get back to the same yearly marginal PDs (as reported in Table 5.4) from CPDs. For example, let us consider CPD(4) NIG borrowers which was estimated as 33.34% and take NIG CPD(3) estimate of 26.96%. Now using Equation 5.9, we can get back marginal PD for NIG borrower at year 4. Thus, MPD4 = 1 – (1 – CPD(4)/(1 – CPD(3))

=1 – (1 – 33.34%) / (1 – 26.96%)
=8.738%.

It is the same marginal PD for NIG for the cohort year 2018–2019 that has been reported in Table 5.4.

This way, the bank can take historical view to derive forward-looking PD curves for ECL estimation.

Statistical Test on Significant Increase in Credit Risk (SICR)

For significant increase in credit risk (SICR) as specified in IFRS 9, a bank may consider down-gradation from high-grade (HG: AAA & AA) to mid-grade (MG: A & BBB) category or to Risky grade (RG: BB & below) in a year as additional indicator besides 30 days past due. This is due to the fact that rating stability may sharply deteriorate and PD also significantly increases as a combined signal for SICR. Risk managers need to be very careful about such early warning signals and take necessary precautions to mitigate the credit risk. As per the accounting standard, with clear indication about SICR, risk analyst will have to now apply lifetime PD instead of 12-month PD for estimation of expected loss-based provision.

A statistical hypothesis test has been conducted, and results are reported in Table 5.13 to demonstrate how hypothesis testing can give more confidence to the risk analyst to prove the happening of significant increase in credit risk in a rated loan portfolio. This has important implications on portfolio management of credit risk as well.

We have performed a statistical *Z* test that demonstrates that PDs of high grade (HG) and mid-grade (MG) are significantly different than PDs of risky grade (RG). In both the tests, the null hypothesis (H0) is that

Table 5.13 Statistical Tests for Determining Rating Migration-Based SICR Criteria

PD of HG vs. PD of RG				PD of MG vs. PD of RG			
PD_{HG}	0.03%	N_{HG}	19	PD_{MG}	0.75%	N_{MG}	795
PD_{RG}	14.53%	N_{RG}	289	PD_{RG}	14.53%	N_{RG}	289
$H_0: PD_{RG} \le PD_{HG}$ $H_1: PD_{RG} > PD_{HG}$				$H_0: PD_{MG} \le PD_{RG}$ $H_1: PD_{MG} > PD_{RG}$			
σ_D	0.0211					σ_D	0.0210
Z_t	6.8706					Z_t	6.5744
$Z_{5\%}$	1.6448					$Z_{5\%}$	1.6449
$Z > Z_{5\%}$	Reject Null					$Z > Z_{5\%}$	Reject Null

Source: Author's own illustration based on internal rating data analysis of a financial institution

PD of RG grade is not statistically higher than PD of HG or MG grades. In both the tests, the null hypothesis is rejected at 5% level of significance and alternate hypothesis was accepted. Thus, we conclude that PD of RG is significantly higher than the PD of HG. Similarly, PD of RG is significantly higher than the PD of MG. Thus, a rating down-gradation from HG or MG to RG will constitute a SICR indicator.

Inverse of Matrix and Solution of Equations

Matrix concept is used to solve regression equations. Many multivariate models are developed based on the concept of matrix. Regression equations in general form can be expressed in terms of matrix form:

$$\begin{bmatrix} y_1 \\ y_2 \\ y_n \end{bmatrix} = \begin{bmatrix} 1x_{21}x_{k1} \\ 1x_{21}x_{k2} \\ 1x_{2n}x_{kn} \end{bmatrix} \begin{bmatrix} \widehat{\beta_1} \\ \widehat{\beta_2} \\ \widehat{\beta_k} \end{bmatrix} + \begin{bmatrix} \widehat{u_1} \\ u_2 \\ u_n \end{bmatrix}$$

$$y = \beta x$$

$$\hat{\beta} = \left(X'X\right)^{-1} X'Y \qquad \text{Eq. 5.10}$$

The inverse and transpose of matrix are solved to get estimate of beta coefficients in multivariate regressions. The beta coefficients are the regression estimates which enables the risk analyst to quantify the relationship between dependent and independent variables. It also helps them to predict the dependent variable. Many statistical packages use the above matrix concept in estimating the regression coefficients.

$\left(X'X\right)^{-1}$ is termed as variance–covariance matrix. This can be solved using matrix properties. The regression methods are discussed in detail in Chapter 7.

Matrix form is generally applied to represent multiple equations. In risk management, it is used to represent weights on different risk factors. Matrix multiplication can be used to estimate portfolio return as well as portfolio volatility.

The variance–covariance matrix is used in solving regression equations and to find out the regression coefficient. It is also used in developing simulation-based VaR models when we need variance–covariance matrix.

In value at risk (VaR) computation, we can estimate portfolio variance through a sum of correlated variables as follows:

$$\sigma_p^2 = w_1 w_1 \rho_{11} \sigma_1 \sigma_1 + w_1 w_2 \rho_{12} \sigma_1 \sigma_2 + \ldots + w_1 w_n \rho_{1n} \sigma_{1n} + \ldots + w_n w_n \rho_{nn} \sigma_{nn} \quad \text{Eq. 5.11}$$

This can be expressed in a general mathematical form:

$$= \sum_{i=1}^{n} \sum_{j=1}^{n} w_{ij} \rho_{ij} \sigma_i \sigma_j \quad \text{Eq. 5.11a}$$

Note that σ is capturing the standard deviation of each assets *i* and *j* and ρ is representing the correlation between assets *i* and *j*.

The above equation can also written in matrix form:

$$\sigma_P^2 = (SR)S^T$$

where S is the standard deviation of assets in the pool matrix; R is the covariance or correlation; and S^T is the transpose of standard deviation matrix.

$$S = \begin{bmatrix} \sigma_1 & \sigma_2 \ldots\ldots & \sigma_n \end{bmatrix}$$

$$R = \begin{bmatrix} \rho_{11} & \rho_{12} & \cdots & \rho_{1n} \\ \rho_{21} & \rho_{22} & \cdots & \rho_{2n} \\ & \cdot\cdot & & \\ \rho_{n1} & \rho_{n2} & \cdots & \rho_{nn} \end{bmatrix}$$

This gives us algebraic expression for variance. Thus, a variance–covariance matrix is a square matrix that contains the variances in the diagonal elements and covariances in the off-diagonal elements. Note that here weights can be adjusted accordingly if standard deviation of returns is estimated as percentage.

When the portfolio has multiple assets and multiple sub-segments, we get a better result through matrix solution to estimate portfolio volatility using variance–covariance matrix. Several statistical packages like Palisade, @Risk can accommodate this matrix pattern and give us portfolio variance which can be further used in estimating VaR and also for measuring portfolio efficiency. Monte Carlo simulation can be run using random numbers to find portfolio profit or loss to obtain VaR. The correlation coefficients can be specified in @RISK using the 'define correlation' function in the toolbar. Note that estimation portfolio volatility enables a risk manager to compare expected return with volatility of its portfolio of instruments. Many portfolio optimization models are based on this analysis.

Summary

This chapter describes the matrix concept and elaborates its applications in measuring PD, CPD, as well as conditional PD which are vital inputs for risk analysis. The transition matrix derived from the concept of matrix algebra has numerous applications in predicting bond valuation, VaR analysis, and loan portfolio monitoring. The Markov chain process used by reputed rating agencies and also the best practiced banks to predict probabilities of rating migration including analysis of default risk. The variance–covariance matrix is used in solving multiple regression equations and to find out the regression coefficient.

Review Questions

1. What is transition matrix? How you can use matrix multiplication to estimate conditional PD?
2. How transition matrix can be used to predict default risk at different horizon?
3. What is the difference between one-year average PD and CPD?
4. How you can obtain marginal PD from CPD?
5. If CPD for BBB-rated borrower in fifth year is 12% and in the fourth year is 10%, then the marginal PD is estimated in the fifth year.
6. How Transition Matrix can be used to monitor asset movement?
7. What is the difference between Conditional PD and CPD?
8. How inverse of matrix is important in risk estimation?

References

Bandyopadhyay, A. (2019), 'The Accuracy of Agency Ratings', *Economic and Political Weekly*, Vol. 44, No. 36, pp. 15–17.

Chakravorty, J. G., and P. R. Ghosh (1972). Higher Algebra, U N Dhar & Sons Pvt. Ltd., Kolkata.

De Servigny, A., and O. Renault (2004). 'Measuring and Managing Credit Risk', Chapter 2.

Hamilton, D. H. (2002). 'Historical Corporate Rating Migration, Default and Recovery Rates', in Credit Ratings: Methodologies, Rationale and Default Risk, ed. Michael K. Ong, Chapter 2, London: RISK publisher.

Hamilton, D. T. and Cantor, R. (2006), 'Measuring Corporate Default Rates', Moody's Investors Service, Global Credit Research.

Morgan, J. P. (1998). 'A One Parameter Representation of Credit Risk and Transition Matrices', Technical Document.

Marrison, C. (2002). 'The Fundamentals of Risk Measurement', Chapter 18, Tata McGraw-Hill, USA

Perederiy, V. (2015). 'Endogenous Derivation and Forecast of Lifetime PDs', working paper, Department of Credit Risk Controlling/Risk Models, Postbank Bonn/ Germany.

Schuermann, T., and S. Hanson (2004). 'Estimating Probabilities of Default', Staff Report no. 190. Federal Reserve Bank of New York.

Standard & Poor (2018). 'Default, Transition and Recovery: 2017 Annual Global Corporate Default Study and Rating Transitions', S&P Global Ratings.

6

Correlation Theorem and Portfolio Management Techniques

Covariance and correlation play important roles in portfolio management of risk. In market risk, it is used as a measure of the dependence between different financial instruments in the calculation of value at risk (VaR). For an equity portfolio to measure the market risk, correlation needs to be addressed to derive diversification benefit in the portfolio. Since all security prices do not always move in the same direction and to the same extent, all segments do not suffer the same degree of losses. The extent of diversification depends on the historical correlations among security returns. Conversely, if the correlations are perfectly positive (= +1), all positions lose to the same degree together. In that case, portfolio variance will be the algebraic sum of sub-portfolio variance. Correlation is concerned with the measurement of strength of association between two variables. It is a crucial parameter in modern portfolio management theory. It is widely used to measure portfolio return volatility as well as computation of portfolio VaR.

Portfolio Measure of Credit Risk

Banks will not be able to manage their loan portfolio credit risk efficiently unless the underlying portfolio credit risks are known. It requires detailed knowledge not only on individual borrower risk but also portfolio specific risks. Total portfolio credit risk has two components: idiosyncratic risk (diversifiable) and systematic risk (undiversifiable). A well-diversified credit portfolio would have a large number of loan assets. The systematic risk cannot be diversified away, and hence, we need to measure the asset correlation to properly understand the portfolio credit risk. The portfolio approach to credit risk is central theme of Internal Rating-Based Approach of Basel Accords (BCBS, 2006, 2017). The Basel Committee has prescribed asset correlation for corporate, SMEs as well as for several retail loan pools (mortgage, personal loan, credit card, etc.). Many globally best practiced banks use Moody's KMV (MKMV) model to actively measure portfolio credit risk. It uses equity return-based correlations or rating-based default correlation measures to derive portfolio unexpected loss. The portfolio unexpected loss formula has been given:

$$UL_p^2 = \sum_{j=1}^{n} w_j^2 UL_j^2 + \sum_{i=1}^{n}\sum_{\substack{j=1 \\ i \neq j}}^{n} w_i w_j UL_i UL_j \rho_{ij} \qquad \text{Eq. 6.1}$$

where UL_p is the standard deviation (in dollar amount) of the loan portfolio. The sign Σ denotes the algebraic sum. The symbol ρ_{ij} captures default correlation. Since many loans are not bought and sold in established market, default correlation can be measured through rating migration history (de Servigny and Renualt, 2003, 2004; Lucas, 1995).

Example

The entire portfolio risk assessment exercises are numerically illustrated in Table 6.1 using a very simple three-asset case. Let us consider that a credit officer in a bank is dealing with three corporate loans: borrower *i*, borrower *j*, and borrower *k*.

One can notice that the unexpected loss in all three loan categories is significantly higher than the expected loss. This is why, capital is needed as a cushion against unexpected loss which can be met through provisions.

As a next level, we have to now assess the portfolio losses. Note that this loan portfolio now consists of three loans. First, we estimate portfolio loss for two assets, and then we extend the analysis for three assets. The entire computation is shown in Table 6.2:

Note that the sum of risk contributions is equal to portfolio unexpected loss of USD 7.47 million. Also notice that the risk contribution

Table 6.1 Portfolio Risk Calculation

Borrower *i* got sanction of a non-amortizing term loan of $ 100 million

For 1 year

At 15% rate of interest (annual)

Credit exposure (E_i)	=	100	Crore
Loss given default (LGD_j)	=	40%	
Credit rating of borrower = AA (say)			
Associated default probability (PD_i)	=	0.50%	

To calculate the expected and unexpected loss of the loan

EL_i	=	$PD_i * LGD_i * E_i$	
	=	0.2	Million$
UL_i	=	$E_i * LGD_i * SQRT\{PD_i * (1 - PD_i)\}$	
	=	2.82	Million$

Borrower *j* received a non-amortizing term loan of $100Million

For 1 year

At 13% rate of interest (annual)

- Credit exposure (E_j)	=	100	Million$
- Loss given default (LGD_j)	=	60%	
- Credit rating of borrower = A (say)			
- Associated default probability (PD_j)	=	1.00%	

To calculate the expected and unexpected loss of the loan

EL*j*	=	$PD_j * LGD_j * E_j$	
	=	0.6	Million$
UL*j*	=	$E_i * LGD_j * SQRT\{PD_j * (1 – PD_j)\}$	
	=	5.97	Million$

(continued)

Table 6.1 Continued

Borrower *k* sanctioned a non-amortizing term loan of \$ 50 Million			
For 1 year			
At 13% rate of interest (annual)			
Credit exposure (E_k)	=	50	Million\$
Loss given default (LGD_k)	=	25%	
Credit rating of borrower = AAA (say)			
Associated default probability (PD_k)	=	0.10%	
To calculate the expected and unexpected loss of the loan			
EL_k	=	$PD_k * LGD_k * E_k$	
	=	0.0125	Million\$
UL_k	=	$E_k * LGD_k * SQRT\{PD_i * (1 - PD_k)\}$	
	=	0.40	Million\$

Table 6.2 Portfolio Risk Position—Two-Assets Case

Say Default Correlation between Borrower *i* and Borrower *j* is given by				
COR_{ij}	=	0.36		
EL_p	=	$EL_i + EL_j$		
	=	0.8	Million\$	
UL_p	=	$SQRT(UL_i^2 + UL_j^2 + 2\,COR_{ij} * UL_i * UL_j)$		
	=	7.47	Million\$	
	<	8.79		crore
	$UL_i*(UL_i+COR_{ij}*UL_j)/UL_p$			
Risk Contribution of Borrower X	=	1.88	Million\$	
	$UL_j*(UL_j+COR_{ij}*UL_i)/UL_p$			
Risk Contribution of Borrower Y	=	5.59	Million\$	
Sum of Risk Contribution of X and Y		7.47	Million\$	

for each borrower is markedly lower than their unexpected losses. This is happening because of correlation benefit that provides room for diversification. The risk contribution of each borrower measures their incremental or marginal contribution to portfolio risk. Accordingly, because of correlation benefit, the unexpected loss charge of an asset will be much lower. This has important implications on risk-based loan pricing. Actually, the unexpected loss charge is much lower due to diversification benefit. A bank cannot practically implement risk-based pricing unless correlation effect is estimated.

One may argue that while portfolio-expected loss is algebraic summation of sub-portfolio-expected losses (i.e. $EL_p = EL_1 + EL_2$), why it is not true for portfolio unexpected loss ($UL \neq UL_1 + UL_2$)? This is a common question generally asked by financial or risk managers. This has been addressed mathematically using expectation theorem.

Let us consider two assets *X* and *Y* in a portfolio. We can re-write the problem as follows:

$$E(X+Y)=E(X)+E(Y);\ \text{but}\ Var(X+Y)\ \text{not equal to}\ V(X)+V(Y)$$

Assume that

$$Var(W)=E\{(W-E(W)\}^2 \tag{1}$$

Let W = X + Y, so (1) becomes

$$Var(X+Y)=E\{(X+Y)-E(X+Y)\}^2 \tag{2}$$

Since E(X + Y) = E(X) + E(Y) and (2) becomes

$$\begin{aligned} Var(X+Y) &= E\{(X+Y)-(E(X)+E(Y)\}^2 \\ &= E\{(X-E(X)+(Y-E(Y)\}^2 \end{aligned}$$

When we expand this, we get

$$E(a+b)^2 = E(a+b)(a+b)$$

where a = X – E(X) and b = Y – E(Y)

$$= E(a^2 + b^2 + 2ab)$$

$$= E[(X - E(X))^2 + (Y - E(Y))^2 + 2(X - E(X))(Y - E(Y))]$$

$$= E(X - E(X))^2 + E(Y - E(Y))^2 + 2E(X - E(X))(Y - E(Y))$$

$$= V(X) + V(Y) + 2Cov(XY)$$

So the answer is false unless cov(x,y) = 0. i.e. x and y are uncorrelated. In general, it holds true and x and y are correlated or dependent, then it holds true.

Hence, it is quite clear that in the presence of correlation, portfolio unexpected loss will be much lower than the sum of the unexpected loss of assets in the portfolio.

The portfolio diversification effect will be more pronounced when we actually consider the three-asset case demonstrated in Table 6.3:

Notice that the portfolio-unexpected loss UL_p amount in 7.58 million USD is much lower that the sub-portfolio level individual asset wise unexpected losses (UL_i, UL_j, and UL_k). Moreover, the portfolio loss volatility (i.e. UL_p) is significantly lower than the sum of unexpected losses of assets ($UL_i + UL_j + UL_k$ = 9.19 Million$).

Table 6.3 Portfolio Risk Estimation—Three-Asset Case

Say Default Correlation between Borrower *i* and Borrower *k* is given by

COR_{ij}	=	0.3

Say Default Correlation between Borrower *j* and Borrower *k* is given by

COR_{ik}	=	0.2
EL_p	=	$EL_i + EL_j + EL_k$
	=	0.8125 Million$
UL_p	=	SQRT(UL_i^2+UL_j^2+UL_k^2+ 2 COR_{ij}*UL_i*UL_j+2COR_{jk}*UL_j*UL_k+2COR_{ik}*UL_i*UL_k)
	=	7.58 Million$
	<	9.19 Million$

It is important to note that if we estimate expected and unexpected losses from average and loss deviations in percentage term, then we have to adjust the portfolio expected and unexpected losses with exposure shares or weights (w_i).

For example, in a two-asset portfolio ($N = 2$), the portfolio risk calculation formula would be

$$\sigma_P = UL_P = \sqrt{w_i^2 UL_i^2 + \ w_j^2 UL_j^2 + 2 w_i w_j COR_{ij} UL_i UL_j} \qquad \text{Eq. 6.2}$$

Note that correlation COR_{ij} is the default correlation between asset i and asset j. It is also denoted by Greek symbol ρ, termed as 'rho'. The symbol w stands for the exposure weights.

Here, w_i is the exposure share of first borrower to the total portfolio and say it is equal to 40%. Accordingly, the 2nd borrower exposure share in the same portfolio of two assets would be 60%.

A bank chooses different portfolio mixes to understand the effect of correlation on portfolio unexpected loss. The above exercise can be extended to multiple assets as well.

If we generalize Equation 6.1 for multiple assets, it may look like

$$UL_P = \sqrt{\sum_{i=1}^{n} \sum_{j=1}^{n} \rho_{i,j}^{d} UL_i UL_j} \qquad \text{Eq. 6.2a}$$

Note that in the above expression, unexpected losses between two exposures (i and j) are measured in terms of absolute \$ unit. Note that i and j can be two different assets or industries.

Because of diversification (i.e. $\rho < 1$), we normally get

$$UL_P \ll \sum_{i=1}^{n} UL_i \qquad \text{Eq. 6.3}$$

Thus, portfolio unexpected loss is significantly lower than the sum of unexpected loss of individual assets in the pool. Normally, correlation ranges between minus 1 and plus 1. For a perfectly concentrated portfolio, correlation (or ρ) would be 1. The higher the correlation of default, the greater is the concentration risk in the loan portfolio. If correlation = 0, it means that two assets are independent.

Correlation Measures

Correlation measures the degree of association between two variables. There are mainly two popular approaches to measure correlation. One is parametric method and another approach uses non-parametric technique. The most popular measure of association between two variables is the Pearson correlation coefficient. It is expressed in the following formula:

$$r_{x,y} = \frac{cov(x,y)}{\sigma_x \sigma_y} \quad \text{Eq. 6.4}$$

The above correlation coefficient *r* is used to denote the degree of association between two variables. The numerator value is covariance between variables *x* and *y*. The respective standard deviations are given in the denominator. Note that the correlation coefficient is a pure number and is independent of the units of measurement. It lies between −1 and + 1.

The above equation can be further expressed as follows:

$$r_{x,y} = \frac{\Sigma(x-\overline{x})(y-\overline{y})}{\sigma_x \sigma_y} = \frac{\Sigma xy - \overline{xy}}{\sigma_x \sigma_y} \quad \text{Eq. 6.4a}$$

It is important to note that the correlation is concerned with measurement of strength of association between two variables. On the other hand, regression is concerned with the prediction of the most likely value of one variable when the value of other variable is known. Correlation does not tell us anything specific about causation.

If we extend the Pearson formula and think in terms of bivariate frequency and joint probabilities, we get the following expression for estimating default correlation (DC):

$$\mathrm{p}_{\mathrm{i,j}}^{\mathrm{D,D}} = \frac{\mathrm{JDP_{i,j}} - \mathrm{PD_i PD_j}}{\sqrt{\mathrm{PD_i}(1-\mathrm{PD_i})\mathrm{PD_j}(1-\mathrm{PD_j})}} \quad \text{Eq. 6.5}$$

The above formula is based on the assumption that there is a constant probability of default (as given by the expected default probability) for a firm or an industry over time and a constant joint default probability (JDP) (as given by the average JDP) over time. However, this does not imply that default probabilities or joint default probabilities are time invariant. It is the limitation of this method.

For example, if the JDP between two borrowers rated A and BBB is estimated as 0.06%, and probability of default of A is 0.70% and BBB is 2%; one can derive their default correlation using Equation 6.5. The estimated value of the default correlation coefficient would be (0.06% – 0.70% × 2%) / SQRT(0.70% × (1 – 0.70%) × 2% × (1 – 2%)) = 3.94%.

Here, the real issue is to estimate JDP. One can use bivariate Gaussian copula function and plug in asset correlation obtained from asset returns and respective probability of defaults to obtain JDP. Another method is to directly obtain it from rating migration history. The formula for JDP is explained below.

For joint default migrations of firms within the same starting rating grade, the following equation is used:

For joint default migration of firms from different starting rating grades, we use the following equation:

$$JDP_{i,j} = \sum_{t=1}^{n} w_{ij}^{t} \frac{T_{i,D}^{t} T_{j,D}^{t}}{N_{i}^{t} N_{j}^{t}} \qquad \text{Eq. 6.6}$$

where the weight is given as follows:

$$w_{ij}^{t} = \frac{N_{i}^{t} N_{j}^{t}}{\sum_{t=1}^{T} N_{i}^{t} N_{j}^{t}} \qquad \text{Eq. 6.6a}$$

where T = total number of years (say 10 years) and t = every year (say year 1, 2, ... 10).

We have illustrated the frequency-based correlation method given in Equation 6.6 with data-based analysis. Table 6.4 presents the yearly rating data obtained from Standard and Poor's Credit Pro.

Note that we can obtain one-year average PD_{IG} = (32/4703) = 0.068%. This is the average probability of default for investment grade (IG) borrower. Similarly, we obtain PD_{NIG} = (1121/33537) = 3.343%.

Table 6.4 Estimation of Frequency-Based JDP and Default Correlation

Year	IG		NIG				
	Rated (N)	Defaulted (D)	Rated (N)	Defaulted (D)	JDF betn. IG & NIG	Weights	Relative Weights (wt)
2003	2875	3	1557	89	0.006%	4476375	0.04223
2004	2987	1	1667	38	0.001%	4979329	0.046975
2005	3070	1	1790	31	0.001%	5495300	0.051842
2006	3117	0	1872	26	0.000%	5835024	0.055047
2007	3075	0	1976	21	0.000%	6076200	0.057323
2008	3144	14	2148	89	0.018%	6753312	0.06371
2009	3125	11	1997	224	0.039%	6240625	0.058874
2010	3046	0	1921	64	0.000%	5851366	0.055201
2011	3074	1	2115	44	0.001%	6501510	0.061335
2012	3096	0	2307	66	0.000%	7142472	0.067382
2013	3134	0	2502	64	0.000%	7841268	0.073974
2014	3248	0	2776	45	0.000%	9016448	0.085061
2015	3340	0	2990	94	0.000%	9986600	0.094213
2016	3338	1	3000	143	0.001%	10014000	0.094472
2017	3354	0	2919	83	0.000%	9790326	0.092361
Total	47023	32	33537	1121			1

Source: Rating Data obtained from S&P Credit Pro published report, 2018.
Note: S&P IG grade consists of rating AAA to BBB; NIG class combines rating BB to CCC.

Standard deviation of PD for IG grade would be

$$SD(PD_{IG}) = \sqrt{0.068\% \times (1 - 0.068\%)} = 2.608\%$$

Similarly, Standard deviation of PD for NIG grade borrowers can be estimated as follows:

$$SD(PD_{NIG}) = \sqrt{3.343\% \times (1 - 3.343\%)} = 17.975\%$$

Weights and relative weights for rated accounts for IG and NIG are estimated using Equation 6.6a.

Now we can estimate JDP by taking weighted sum of joint default frequency (JDF) and relative weights (wt). For this, we have taken sum product of these two series in excel and obtain value of $JDP_{IG\&NIG} = 0.0040\%$.

Now if we multiply PD_{IG} with PD_{NIG} values, we get

$$0.068\% \times 3.343\%$$
$$= 0.0023\%$$

Notice that our estimated JDP value is higher than the product of their respective PDs.

Hence, we can comment that there is a presence of positive correlation between IG default and NIG default. This correlation may arise due to some common factors (geographic or macroeconomic).

We can now estimate default correlation by Equation 6.5. This is shown as follows:

$$DC = \{JDP_{IG\&NIG} - PD_{IG\times}PD_{NIG})\} / \{(SD(PD_{IG}) \times SD(PD_{NIG})\}$$
$$= (0.0040\% - 0.0023\%) / (2.608\% \times 17.975\%)$$
$$= 0.363\% \text{ approximately.}$$

Default correlation is very crucial for estimation of portfolio unexpected loss and economic capital. Capturing simultaneous defaulting events and estimation of correlation enables a risk manager to understand portfolio concentration and diversification. Correlation of joint credit quality movement has significant influence on the market value of a credit portfolio. Many portfolio models designed by like Credit Suisse and MKMV allow correlations in modelling default events. The default correlation estimation technique and its implications on overall credit portfolio management has been elaborated in Bandyopadhyay (2016).

For operational risk modelling, Spearman rank correlation is also used to measure the strength of association between two variables. But unlike Pearson correlation, it uses ranks of the values, and hence, it is a non-parametric measure. If X and Y variables are ranked in such a manner, the coefficient of rank correlation, or the Spearman's formula for rank correlation is given by

$$R = 1 - \frac{6\sum d^2}{n^3 - n} \qquad \text{Eq. 6.7}$$

where the term d is the difference in rank orders.

The tie-adjusted rank correlation coefficient is

$$=1-\frac{6\left\{\Sigma d^2+\Sigma(t^3-t)/12\right\}}{n^3-n} \qquad \text{Eq. 6.7a}$$

where t is the number of individuals involved in a tie either in the first or second series.

Spearman rank correlation is also used in model validation where the analyst can compare external ratings with internal rating or predicted score with actual default rates.

Steps for Computation of the Spearman Rank Correlation

Step1: Convert rating symbols to rating categorical numbers awarded by RAM models as well as credit rating agencies (CRAs). For example, if the customer is rated BR4, we convert it to numerical number 4, BR5 to 5 in the same order as given in rating symbols. Similarly, for external ratings, AAA is given 1, AA, 2, A, 3, BBB 4, . . . and C as 7.

Step 2: We rank the customers in terms of internal ratings (RAM) first using rank option in excel and then rank them in terms of CRA ratings both in ascending orders. We preserve these rankings in column L and M.

Step 3: We obtain the difference square in ranks between CRA and Internal rating for each customer, i.e. d^2=(Rank of RAM – Rank of CRA)^2. This has been done in column N.

Step 4: As a final step, we estimate the Spearman Rank Correlation (R) using the following standard formula mentioned in Equation 6.7.

We illustrate this exercise with a limited number of observations to conserve space. It may be extended to a larger number of observations as well.

The following table presents recorded data showing the test scores made by 7 borrowers rated by RAM as well as CRISIL scores.

Here, n = number of customers = 6

$\Sigma d^2 = 20$

$$\text{Therefore, } R = 1 - \frac{6\sum d^2}{\left(n^3 - n\right)}$$

$$= 1 - \frac{6 \times 20}{\left(7^3 - 7\right)}$$

$$= 0.6429.$$

We can take the data to STATA and can perform the same test using following command:

spearman ram crisil

Number of obs = 7
Spearman's rho = 0.6429

Here, we do not have any ties; otherwise, we would have to adjust the ties.

Similarly, we can estimate rank-based asset correlation for various losses or return series when we estimate portfolio VaR.

Note that the rank correlation is used as a measure of degree of association between two attributes, where measurements on the characters are not available, but it is possible to rank the individual in some orders. It uses ranks of the original data rather than their actual values. It is a non-parametric measure and, hence does not get influenced by presence of large numbers. Unlike Pearson correlation, it does not make any assumption about the joint distribution of the variables.

Spearman's rank correlation is used to estimate portfolio VaR for operational risk where we combine losses of different events across business lines. We can find correlation between operational risk and gross income of business lines. One can also use it to establish relationship between risk and return in several sub-portfolios.

Measurement of Portfolio Market Risk

In market risk, the variance–covariance VaR (VCVaR) method captures the diversification benefits in the portfolio. In particular, standard deviation (variance) is used as a measure of shocks to individual securities; correlations (covariance) are employed to compute portfolio losses; and the normal distribution is included to add an element of uncertainty. Since all these concepts are so popular in statistics, the variance–covariance method has been widely used, to predict market risk losses. The VC VaR method assumes that daily returns follow a normal distribution.

The portfolio VaR at 99% confidence level, if estimated at USD 1023.782 for example, is actually less than the sum of the individual security VaR at the same confidence level, which is USD 1034.563. Therefore, because all security prices do not always move in the same direction and to the same extent, all segments do not suffer the same degree of losses.

If portfolio daily VaR at 99% confidence level in is estimated as USD 1023.783. Thus, we can say that there is a 1% chance that losses on the portfolio, as on 31 March 2019 will exceed USD 1023.782 (or 2.27% of Portfolio Value) on the next day. This way it is interpreted.

Portfolio VaR model generally used the Pearson correlation matrix obtained from equity or bond or forex returns.

Portfolio Optimization

Correlation plays important in portfolio optimization as well. This has been illustrated below. Assume that the analyst wishes to estimate risk as well as return using equity of five stocks. Correlation matrix gives out the pairwise association between any two stocks in the portfolio. Correlation between stock M and stock N is the same as the correlation between stock N and M since correlation does not specify any causation. Equity correlation of a stock (or asset) within itself is 1. The diagonals of a correlation matrix represent within correlation. The between correlations are presented in off-diagonal cells of the matrix. For any given value of standard deviation (or portfolio volatility), a risk manager would like to choose an equity (or investment) portfolio that yields the greatest possible expected

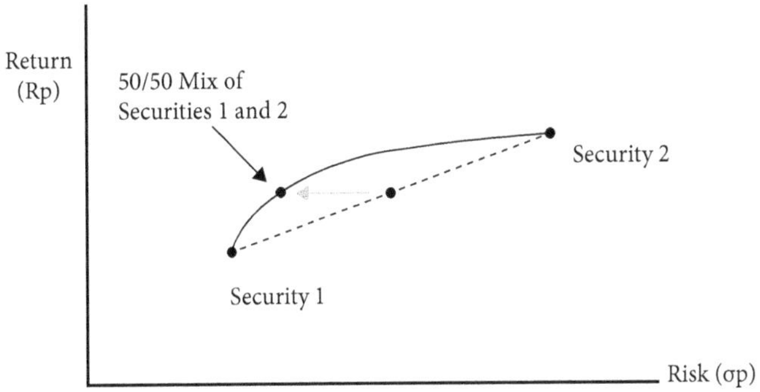

Figure 6.1 Efficient Frontier Concept
Source: Author's illustration adopted from Efficient Frontier concept

Table 6.5 Estimation of Spearman Rank Correlation

Borrower	RAM Score x	CRISL Score y	$D = x - y$	d^2
A	2	3	−1	1
B	1	4	−3	9
C	4	2	2	4
D	5	5	0	0
E	3	1	2	4
F	7	6	1	1
G	6	7	−1	1
Total			0	20

Source: Author's own illustration

rate of return. In this context, an efficient frontier analysis would guide the risk manager to improve reward to risk. It is important to note that the standard deviation of returns of the 50:50 allocation will be actually less than the average of standard deviations of the two securities. This is effect is due to the presence of covariance. Figure 6.1 illustrates this with two securities.

Suppose that the portfolio manager holds two bonds with the following characteristics:

The correlation between Bond 1 and Bond 2 = −0.75.

The expected return on the bond portfolio is

$$R_p = 0.40(10\%) + 0.60(12.5\%) = 11.5\%$$

The variance is

$$\sigma_p^2 = (0.40)^2(0.0815)^2 + (0.60)^2(0.1020)^2 + 2(0.40)(0.60)(-0.75)(0.0815)(0.1020) = 0.001816 \qquad \text{Eq. 6.8}$$

Thus, portfolio volatility or risk $= \sigma_p = \sqrt{0.001816} = 4.26\%$.

Note that, because of the negative correlation, the portfolio manager is able to derive enough diversification benefit. Because of this, the portfolio standard deviation is much lower than the risk of either individual bonds.

For multiple assets, the portfolio risk manager will have to derive asset return correlations, standard deviation of returns and choose different combinations of assets mix (i.e. exposure share) to derive the portfolio volatility. By appropriately utilizing correlation coefficients among assets, the manager can significantly reduce risk in asset portfolio and improve the portfolio's risk return trade-off. A ranking of various portfolio combinations with target return with respect to given risk or minimize return subject to given target return will enable him to find out the optimal portfolio combination through the efficient frontier curve. This is the modern portfolio theory which is being adopted by many best practiced banks.

When we hold multiple stocks (say five securities or more), then we have to bring variance–covariance matrix in the portfolio return and risk analysis. Covariance is basically the numerator portion of the correlation formula. It measures the directional pairwise relationship between the returns of assets. A positive covariance implies that asset or bond returns are moving together while a negative covariance means that they move inversely. Covariance is estimated by assessing standard deviations from the expected returns (within group) or by multiplying the correlation between the pairwise variables by the standard deviation of each variable.

For example, assume that the variance–covariance matrix suggests that the covariance between W and P asset return is 0.0000394. This is the same covariance between P and W. The first element in the matrix is X_{11} which corresponds to C and C which is the stock. This represents covariance between Security C with itself, which is nothing but the variance. This is the reason why the matrix is termed as variance–covariance matrix. In the denominator of the correlation equation, standard deviations are estimated by product of the standard deviation of all possible portfolio combination. Then the calculations shown in Equation 6.7 get extended to a Bernoulli form. We resort to matrix multiplication for this. This can be achieved by multiplying the standard deviation array with the transpose of itself.

The software @Risk is capable of entering the entire correlation matrix and can run simulation and perform portfolio optimization.

It estimates this way: Portfolio Variance = Sqrt (Transpose (Wt.SD) * Correlation Matrix * Wt. SD)

SD = standard deviation; Sqrt = square root; Wt: portfolio share or weights.

Integration of Risk and Estimation of Bank Capital

The risk capital can be calculated for the bank as a whole if we can include the correlation between various risks. For this, we use variance equation to get the variance for the whole bank based on the variance and covariance of the individual risk types.

The historical time series of loss data for each type of risk will enable us to derive the correlations. Kuritzkes, Schuermann, and Weiner (KSW) (Wharton, 2003), Rosenberg & Schuermann (JFE, 2006) in their risk aggregation exercise examine a broad range of correlations gathered from several academic and industry studies. These correlations would enable a risk manager to obtain total risk capital required by a financial institution. For example, Rosenberg and Schuermann (2006) study has estimated correlation between credit risk and market risk as 0.50. Similarly, the same study provides correlation estimate between credit risk and operational risk as 0.20. An integrated VaR framework was suggested in the paper. Using correlations, one can derive aggregate bank level portfolio risk. A bottom approach is essential to measure and understand the effect of risks on bank's overall business.

Summary

Practically, a commercial bank holds many assets in their credit portfolio with different degrees of risks. Therefore, finding those many asset-wise correlations is a challenge for the bank. This why, assets are finally grouped into various sub-pools depending upon their common risk characteristics. For example, a bank can create rating grade-wise pool, industry pool, loan to value ratio-wise pools, and region-wise pools (zone-wise or rural, urban, semi-urban) and can estimate default correlations. The methods for estimation of such correlations are explained in subsequent chapter. A portfolio approach is essential to identify specific and vulnerable sectors and credit asset categories which may face systematic/cyclical impact severely.

It is quite clear from the examples in this chapter that correlation contributes significantly in the assessment of portfolio risk. Correlated and interrelated risk events and indicators need to be highlighted for better portfolio management. As you diversify your portfolio, the portfolio risk reduces depending upon the correlation of portfolio components. The lower the correlation, the greater the diversification and the lower the portfolio risk. Accordingly, while constructing or managing a portfolio, correlation analysis is required to create a relatively shockproof credit portfolio. Combining the credit or investment assets with lower correlations tend to reduce the overall portfolio risk. Modern portfolio theorem suggests effective ways to allocate assets and utilize correlations to maximize gains through diversification.

Review Questions

1. Suppose that the two assets in a hypothetical loan portfolio have an identical credit risk grade, and hence, same probability of default (PD) = 2.16%. However, the assets are from two different sectors: sector auto (A) and sector building materials (B). A study of external risks points out that there is a potential external risk that may impact the portfolio adversely. Hence, there is a risk of downgrade (or migration risk) of portfolio components if this external event occurs. The volatility risk (standard deviation) in asset A is 5%

Table 6.6 Bond Portfolio Returns

Bond	Share	Return (R)	Volatility (SD)
1	0.40	10%	8.15%
2	0.60	12.5%	10.20%

and unexpected risk (standard deviation) in asset B is 6%. A correlation between both sectors is stated to be 50%. Which combination (or mix) of asset A and asset B ratio amongst the following options will provide the least risky credit portfolio (or lowest ULp)?

a) 0:100
b) 50:50
c) 60:40
d) 100:0

2. Assume that an FI holds two loans with the following return and risk characteristics:
   a) Estimate the return and risk on loan 1
   b) Estimate the return and risk on loan 2
   c) Estimate the return and risk of the portfolio
3. Why correlation analysis is important for a risk manager?

If the JDP between asset X and asset Y is 0.0085% and PD of asset X is 0.80% and PD of asset Y is 0.25%, the default correlation between two assets would be

a) <=0%
b) >0% but <=1%
c) >1% but <=5%
d) >5%

4. If the JDP between two borrowers A and B is lower than the product of their respective individual default probabilities, the default correlation between them would be
   a) Zero
   b) Negative
   c) Positive
   d) Infinity

Table 6.7 Portfolio Risk and Return

Loan Type	Exposure Share	Annual Spread between Loan Rate & FI's cost of funds	Annual Fees	LGD	PD	Default Correlation
Term loan 1	60%	5%	2%	25%	3%	−0.25
Term loan 2	40%	4%	1.5%	20%	2%	
Total	100%					

5. Is there any correlation between credit risk and market risk? Why there will be any correlation?
6. Which correlation is higher? Between credit risk and operational risk or between credit risk and market risk?
7. How correlation can be measured? How does it contribute to portfolio management?
8. How risk aggregation can be done on an integrated basis?
9. Which unexpected loss (UL) is highest amongst the following scenarios?
   a) PD volatile and LGD constant
   b) LGD volatile and PD constant
   c) Both PD and LGD are constant
   d) Both PD and LGD are volatile
10. The lower the default correlation in a credit portfolio,
    a) The Lower the unexpected loss will be.
    b) The higher the expected loss will be.
    c) The higher the unexpected loss will be.
    d) The lower the expected loss will be.

References

Bandyopadhyay, A. (2016). 'Managing Portfolio Credit Risk in Banks', Cambridge University Press. Chapter 6.

BCBS (2006). 'International Convergence of Capital Measurement and Capital Standards: A Revised Framework', Publication No. 128, Basel Committee on Banking Supervision, Bank for International Settlements, Basel, June.

BCBS (2017). 'Basel III: Finalising Post Crisis Reforms', Bank for International Settlements, Basel, December.

De Servigny, A., and O. Renault (2003). 'Default Correlation Evidence', *RISK*, Vol. 16, Issue 7, July, pp. 90–94.

De Servigny, A., and O. Renault (2004). 'Measuring and Managing Credit Risk', McGraw-Hill, Chapter 5.

Lucas, D. J. (1995). 'Default Correlation and Credit Analysis', *Journal of Fixed Income*, Vol. 4, Issue 4, pp. 76–87.

Kuritzkes, A., T. Schuermann, and S. M. Weiner (2003). 'Risk Measurement, Risk Management and Capital Adequacy of Financial Conglomerates', Wharton working paper.

Marrison, C. (2002). 'The Fundamentals of Risk Measurement', Tata McGraw-Hill Edition, Chapter 20.

Rosenberg, J. V., and T. Schuermann (2006). 'A General Approach to Integrated Risk Management with Skewed, Fat-tailed Risks', *Journal of Financial Economics*, Vol. 79, Issue 3, pp. 569–614.

7
Multivariate Analysis to Understand Functional Relationship and Scenario Building

Multivariate analysis takes into consideration of many factors in analysing risks. It allows portfolio manager to capture multiple drivers and mitigate risks detected through the analysis. Multivariate models are popularly used to predict the variability in the dependent variable based on its covariance with set of independent variables. This has widespread applications in developing credit rating models. Risk analysts use multivariate techniques to forecast default risk or investment outcomes to understand the role of key contributing factors. It has wider application in scorecard development, portfolio selection (profit vs. risk), risk integration, and generating stress testing scenarios for capital analysis. Multivariate regression models are also used in predicting losses.

Regression Basics

Regression analysis helps a risk manager to solve problems involving sets of variables when it is known that there exists some inherent relationship among variables. Before running the analysis, one has to know what are the dependent variables of the problem and set of independent variables that influence the dependent variables. A reasonable form of a relationship between the dependent y and the regressor x can be defined through a linear relationship.

$$y = \alpha + \beta x + u_i \qquad \text{Eq. 7.1}$$

where the alpha is the intercept and beta is the coefficient or slope. The term u_i is the error term. It is assumed that the error term is normally distributed. One can perform Ordinary Least-Square (OLS) Regression to fit the above model. This is done by minimizing the error term. This will give us the estimated value of the slope and the coefficient.

The following is an estimated equation:

$$\hat{y} = 3.8296 + 0.9036x \qquad \text{Eq. 7.2}$$

Using the above regression model, one can predict the value of *y*. For this one must also check whether the fitness of the model is good. This is confirmed by the statistic R^2 which provides explanatory power of the model (it is explained sum squares/total sum squares).

Note that the coefficients will have to be statistically significant to claim meaningful relationship between *x* and *y* variables. This is confirmed by coefficient significance *t*-test. Here, the *t* statistic = coefficient/standard error. Standard error = Standard deviation/number of observations. If the *t*-value is higher than the table value of *t* (or critical *t*) at a confidence interval of 95% and with a certain degrees of freedom (number of observations-number of factors or parameters), then we say that the coefficient value is statistically significant. The *t*-table is given in the Appendix.

The following estimated equations are used to solve the regressions:

$$Y_j = a + b \cdot X_j + \varepsilon_j$$

$$\hat{b} = \frac{\sum (X_i - \bar{X})(Y_i - \bar{Y})}{\sum (X_i - \bar{X})^2} \qquad \text{Eq. 7.3}$$

$$\hat{a} = \bar{Y} - \hat{b}\,\bar{X}$$

The expression *b* hat is the estimated beta coefficient (like the 0.9036 in the previous equation. Similarly, a hat is the estimated intercept (3.8296). *Y* bar is the mean value of dependent variable and *X* bar is the mean value of independent variable. The symbol ε_j denotes the regression error term. Regression coefficients are derived by fitting regression line and minimizing the error sum square or Residual Sum of Squares (RSS).

Above Equation 7.3 for regression coefficient b (or beta hat) can be expressed as:

$$\hat{b} = \frac{\operatorname{Cov}(X,Y)}{\sigma_X^2}$$

$$= r \times \frac{\sigma_Y}{\sigma_X}$$

Note that in regression, the explanatory power of the model (or goodness of fit) is checked through the R-square value. The expression for R-square is

$$R^2 = \frac{\sum(\hat{Y}_i - \bar{Y})^2}{\sum(Y_i - \bar{Y})^2} = (\text{correlation})^2$$

$$\text{S.E}(\hat{b}) = \sqrt{\frac{\sum(Y_i - \hat{Y}_i)^2/(n-2)}{\sum(X_i - \bar{X})^2}} = \sqrt{\frac{\text{RSS}/(n-2)}{\sum(X_i - \bar{X})^2}} \qquad \text{Eq. 7.4}$$

$$\text{S.E}(\hat{a}) = \sqrt{\text{Variance}(\hat{a})} = \sqrt{\frac{\text{RSS}}{n-2}\left[\frac{1}{n} + \frac{\bar{X}^2}{\sum X_i^2}\right]}$$

Here, the R-squared is a measure of the goodness of fit of our model, while the standard error or deviation of b gives us a measure of confidence for our estimate of b.

Standard errors (S.E) are important to test the statistical significance of the coefficients. RSS is the residual sum square. The term n is the number of observations. Higher the R^2, better is the fitness of the model.

These regressions can be run in Excel using statistics. For better estimates they can be run in statistical packages like STATA, SPSS, SAS, etc.

If there is a non-linearity in the relationship between variables, one can use log transformation to run simple regressions.

The statistical significance of the regression coefficients is checked through *t*-test.

T-test in regression exercise helps us to examine the whether there is any significant effect of regression parameters on dependent variable.

For example, if the risk manager wants to examine the effect of system downtime on the amount of operational risk or fall in GDP growth on default %.

The hypotheses are set like:

H_0: $b = 0; a = 0$
H_a: $b \neq 0; a \neq 0$

Test Statistics: F-statistics for overall significance and *t*-statistics for individual coefficient significance

The *t*-statistic is given as:

$$t_{\hat{a}} = \frac{\hat{a} - 0}{S.E(\hat{a})} \qquad t_{\hat{b}} = \frac{\hat{b} - b}{S.E.(\hat{b})} \qquad \text{Eq. 7.5}$$

Rule of thumb: If estimated *t* is greater than tabulated t at a certain d.f., i.e. $P(|t_{computed}| > t_{critical})$ is < 0.05; we reject the null hypothesis and conclude that independent variable (*X*) significantly affect the dependent variable (*Y*).

In this context, ANOVA will help us the read the regression results better. It reports the following test statistics

- R^2 = ESS/TSS measures explanatory power of regression model. ESS is the explained sum square and TSS is the total sum of squares.
- R^2 (Adj) = $1 - [(RSS/n-k) / (TSS/n-1)] = 1-(1-R^2) \times (n-1/n-k)$
  n = no. of obs.; k = no. of parameters; Adjusted R-square is degrees of freedom adjusted measure of model's explanatory power.
  Here, F-test examines the goodness of fit of the model
  H_0: $\beta_1 = \beta_2 = \beta_3 = \ldots. = \beta_n = 0$
- $F = (R^2/k-1) / (1-R^2)/n-k = (R^2/1-R^2) \times (n-k/k-1)$

Rule of Thumb: A high F value and low *p* (less than 5%) rejects the hypothesis and then model fits well.

An example of regression analysis is documented below:

Suppose a risk analyst wants to fit a loss given default prediction model. He runs the following regression model in Excel:

Table 7.1 Loan Loss Regression Result and ANOVA

Y = Loan Loss
X_1 = Guarantee (dichotomous)
X_2 = Margin (interval)
X_3 = Security (dichotomous)
X_4 = Seniority (interval, 0–4)

Model Summary

Model	R	R Square	Adjusted R Square	Std. Error the Estimate
1	0.393[a]	0.155	0.153	0.838

a. Predictors; (Constant, Guarantee, Collection, Security, and Seniority)

ANOVA[b]

Model	Sum of Squares df	Mean Square	F	Sig.		
1	Regression	251.358	4	62.840	89.437	0.00
	Residual	1373.601	1955	0.703		
	Total	1624.959	1959			

a. Dependent variable: Loan Loss
b. Overall Model Explanatory Power Test Results

The estimated coefficients are reported below:

Model	Coefficients[a]				
	Unstandardized coefficients		Standardized coefficients		Sig
	B	Std. error	β	*t*	
1 (Constant)	3.721	0.115		32.373	0.00
Guarantee	4.821E-02	0.38	0.026	1.257	0.209
Margin	−0.361	0.024	−0.316	−14.772	0.00
Security	−0.207	0.042	−0.104	−4.906	0.00
Seniority (scale)	5.131E−02	0.006	0.169	7.912	0.00

[a]Dependent variable: Loan Loss

Interpretation

- Loss does not seem to be dependent on Guarantee (Yes or No) ($P = 0.209 > 0.05$).
- Margin, Security and Seniority have significant effect on Loss.
- Margin has the strongest effect (Beta = − 0.316). The higher the margin, the better the recovery and lower the loss. Presence of Security has a negative effect and Seniority positive effect on Loan Loss.
- In total the model is statistically significant and explains 15.5% of total variation in loss experience.

The same regression can also be run in statistical packages like STATA or SPSS.

Let's take another example where a market risk analyst has run the following regression using STATA:

reg stockreturn market return

The regression results and ANOVA are reported below Table 7.2.

The above regression results have reported many statistical results. First look at the R-squared, Adjusted R-squared and F value. These test statistics measure the explanatory power of a regression model. All the values are high and F value is significant (since Prob > F = 0.000). These statistics reveal that model is a good fit and the model makes much sense.

The coefficient value of factor 'Marketreturn' is popularly termed as equity beta and the value is 1.1056. It signifies that if the market return goes up by 100%, the return of the stock increases by 110.56%. The coefficient is also statistically significant. The $P > |t| = 0.000$ indicates that the probability of type I error is lower than 1%. It says that we can confidently reject the null hypothesis of zero coefficient (of no impact) at one percent or event better level of significance. The constant (_cons) term is statistically insignificant and we can say that we cannot reject the null hypothesis. Moreover, R-squared provides the measure of systematic risk and $1-R^2$ counts the idiosyncratic (specific volatility of the stock itself).

It is important to note that the above regression estimation formulas given in expression 7.3 can also be expressed in terms of matrix form. The matrix approach works better when we perform multiple regression where we consider multiple factors in fitting a regression model. This is

Table 7.2 Regression Results and ANOVA

Source |	SS	Df	MS		Number of obs = 2492
					F(1,2490) = 1487.25
Model |	0.9619	1	0.9619	Prob>F = 0.000	
Residual |	1.6105	2490	0.0006	R-squared = 0.3739	
			Adj R-squared = 0.3737		
Total |	2.5724	2491	0.00103	Root MSE = 0.02543	
Stockreturn |	Coef.	Std.Err.	t	P>|t| [95% Conf. Interval]	
Marketreturn | 1.1056	0.02867	38.56	0.000	1.0494	1.1618
_cons | 4.62e-06	0.00051	0.01	0.993	−0.001	0.0010

very useful for risk analysts for predicting risk drivers and linking other factors to perform scenario analysis.

A multivariate regression model can be expressed in general form as given below:

$$y = X\beta + u \qquad \text{Eq. 7.6}$$

Where y is the dependent variable, x is the set of regression factors and u is the error term.

In matrix form, it can be shown as:

$$\begin{bmatrix} y_1 \\ y_2 \\ .. \\ y_n \end{bmatrix} = \begin{bmatrix} 1\ x_{11} & x_{12} \cdots & . x_{1k} \\ 1\ x_{21} & x_{22} \cdots & . x_{2k} \\ & \cdots \cdots & \\ 1\ x_{n1} & x_{n2} \cdots & . x_{nk} \end{bmatrix} \begin{bmatrix} \beta_1 \\ \beta_2 \\ .. \\ \beta_k \end{bmatrix} + \begin{bmatrix} u_1 \\ u_2 \\ .. \\ u_n \end{bmatrix} \qquad \text{Eq. 7.7}$$

$$n\times 1 \qquad (n\times k) \qquad (k\times 1) \quad (n\times 1)$$

The matrix dimensions are given (row and columns).

The regression coefficients of k parameters can be estimated by solving:

$$\hat{\beta} = \begin{bmatrix} \hat{\beta}_1 \\ \hat{\beta}_2 \\ .. \\ \hat{\beta}_k \end{bmatrix} = \left(X'X\right)^{-1} X'Y \qquad \text{Eq. 7.8}$$

This can be solved using matrix multiplication and matrix inverse formula.

The above expression is obtained through residual sum square (RSS) minimization with respect to all the elements of β in a multiple regression framework using optimization technique.

For simplicity, in a two variable case, it can be shown that by solving:

$$(X'X)\beta = X'Y \qquad \text{Eq. 7.9}$$

$$=> \begin{vmatrix} n & \Sigma x \\ \Sigma x & \Sigma x^2 \end{vmatrix} \begin{vmatrix} \beta_1 \\ \beta_2 \end{vmatrix} = \begin{vmatrix} \Sigma y \\ \Sigma xy \end{vmatrix} \qquad \text{Eq. 7.10}$$

This gives us:

Two linear equations to solve for the regression coefficients:

$$n\beta_1 + \beta_2 \sum x = \sum y \qquad \text{Eq. 7.11}$$

$$\beta_1 \sum x + \beta_2 \sum x^2 = \sum xy \qquad \text{Eq. 7.12}$$

So, if we have values of y and x from data, we can solve for β_1 and β_2 through optimization method and we obtain intercept and the coefficient values as given in 7.3 (value of a and b). It can also be solved using Cramer's Rule. Hence, from the above steps, we can get back the basic regression estimated equations which can be further solved to obtain the intercept as well as beta coefficient. Basics about regression methods are discussed in Nagar and Das (1983), Stock and Watson (2003), and Walpole et al. (2012).

Applications of Multiple Regressions in Risk Analysis

The above regression model has lot of applications in risk management. It enables a risk manager to create and select the key risk indicators in operational risk.

In such case, the regression function would be:

$$\begin{aligned} \textit{Operational Loss} = f\,(&\textit{system downtime, no. of trainees working,}\\ &\textit{no. of experienced staff, volume of transactions,}\\ &\textit{no. of transaction errors}) \end{aligned}$$

Through regression analysis, one can check whether these factors are significantly contributing to operational loss. This way, a bank can develop key risk indicators (KRIs) to link risk indicators with operational loss.

To apply this technique, one can devise a risk map that encompasses all types of operational risk (legal, compliance, operations, security, system, etc.) and then the key qualitative as well as quantitative factors may be selected through MDA or regression analysis to develop risk level of operational process of a Bank (e.g. transaction processing in each business). Such exercise would also help the bank to understand the key factors that affect the op-risk rating.

Multiple Discriminant Analysis (MDA)

Multiple Discriminant Analysis is a multivariate form of ANOVA. The primary objective is to predict an entity's likelihood of belonging to a particular class or group based on several predictor variables. Multiple discriminant function analysis (MDA) is used when the dependent has three or more categories. It has popular application in building credit scorecard. Altman Z score (1968, 1995) is based on MDA that evaluates the companies based upon a number of financial indicators and companies are classified into sick company or healthy company. A prospective client for granting loan has to be rated as good credit risk or bad credit risk. Further, it may be of interest to assess the relative importance of the variables for discrimination purposes. Similarly, from the investor's point of view, it is necessary to discriminate between the shares based upon financial and other results into 'Good Buy' or 'Bad Buy'. The purpose of MDA is to maximally separate the mutually exclusive groups and to determine the most parsimonious way to separate group.

MDA derives an equation as linear combination of the set of independent variables that will discriminate best between the groups of dependent variables (say solvent vs. defaulted).

The weights are assigned to each independent variable are corrected for the interrelationships among all variables. The weights are referred to as discriminant coefficients.

Discriminant Function:

$$Z = W_1 X_1 + W_2 X_2 + \ldots\ldots + W_n X_n \qquad \text{Eq. 7.13}$$

where Z = discriminant score for each respondent/individual; W_n = discriminant weights and X_n are the explanatory factors.

The cut off Z-score is the combined benchmark for identified independent variables to classify the prospective borrower into defaulted or solvent category.

The discriminant function coefficients (W_s) are partial coefficients, reflecting the unique contribution of each variable to the classification of the criterion variable.

The objective of MDA is to choose a set of Ws such that the average score for group I (good) be as far away as possible from the average score for group II (bad or poor). This has been illustrated in the above two Figures (7.1 and 7.2).

Take a look at the above two figures showing score-wise distribution of bankrupt and non-bankrupt category of borrowers. The first graph has substantial overlapping of observations making it difficult to predict failure of large number of borrowers, while the second graph has very less overlapping area between the two categories. MDA attempts to find

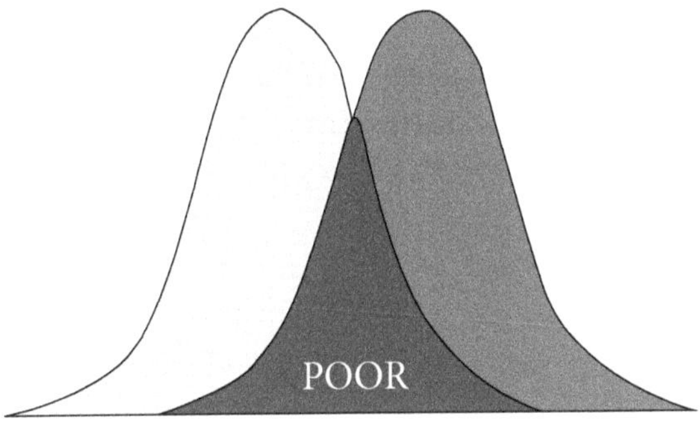

Figure 7.1 Scoring Distribution from Poorly Fitted Rating Model

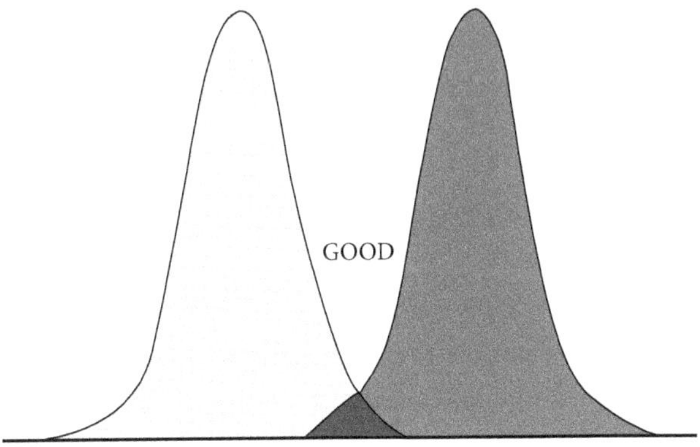

Figure 7.2 Good-Fitted Rating Model and Separation Power

maximum distance in mean between two groups with respect to each variable and their combinations.

The standardized discriminant coefficients are like beta weights in regression, are used to assess the relative classifying importance of the independent variables. In choosing the weights (W_s), our objective is to maximize the ratio of 'Between Group Variations' to 'Within Group Variations'.

The vector of coefficients of discriminant functions is obtained as the matrix product of the inverse of dispersion (or covariance) matrix and vector of difference (d) of means:

$$W = S^{-1} \times d$$

This method also applies in standard multivariate regression models. MDA can be done in SPSS statistical package using tool bar Analyse, Classify, Discriminant and using classification (prior probabilities, summary table, use covariance matrix-within group) specification and statistics (means, univariate ANOVA, Box's M, Fishers and Unstandardized) options.

Key Test Statistics for MDA

An 'F test (Wilks' lambda) is used to test if the discriminant model as a whole is significant,

If the F test shows significance, then the individual independent variables are assessed to see which differ significantly in mean by group and these are used to classify the dependent variable.

Tests of Significance

Wilks's lambda (WSS/TSS) is used in an ANOVA test of mean differences in DA, such that the smaller the lambda for an independent variable, the more that variable contributes to the discriminant function.

The F test (BSS/WSS with adjustment of degrees of freedom) of Wilks lambda checks which variables' contributions are significant. The

F statistic is a ratio of between-groups variability to the within groups variability.

Both these test statistics are checked to identify significant variables to be included in the multivariate model.

The test statistics has been further elaborated with an example. We have used various financial ratios to develop a corporate scorecard. For this, we have collected financial data from CMIE Prowess of 137 firms over 2005 to 2010. The yearly rating data of these companies are obtained from CRISIL's published rating scan. There are total 67 defaulted companies present in the pool. We have run MDA in SPSS on selected ratios. We first report the summary statistics in Table 7.3.

It is quite evident that there is a clear difference in performance in terms of key financial ratios between solvent (dsolv = 1) and defaulted (dsolv = 0) group. The factors tested are: cr = current ratio, mve_bvl = market value of equity to book value of liability, cprof_ta = cash profit to

Table 7.3 Summary Statistics about Discriminant Factors

Group Statistics					
dsolv		Mean	Std. Deviation	Valid N (Listwise)	
				Unweighted	Weighted
0	cr	1.629403669724770	3.129091402756838	218	218.000
	mve_bvl	.540453022264869	1.465333268079680	218	218.000
	cprof_ta	.041125647553356	.073056901108418	218	218.000
	sales_ta	.848597731535225	.492575228535643	218	218.000
	tbor_tnw	2.509333283744332	6.385493150897490	218	218.000
1	cr	1.606291793313070	.833764011451801	329	329.000
	mve_bvl	1.497905387823995	1.245969298908796	329	329.000
	cprof_ta	.120287957383471	.072040579436131	329	329.000
	sales_ta	1.123481145916347	.726820433300894	329	329.000
	tbor_tnw	.655488195727985	.891145175516745	329	329.000
Total	cr	1.615502742230347	2.075840681787653	547	547.000
	mve_bvl	1.116324737564600	1.416375643917792	547	547.000
	cprof_ta	.088738810138563	.082120971251966	547	547.000
	sales_ta	1.013929803439044	.657208727318622	547	547.000
	tbor_tnw	1.394314940129381	4.184213050158209	547	547.000

Table 7.4 MDA Results in SPSS: Group Mean Comparison Tests

Tests of Equality of Group Means					
	Wilks' Lambda	F	df1	df2	Sig.
cr	1.000	.016	1	545	.899
mve_bvl	.890	67.178	1	545	.000
cprof_ta	.777	156.553	1	545	.000
sales_ta	.958	23.900	1	545	.000
tbor_tnw	.953	26.962	1	545	.000

total asset, sales_ta = sales to total assets and tbor_tnw = total borrowings to total net-worth. These ratios are generated from the balance sheet data of this panel of companies.

The discriminatory results and key test statistics are reported in Table 7.4.

Notice that the group comparison test has reported Wilk's lambda and F test results. In all financial ratios except current ratio (cr), F values are statistically significant (since in Sig. column, p-values are lower than 0.01). Therefore, in developing scorecard, we can retain all these four ratios. Accordingly, we have dropped the current ratio and re-run the MDA analysis in SPSS.

The summary of canonical function based on the five factors has been summarized in Table 7.5. The larger the eigen value (SSB/SSW), the more of the variance in the dependent variable (i.e. dsolv = 1, if the borrower is solvent and = 0 if defaulted) is explained by the function. The canonical correlation (CC) is the measure of association between the discriminant function and (or z score obtained through estimated model coefficients) and the dependent variable (solvency dummy dsolv). $CC = \sqrt{\frac{SSB}{SSW}}$; higher the value, greater the predictive power of the estimated model. Thus, the square of the CC coefficient is the percentage of variance explained in the dependent variable.

Note that the canonical correlation coefficient is 0.505. Hence, the model has slightly above 50% explanatory power.

Wilk's lambda is a measure of how well each function separates cases into groups. Smaller values of Wilk's lambda (means lower error rate) indicate greater discriminatory power of the estimated function.

Table 7.5 Summary of Canonical Discriminant Function

Eigen Values				
Function	Eigen Value	% of Variance	Cumulative %	Canonical Correlation
1	0.343[a]	100.0	100.0	0.505

a. First 1 canonical discriminant functions were used in the analysis.

Table 7.5a Fitted Model's Separation Power

Wilks' Lambda				
Test of Function(s)	Wilks' Lambda	Chi-square	df	Sig.
1	.745	160.144	4	.000

Table 7.6 Standardized Discriminant Coefficients

Standardized Canonical Discriminant Function Coefficients	
	Function
	1
mve_bvl	.288
cprof_ta	.724
sales_ta	.244
tbor_tnw	-.204

The standardized discriminant function coefficients reported in the Table 7.6 serve the same purpose as beta weights in multiple regression (partial coefficient). Higher the beta, greater is the weightage. It helps the risk manager to identify which ratio has greater impact on the discriminant score. It allows him/her to compare variables measured on different scales.

Discriminant function reported in Table 7.7 is a latent variable that is created as a linear combination of independent variables. As a next step, we look at the discriminant Functions (Classification Functions).

Table 7.7 Classification Z Score Equation Separating Two Groups

Classification Function Coefficients			
	dsolv		Zscore
	0	1	
mve_bvl	.222	.479	0.257
cprof_ta	5.657	17.596	11.939
sales_ta	1.960	2.412	0.452
tbor_tnw	.181	.122	−0.059
(Constant)	−2.155	−3.321	−1.166

Fisher's linear discriminant functions

Two sets (one for each dependent group) of unstandardized linear discriminant coefficients are calculated, which can be used to classify cases and build the Z score.

Use the Z scores to predict the group: $Z = Z(1) - Z(0)$.

The model has been presented in the last column of Table 7.7.

Now, using the Bayes' probability theorem, we obtain the predicted probability that a corporate borrower will belong to defaulted (1) or solvent group (0). The prior probabilities are worked out based on the proportion of defaulted and solvent companies in each group. Here it is 40% for dsolv = 0 and 60% for dsolv = 1.

SPSS reports the group counts for each observations. Otherwise, use $EPS = 1 / (1 + \exp(-z))$ and use $EPS = 0.50$ as cut-off point.

Next, look at the Classification Statistics (check the classification that reports the overall predictive accuracy of the model).

Diagnostic Checks

Confusion Matrix

The discriminant function is used to find out how well it discriminates the sample data. This gives rise to the confusion matrix. There are four elements in this matrix, corresponding to the four cases generated by the combination of Actual Group I and Group II and Predicted Group I and

Table 7.8 Confusion Matrix

Classification Results[a,c]					
		dsolv	Predicted Group Membership		Total
			0	1	
Original	Count	0	139	79	218
		1	45	284	329
	%	0	63.8	36.2	100.0
		1	13.7	86.3	100.0
Cross-validated[b]	Count	0	139	79	218
		1	46	283	329
	%	0	63.8	36.2	100.0
		1	14.0	86.0	100.0

a. 77.3% of original grouped cases correctly classified.

b. Cross-validation is done only for those cases in the analysis. In cross-validation, each case is classified by the functions derived from all cases other than that case.

c. 77.1% of cross-validated grouped cases correctly classified.

Group II. If the overall correct classification is more than 80%, it is considered that the model has good separation power.

The confusion matrix is given in Table 7.8. The total of off diagonal elements is the number of misclassification.

The confusion matrix generated from the above model has been reported below.

- Count % correction prediction (True Positive and True Negative)
- Check Sensitivity-True positive rates or hit rates: TP / (TP + FN)
- Also check Specificity-True Negatives: TN / (TN + FP)
- Count Type I error rate: False + ve: FP rate= and Type II error: False –ve: FN Rate (also termed as 1-specificity)

The overall classification power of the model is 77.3%. The type I error rate is 36.2%. Similarly, type II error rate is 13.7%. However, the model accuracy can be further improved by experimenting more ratios or factors that the analyst wants to examine. For example, the analyst may want to add interest coverage ratio, networking capital to total assets instead of current ratio as well. This is a step-wise process and the entire process need to be repeated to take a final decision on the model. Finally, it has to be tested on a holdout sample as well. There should be proper balance between type I and type II error rate.

Plot ROC Curve

Using the obtained z score, compare predicted group with actual group using Receiver Operating Characteristic Curve. If the curve is smooth concave and covers greater area above the diagonal 45 degree line, higher would be the predictive power of the model.

The following figure displays the model accuracy power result. It plots the Sensitivity vs. 1-Specificity-greater the area above diagonal 45^0 line, better the predictive power of the model.

For constructing the confusion matrix and ROC plot, we predict the borrower risks by computing the Z scores. For this, we generate following equation:

```
COMPUTE Zscore
  = -1.166+0.257*mve_bvl+11.939*cprof_ta
  +0.452*sales_ta-0.059*tborr_tnw
As a next step, we predict expected probability
  of solvency
COMPUTE EPS=1/(1+exp(-Zscore))
```

Next, we compare the predicted EPS with actual state (dsolv). Note that dsolv is a dummy variable that represents solvency status of a company.

If the company is solvent, dsolv = 1 and if the company has defaulted the dummy value dsolv = 0. Here, Solvent group (dsolv = 1) has been considered as treatment group and dsolv = 0 has been taken as control group. Therefore, while drawing the ROC curve to assess the discriminatory power of the *Z* score model, we take EPS as test variable and dsolv as state variable, where value of the state variable is set as 1. The ROC plot is reported in Figure 7.3.

The area under ROC measures the discriminatory power of the model. The area under the curve = 0.827. The fitted graph based on the predicted z scores is well above the 45 degree diagonal line. Hence, the model has separation power. The predicted ranks are matching with actual position of risk of the borrowers. The riskier borrowers are located in the lower panel of the graph and safer companies are in the upper side of the graph.

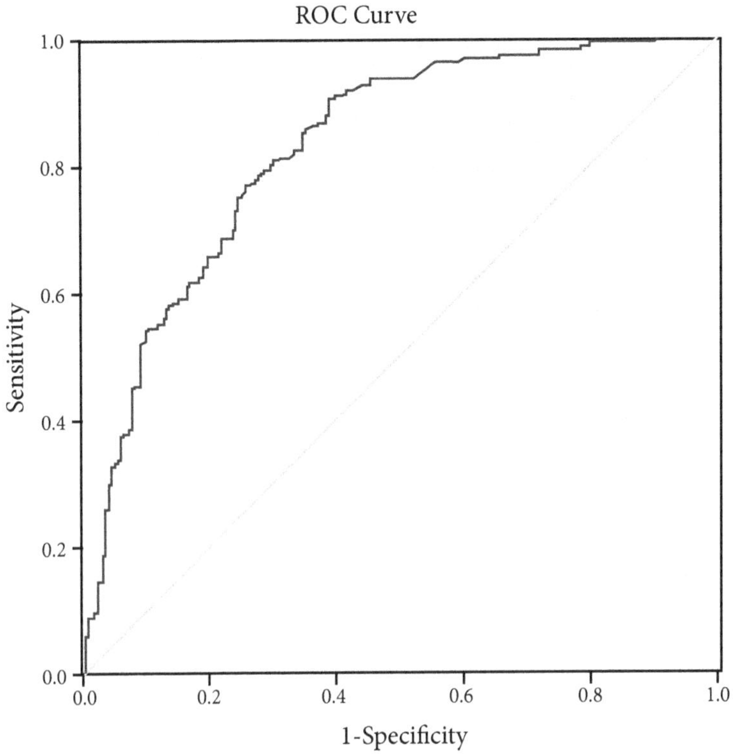

Figure 7.3 ROC plot

Application of MDA Technique

Statistical techniques like MDA methods may be applied to design Qualitative Risk Rating of Operational Risk Management Process in a Bank (as part of QLA).It is popularly used to develop Credit Scoring Models (Both Corporate as well as Retail)-Good borrower vs. Bad borrower. Further it may be of interest to assess the relative importance of the variables for discrimination purposes. From the investor's point of view, it is necessary to discriminate between the shares based upon financial and other results into 'Good Buy' or 'Bad Buy'. This helps in Portfolio selection.

Altman (1968) had developed the bankruptcy predictor model using MDA analysis. The discriminant scoring model was developed for publicly traded manufacturing firms in the United States. The indicator Z score is an overall measure of default risk of a borrower. The weighted importance of these ratios are based on the past observed experience of 33 defaulting vs. 33 similar set of non-defaulting companies over many years. Altman's statistically derived discriminant function (Z-score credit classification model) takes the form of:

$$Z = 1.2X_1 + 1.4X_2 + 3.3X_3 + 0.6X_4 + 0.999X_5 \qquad \text{Eq. 7.14}$$

where X_1 = working capital/total assets; X_2 = Retained earnings/total assets; X_3 = Earnings before interest and taxes/total assets; X_4 = Market value of equity/book value of total liabilities; and X_5 = Sales/total assets. Working capital is current assets minus current liabilities.

The higher the value of *Z* score, lower is the chance that a corporate will default. If Z > 2.99, borrower is considered safe. A borrower with Z score below 1.81 is classified as risky. Hence, a bank should not sanction a loan to this borrower until it improves its earnings. Note that the third variable, EBIT to total assets ratio has the highest importance in the above *Z* score model.

Suppose a risk manager has collected following financial information about the company using its latest audited balance sheet report. The financial data is given in Table 7.9 below:

Table 7.9 Company Financials (Selected)

Items	**Unit in $ Million**
Total assets	100
Current assets	40
Current liabilities	35
Long-term debt (book)	50
Total stockholders' equity (book)	15
Retained earnings	10
Sales	150
EBIT	8
Market value of equity	30

Source: Author's own illustration.

Table 7.10 Financial Ratios

Ratios	Variables	Values
X1	NWC/TA	0.05
X2	RE/TA	0.1
X3	EBIT/TA	0.08
X4	MVE/BVL	0.352941
X5	Sales/TA	1.5

Source: Author's own

Based on the financial data, all the five ratios used by Altman' model has been estimated.

Applying these financial ratios, the analyst obtains the Z score value using Equation 8.5. The value of obtained Z score = 2.17. As per the Altman's benchmark, it indicates the company is in a Gray zone and risk is moderate. The expected probability of default of the borrower (EPD) = 1 / (1 + exp(2.17)) = 10.21%.

Non-Linear Probability Models-Logistic Regression

In logistic regression, we want to be able to model the probability of the event occurring with an explanatory variable '*X*', but we want the predicted probability to remain within the [0,1] bounds. Logistic function enables us to address nonlinear relation and brings probability to be bounded between 0 and 1.

The Logistic Curve will relate the explanatory variable X to the probability of the event occurring. In our example, it will relate the number of study hours with the probability of passing the exam. Similarly, it can related debt equity ratio or loan to value ratio of a borrower to its probability of default.

We could use the Normal Cumulative Distribution instead of the Logistic Curve. This would lead us to Probit Models. Basically, then, the difference between probit and logit models in theoretical terms has to do with the probability distribution we assume for the underlying process.

In the logistic regression, we will be interested in finding estimates for α and βsso that the Logistic Function best fits the data. This is done through using Maximum Likelihood Estimation (MLE) method:

$$LL = \ln L = \sum_{i=1}^{n} [y_i \ln p_i + (1 - y_i)\ln(1 - p_i)] \qquad \text{Eq. 7.15}$$

In a nutshell, Logistic regression is a multiple regression with an outcome variable (or dependent variable) that is a categorical dichotomous (or binary) and explanatory variables that can be either continuous or categorical. In other words, the interest is in predicting which of two possible events are going to happen given certain other information.

Pseudo R2 measures for logistic regression, which is one approach to assessing model fit.

Logit regression technique is popularly used in developing credit scoring models for Corporate/SMEs/Retail Loans.

The logit model overcomes the weakness of 'un-boundedness' problem of MDA and Linear Probability Models by restricting the estimated range of default probabilities to lie between 0 and 1.

Essentially this is done by plugging the estimated values of Z from LPM into the formula: $F(z) = 1/(1 + \exp(-z))$.

Application of Logit Model in Risk Management

Logistic regression is a simple and appropriate technique for estimating the log of the odds of default as a linear function of loan application attributes:

$$\ln\left[\frac{\text{Prob(Default)}}{\text{Prob(Solvency)}}\right] = \beta_0 + \beta_1 X_1 + \beta_2 X_2 + \beta_3 X_3 + \ldots + \beta_k X_{k.} \qquad \text{Eq. 7.16}$$

where (1−p) is the 'odds ratio & ln[p/(1−p)]' is the log odds ratio, or 'logit'

An interpretation of the logit coefficient which is usually more intuitive is the 'odds ratio'.

Since:

$$[p/(1-p)] = \exp(\alpha+\beta X)$$

$\exp(\beta)$ is the effect of the independent variable on the 'odds ratio'

A logistic model has the flexibility of incorporating both the qualitative and quantitative factors and is more efficient than the linear regression probability model.

In logistic regression exercise, we are actually predicting the probability of a loan default based on the financial, non-financial (qualitative borrower characteristics), situational factors (location and local factors) obtained from the credit files of the Bank and external macro-economic conditions.

Suppose the modelling team in the bank has developed a corporate default predictor model using logistic regression in STATA.

The model has been expressed in the following equation:

$$Z = -0.81X1 + 0.15X2 + 1.25X3 - 0.45X4$$

The factor information for LMN Company Ltd. is given below:

All factors are statistically significant. The overall explanatory power (R-square) = 0.60.

Based on the values of the ratios, we can obtain Z score for the LMN Company. The obtained Z score = −1.5655. Now using the exponential function, we derive the expected PD for the company. The estimated EPD = 1/((1 + exp(−Z)) = 1/(1 + exp(1.5655)) = 17.29%.

This expected PD then can be compared with the actual default rates for calibration purpose. The same exercise should be repeated for good

Table 7.11 Financial Ratios of LMN Company Ltd.

Factors	Ratios	Values
X1	Liquidity ratio	2.15
X2	Debt to Assets ratio	45%
X3	Volatility in earnings	0.13
X4	Profit margin	12%

Source: Author's own illustration

Table 7.12 Logit Regression Log

. logit default linc employ debtinc creddebt address

Iteration 0: log likelihood = −984.63781
Iteration 1: log likelihood = −721.76856
Iteration 2: log likelihood = −690.08537
Iteration 3: log likelihood = −688.92442
Iteration 4: log likelihood = −688.9225
Iteration 5: log likelihood = −688.9225

Logistic regression Number of obs = 1500
LR chi²(5) = 591.43
Prob > chi² = 0.0000
Log likelihood = −688.9225 Pseudo R2 = 0.3003

default |	Coef.	Std. Err.	z	P>|z|	[95% Conf. Interval]	
linc |	0.011831	0.1650405	0.07	0.943	−0.3116425	0.3353044
employ |	−.2217707	0.0204973	−10.82	0.000	−0.2619446	−0.1815968
debtinc |	0.1044247	0.0126975	8.22	0.000	0.079538	0.1293113
creddebt |	0.4852114	0.0559389	8.67	0.000	0.3755731	0.5948497
address |	−0.0769442	0.0190054	−4.05	0.000	−0.1141941	−0.0396942
_cons |	−1.031523	0.5766316	−1.79	0.074	−2.161701	.0986538

companies (better rated) as well as bad companies (defaulted or lower rated). For corporates, financial data can be obtained from CMIE Prowess source or Ace Equity. For default information, one can check the published rating given by Credit Rating Agencies. Internally, banks can use their past default data for predicting future defaults. This way, logit model works.

We have run similar model on retail loan accounts as well. A 1500 account level cross section data was used to run logit regressions in STATA to predict default risk. The MLE based logit regression output has been reported in Table 7.12:

Variable Description

Default: dependent variable is a dummy (default = 1 if the account has defaulted on loan payments and default = 0 if the account is solvent).

linc: log of income
employ: number of years in the present job
debtinc: debt to income ratio (or burden) in %
creddebt: credit card debt in '000$
address: number of years in the current address
_cons: intercept term

Note that in the above logistic regression result, all the independent factors except 'linc' are statistically significant (since z values are higher and p values < 0.01). The intercept value is statistically significant. This means influence of other factors are insignificant. The sign of significant factors helps us to relate the factor with probability of default. For example, an increase in employment year as well as number of years in the current address reduce default risk. On the other hand, an increase in debt to income ration significantly increases default probability of the personal loan borrower.

We can also measure the effect of one unit change in factor on default risk. For this, if we take employ variable, we use $\{exp(\beta)\text{-}1\}\times 100$ and obtain value -19.8901. This value captures the effect of one unit change in the regression factor on odd ration in favour of default. That means, with a 10% increase in x factor (i.e. employment year), the odds of default gets reduced by 1.9%.

The 'economic significance' of each factor can be checked through estimating beta factor. Let's consider independent variable 'employ'. From the estimated coefficient (= – 0.2217707), we obtain $\beta = (\text{coeff}) \times \left(\dfrac{\sigma_x}{\sigma_y}\right)$

By plugging in standard deviation of x factor (σ_x = 8.977644) and standard deviation of y – 0.4816841, we get $\beta = -4.13337$.

This can be interpreted as: with one standard deviation increase in employment year, odd to default reduces by 4 standard deviation.

After regression, we can predict the expected probability of default using the above equation.

For this, we write following command in the STATA:

. predict epd

(option pr assumed; Pr(default))

Validation of Predictive Power of Logit Models

There are several statistics which can be used for comparing alternative models or evaluating the performance of a single model:

- Model Chi-Square (Fitness)
- Percent Correct Predictions
- Pseudo-R^2

Model Chi-square:

The model likelihood ratio (LR), statistic is

$$LR[k] = -2[LL(\alpha) - LL(\alpha, \beta) \qquad \text{Eq. 7.17}$$

From the STATA regression results, we can compute the LR chi^2.

$$LR[i] = [\{-2LL\,(of\ beginning\ model)\} - \{-2LL\,(of\ ending\ model)\}]$$

The LR statistic is distributed chi-square with k degrees of freedom, where k is the number of independent variables. One has to use the 'Model Chi-Square' statistic to determine if the overall model is statistically significant.

Based on the regression results reported in Table 7.12, one can use Equation 8.8 to verify whether we are getting the same LR chi^2 value.

Let's check this. Our obtained $LL(\alpha) = -984.63781$ and $LL(\alpha, \beta) = -688.9225$. Using these two estimates, we get LR chi^2=

$$[\{-2LL\,(-688.9225)\} - \{-2LL\,(-688.9225)\}]$$
$$= 591.43$$

The degrees of freedom for chi-square test is $k-1 = 5+1-1 = 5$

Prob > $chi^2 = 0.0000$ indicate that the null hypothesis of all coefficients of factors including intercept = 0 is being rejected and the model fits well.

For more advanced analysis, A Hosmer Lemeshow Goodness of Fit Test is conducted to check the validity of the model. This has been discussed with examples in Validation chapter. The detailed test statistics about logistic regressions are also elaborated in Hendry and Nielsen (2007).

Percent Correction Predictions

The 'Percent Correct Predictions' statistic assumes that if the estimated p is greater than or equal to 0.5 then the event is expected to occur and not occur otherwise. By assigning these probabilities 0s and 1s and comparing these to the actual 0s and 1s, the % correct Yes, % correct No, and overall % correct scores are calculated. A Hosmer Lemeshow Goodness of Fit Test is conducted to check the validity of the model.

c. Pseudo R2: It is also termed as Mc Fadden's R-square statistic to check the validity of the logistic regression model.

$$\text{McFadden's-R}^2 = 1 - [\text{LL}(\alpha, \beta)/\text{LL}(\alpha)]$$
$$= [1 - \{-2\text{LL}(\alpha, \beta)/ -2\text{LL}(\alpha)\}]$$

where the R^2 is a scalar measure which varies between 0 and (somewhat close to) 1 much like the R^2 in a LP model.

Using the LL estimates obtained in Table 7.6, we can again check the McFadden's-R^2.

$$= [1 - \{-2 \times -688.9225) / (-2 \times -984.63781)\}]$$
$$= 0.3003$$

There are other validation test as well to be sure about predicted model accuracy. This has been discussed in Chapter 9.

Panel Regression Methods

In panel data, cross section units/individuals (persons, companies, banks, states, countries etc.) are observed at several points in times (quarters, years, before and after treatment etc.). These are repeated observations on the same cross-section units. For this reason, it is also known as longitudinal or cross sectional time series data. Panel data basically pools both cross section as well as time series observations and behaviour of entities are observed across time. These entities could be states, companies, individuals, countries etc. By combining time series of cross section observations, panel data provide more data observations, greater variability, less collinearity among variables, more degrees of freedom and more efficiency. Panel data are most useful when we suspect that the outcome variable (*Y*) depends on explanatory variables which are not observable but correlated with the observed explanatory variables. If such omitted (unobserved) variables are constant over time (or time invariant), panel data estimators allow to consistently estimate the effect of the observed explanatory variables. Panel data allows a researcher to control for variables that cannot be observed or measured like cultural factors or difference in business practices across companies (or banks). This is, it accounts for individual heterogeneity.

The Panel Econometric Model

Let's consider the dependent variable y_{it} is the value of the variable for cross section unit *i* and time *t* where $i = 1, \ldots, n$ and $t = 1, 2, \ldots, T$

X^j_{it} is the value of the *j*th explanatory variable for unit *i* at time *t*. There are *K* explanatory variables indexed by $j = 1, 2, \ldots, K$.

We are mainly considering balanced panels. That is, we have the same number of observations on each cross-section unit, so that the total number of observations is $n \times T$. Normally in a standard panel data structure, the number of observations *N* is large relative to the number of time periods *T*. It is generally recommended that the *T* should be at least 6 to remove any biasness in the panel estimation.

The basic equation for panel data analysis may be characterized by the following equation:

$$y_{it} = \beta X_{it} + u_{it} \qquad \text{Eq. 7.18}$$

where β is the coefficient for the set of explanatory variables X_{it}.

The error term ε_{it} is the stochastic term that captures time varying and bank (or firm) specific random components. Where the error term u_{it} can be expressed as:

$$u_{it} = \alpha_i + \varepsilon_{it} \qquad \text{Eq. 7.18a}$$

for $i = 1, N$ and $t = 1, T$.

The error term ε_{it} thus represents the effects of the omitted variables that are particular to individual units α_i s and time periods.

Let $E(\alpha_i) = E(\varepsilon_{it}) = 0$, $Var(\alpha_i) = \sigma_\alpha^2$, $Var(\varepsilon_{it}) = \sigma_\varepsilon^2$, and $E(\alpha_i, \varepsilon_{it}) = 0$.

The presence of α_i leads to serial correlation in the u_{it}, $E(u_{it}u_{is}) = \sigma_\alpha^2$ for $t \neq s$; thus, failure to account for α_i leads, at a minimum, to incorrect standard errors and inefficient estimation. Moreover, if α_i is correlated with x_{it}, failure to account for α_i leads to heterogeneity (omitted variables) bias in the estimate of β.

The Simplest Case-Pooled Estimation

The simplest estimation method is to stack the data and use it as a linear model and apply Ordinary Least Squares (OLS). The mode will look like:

$$y = \beta X + \varepsilon \qquad \text{Eq. 7.19}$$

STATA Command:

```
Option 1: OLS
reg y x1 x2 x3
```

However, this method has limitation and is less efficient since the panel structure is not properly used and the unobserved individual effect may be correlated with the regressor term.

The Fixed Effect Model

Fixed-effects (FE) specification is used whenever researcher only interested in analysing the impact of variables that vary over time. FE explores the relationship between predictor and outcome variables within an entity (country, person, company, etc.). Each entity has its own individual characteristics that may or may not influence the predictor variables. For example, being a male or female could influence the opinion toward certain issue; or the political system of a particular country could have some effect on trade or GDP; or the business practices of a company may influence its stock price.

When using FE we assume that something within the individual may impact or bias the predictor or outcome variables and we need to control for this. This is the rationale behind the assumption of the correlation between entity's error term and predictor variables. FE removes the effect of those time-invariant characteristics so we can assess the net effect of the predictors on the outcome variable.

The equation for the fixed effects model used is

$$y_{it} = \beta_k X_{it} + \alpha_i + \varepsilon_{it} \qquad \text{Eq. 7.19a}$$

where

α_i (i = 1, . . . , n) is the unknown intercept for each cross section unit (say firms, banks, countries etc.)

y_{it} is the dependent variable where i = entity and t = time.

X_{it} represents the set of independent variables

β_k is the set of coefficients

ε_{it} is the error term

The key insight is that in the fixed effect model, the individual specific effect 'α_i' is a random variable that is allowed to be correlated with the explanatory variables.

LSDV Model

The least-square dummy variable model (LSDV) provides a good way to understand panel fixed effects. The effect of x1 is mediated by the differences across countries or states or industries. By adding the dummy for each country/state/industry we are estimating the pure effect of x1 (by controlling for the unobserved heterogeneity). Each dummy is absorbing the effects particular to each country/industry/state. Thus, the LSDV estimator is pooled OLS including a set of N−1 dummy variables which identify the individuals and hence an additional N−1 parameters. Note that to avoid dummy trap, one of the individual dummies is dropped because we include a constant. The time invariant explanatory variables are dropped because they are perfectly collinear with the individual dummy variables. You can generate multiple dummies in STATA package.

The LSDV estimator of β is numerically identical with the FE estimator and therefore consistent under the same assumptions. The SDV estimators of the additional parameters for the individual-specific dummy variables, however, are inconsistent as the number of parameters goes to infinity as $N \rightarrow \propto$. A more detailed discussions on panel data regression methods are explained in Hsiao (1986), Baltagi (2008), and Wooldridge (2010).

STATA Command:

Option 2: OLS with dummies

```
xi: regress y x1 x2 x3 i.country
estimates store ols

Option 3: LSDV model using areg
areg y x1 x2 x3, absorb(country)
estimates store areg
```

Limitations of Fixed Effect Approach

Fixed effect model cannot estimate effects of variables which vary across individuals but not over time. One cannot use dummies to control for omitted variables. Use of fixed effects is inefficient if α_i is uncorrelated with X_{it} (i.e. if appropriate model is random effects).

Random Effect Model

In the random effects model, the individual specific effect is a random variable (α_i) that is uncorrelated with the explanatory variable (X_{it}). The random effect estimator is the feasible generalized least-squares (GLS) estimator.

Fixed Effect vs. Random Effect Specification

Key consideration is the orthogonality of α_i. If omitted variable (or fixed effect) α_i is uncorrelated with the explanatory variable X_{it}, (i.e. E(X_{it}, α_i) = 0), then random effects is the appropriate estimator. However, if α_i is correlated with the variables in X_{it}, then the fixed effects model is appropriate.

This can be examined using Wu-Hausman Test. For this, run both FE and RE models and compute the test statistic.

$$[\hat{\beta}_{FE} - \hat{\beta}_{RE}]' [\mathrm{Var}(\hat{\beta}_{FE}) - \mathrm{Var}(\hat{\beta}_{RE})]^{-1} [\hat{\beta}_{FE} - \hat{\beta}_{RE}] \sim \chi_k^2 \qquad \text{Eq. 7.20}$$

This test is based on the difference of the two estimated covariance matrices and the difference between the fixed effects and random effects vectors of slope coefficients.

The Hausman test's null—difference in coefficients not systematic.

To decide between fixed or random effects we have to run a Hausman test where then null hypothesis (H_0) is that the preferred model is random effects vs. the alternative the fixed effects (Green, 2008, chapter 9). It basically checks whether the unique errors (α_i) are correlated with the regressors (X_{it}), the null hypothesis is they are not (i.e. E(X_{it}, α_i) = 0).[1]

In the Hausman test, the null is that the two estimation methods are both OK and that therefore they should yield coefficients that are 'similar'. The alternative hypothesis is that the fixed effects estimation is OK and

[1] The crucial distinction between fixed and random effects is whether the unobserved individual effect embodies elements that are correlated with the regressors in the model, not whether these effects are stochastic or not (Green, 2008, p.183).

the random effects estimation is not; if this is the case, then we would expect to see differences between the two sets of coefficients.

This is because the random effects estimator makes an assumption (the random effects are orthogonal to the regressors, i.e. $E(X_{it}, \alpha_i) = 0$) that the fixed effects estimator does not. If this assumption is wrong, the random effects estimator will be inconsistent, but the fixed effects estimator is unaffected. Hence, if the assumption is wrong, this will be reflected in a difference between the two set of coefficients. The bigger the difference (the less similar are the two sets of coefficients), the bigger the Hausman statistic.

We are actually comparing the coefficients estimated by both the techniques. If there is a large difference, then fixed effect specification is correct. If there is no significant difference, then fixed effect specification is incorrect and random effect specification is correct. The observed difference mainly occurs due to the zero correlation between α_i and X_{it}.

The Hausman test statistic is asymptotically distributed as Chi-Square with k degrees of freedom under the null hypothesis that the random effect estimator is correct i.e. if the random effect model is correctly specified and alpha i is uncorrelated with the regressor X_{it}. In such a case the coefficient estimated by fixed effect estimator and same coefficient that are also estimated by random effect should not statistically differ (i.e. null hypothesis). The significance of the Chi-Square statistic of the Hausman test enables us to make a choice between Fixed Effect and Random Effect Models. If the p value reported in the Hausman Chi-Square test is less than 5%, we reject the null hypothesis and hence fixed effect model is more appropriate than random effect estimator. If the p value is higher than the 5%, we select random effect specification.

Thus, a large and significant Hausman statistic means a large and significant difference, and so you reject the null that the two methods are OK in favour of the alternative hypothesis that one is OK (fixed effects) and one isn't (random effects).

It is worthwhile to mention that many researchers use Breusch-Pagan Lagrange Multiplier (LM) test to check the validity of Random Effect Model vis-à-vis Simple Pooled Robust Regression. It checks whether there is any significant difference across units. A lower chi-square or higher p-value (> 0.05) would fail to reject the null (no panel effect) and conclude that the random effect is not appropriate.

To take a final decision on the specification of panel model structure, they go by Hausman (1978) test and then check LM test to decide the suitability of Fixed Effect or Random Effect or simple regression model.

Following STATA commands may be used for different specifications:

STATA Command:

```
Option 4: pure fixed effect regression
xtreg y x1 x2 x3, fe
estimates store fixed

xtreg y x1 x2 x3, re

estimates store random
```

As a next step, perform Hausman test in STATA. This has been shown in the following example:

Example of Panel Regression in STATA: Factors Determine Refinancing by Housing Finance Companies (HFCs)

Step 1

```
. xtreg nhbborr_tbor lta costincr hc_car,fe
```

Description of Variables used:

Note that Dependent variable (nhbborr_tbor) is Borrowings from National Housing Bank (NHB) to total borrowings

The independent variables are:

lta = natural log of total assets proxy the firm size

constincr = cost to income ratio

hc_car = capital adequacy ratio of the HFCs

The overall R2 is 0.25 and model fits well

Table 7.13 Fixed Effect Regression Output in STATA

Fixed-effects (within) regression	Number of obs = 55
Group variable (i): hfccode	Number of groups = 9
R-sq: within = **0.2314**	Obs per group: min = 2
between = 0.0991	avg = 6.1
overall = 0.2501	max = 7
	F (3,43) = **4.31**
corr(u_i, Xb) = **0.0205**	Prob > F = **0.0096**

nhbborr_ tbor |	**Coef.**	**Std. Err.**	**t**	**P > |t|**	**[95% Conf. Interval]**	
lta |	−0.0428185	0.0214825	−1.99	0.053	−0.086142	0.0005051
costincr |	0.80406	0.3405904 2.36	0.023	0.117194	1.490926	
hc_car |	−0.0048049	0.0025335	−1.90	0.065	−0.0099143	0.0003044
_cons |	0.1106996	0.2719528	0.41	0.686	−0.4377454	0.6591446
sigma_u |	0.16060138					
sigma_e |	0.0642141					
rho |	0.8621669				(fraction of variance due to u_i)	
F test that all u_i = 0:		F(8, 43) = 17.20			Prob > F = 0.0000	

Finally it has 9 HFCs (number of groups) and 6 years data (time dimension).

The above analysis is based on 9 Housing Finance Company's data over 6 years.

Interpretation: The F statistics tests whether all the coefficients in the model are different than zero. If the reported p value is < 0.05, then your model is ok. In fixed effect regression, you must check the within R2 since it uses within estimator. In terms of goodness of fit, the R2 between is directly relevant; our R2 is 0.099. Check the errors u_i are correlated with the regressors in the fixed effects model.

Step 2

```
. estimates store fixed
```

Step 3

Now we Run Random Effect Model in our panel data. For this, we first save the estimates of fixed effect model. Then we run random model and also save the estimates, after this, we perform the Hausman test.

```
. xtreg nhbborr_tbor lta costincr hc_car,re
```

Step 4

```
. estimates store random
```

Table 7.14 Random Effect Regression Output in STATA

Random-effects GLS regression				Number of obs = 55		
Group variable (i): hfccode				Number of groups = 9		
R-sq: within = 0.1903				Obs per group: min = 2		
between = 0.2589				avg = 6.1		
overall = 0.3754				max = 7		
Random effects u_i ~ Gaussian				Wald chi² (3) = 14.50		
corr(u_i, X) = 0 (assumed)				Prob > chi² = 0.0023		
nhbborr_ tbor |	**Coef.**	**Std. Err.**	**z**	**P>|z|**	**[95% Conf. Interval]**	
lta |	−0.0535556	.0166155	−3.22	0.001	−0.0861214	−0.0209898
costincr |	0.4493765	.3251626	1.38	0.167	−0.1879304	1.086683
hc_car |	−0.0032995	.0027549	−1.20	0.231	−0.008699	0.0021001
_cons |	.4900928	.2871467	1.71	0.088	−0.0727044	1.05289
sigma_u |	0.08470031					
sigma_e |	0.0642141					
rho |	0.63501518		(fraction of variance due to u_i)			

Finally Perform Hausman Test in STATA by writing following command:

```
. hausman fixed random, sigmamore
```

	Coefficients			
	(b)	(B)	(b-B)	sqrt(diag (V_b-V_B))
	fixed	random	Difference	S.E.
lta	-.0428185	-.0535556	.0107371	.01773
costincr	.80406	.4493765	.3546835	.2065903
hc_car	-.0048049	-.0032995	-.0015055	.000789

```
b = consistent under Ho and Ha; obtained from xtreg
B = inconsistent under Ha, efficient under Ho;
  obtained from xtreg

Test: Ho: difference in coefficients not systematic

      chi2(3) = (b-B)'[(V_b-V_B)^(-1)](b-B)
              = 13.38
    Prob>chi2 = 0.0039
It confirms that Fixed effect model specification
  is right (since p < 0.05).
```

Note

STATA report three R-squares are:

(1) Within: The R-squared from the mean-deviated regression; i.e. the ordinary R-squared from running OLS on the transformed data.
(2) Between: first, this computes the fitted values using the fixed-effects parameter vector and the within-individual means of the independent variables. Then calculates the R-squared as the squared correlation between those predicted values and the within-individual means of the original y variable.
(3) Overall: first, this computes the fitted values using the fixed-effects parameter vector and the original, untransformed independent

variables. Then calculates the R-squared as the squared correlation between those predicted values and the original, untransformed y variable.

For fixed effects, we report within R-squared since it uses the within estimator. The fixed effect estimation subtracts the time averages from the initial model. The fixed effect estimator or within estimator of the slope coefficient β estimates the within model by OLS. Panel data regression applications are further elaborated in Reyna (2007) and Schmidheiny (2015).

Such Panel regression method is very useful in studying the effect of various risk factors (idiosyncratic as well as systematic) on performance of banks. It also enables an analyst to study the interlink age between credit risk, liquidity risk and market risk factors on bank performance. Many researchers have developed integrated risk management capital solutions based on panel regression methods.

To further demonstrate the application of multivariate panel regression method in risk management research, another example has been worked out. Table 7.15 the multivariate Panel Regression results based on ownership type of the banks. Our two set of multivariate models capture the relationship between the identified bank specific factors (including capital infusion) and with bank performance indicators as expressed by Return on Assets and Net Interest Margin for PSBs. Table 7.15 also demonstrates how panel regression results with proper diagnostic checks should be presented systematically.

A Hausman (1978) test has been employed to determine if a fixed effect or a random effects estimator was appropriate. Further, the LM test is employed on the residuals to check whether simple robust regression (OLS with robust standard error) or a random effects estimator was appropriate. We have also performed variance inflation (VIF) test to check if there is any multi-collinearity problem. In all our models, there is no multicollinearity issue. We first go by Hausman test and then check LM test to finally decide the suitability of appropriate panel regression model.

In the panel regression model reported in Table 17.15, we examine various bank specific factors including capital infusion on the bank performance. Return on Assets (ROA) of a bank is a financial ratio which measures net income as a percentage of average total assets of the bank. It indicates how efficient the management of the bank is, at employing its assets to generate profits.

Table 7.15 Panel Regressions Results of Two Models representing Determinants of Bank Performance

Dependent Variables:	Model 1: ROA	Model 2: NIM
Independent Variables		
GNPA	−0.117*** (−14.02)	−0.064*** (−5.75)
CASA	0.048*** (4.14)	0.052*** (4.21)
Credit/Deposits	−0.009*** (−2.65)	0.021** (1.97)
FeeInc/TI	--	−0.048 (−1.51)
CostInc	−0.012 (−1.63)	--
IntInc/WF	−0.003 (−0.08)	--
Cap/NW	−0.0017 (−0.57)	0.007* (0.08)
Constant	0.0097 (1.18)	−0.0001 (−0.02)
No. of Obs.	189	189
$AdjR^2$	0.8246	0.4164
F or Wald chi^2 Statistics	F(6,20): 101.77***	Wald chi^2 (5): 47.22***
Hausman Test#	chi^2 (6) = 30.33***	chi^2 (5) = 3.20
LM Test$	0.7086	0.0000***
Panel Model Chosen	Fixed Effect (FE) Model	Random Effect (RE) Model

Note: The above result is based on panel data analysis of 21 public sector banks over 9 years (2009 to 2018) Figures in the parentheses are *t*-values in Model 1 and Model 2. They are heteroskedasticity robust. ***: Significant at 1% or better level; **: Significant at 1–5%level; *: Significant at 5–10% level.

#: Hausman test checks the validity of fixed effect regression. $: Breusch-Pagan Lagrange Multiplier (LM) test checks the validity of Random Effect Model vs. Simple Regression.

In line with our expectations, the credit risk captured by gross non-performing assets to gross advances ratio (GNPA) has a significant negative effect on the profitability ratio i.e. ROA of PSBs. The loss assets increase the provisioning costs of the banks, which exert pressure on their profits.

Further, we have also estimated the economic significance of GNPA ratio on profitability of public sector banks. We find that a one unit change in Gross NPA ratio (e.g. 1 percentage point) significantly reduces the Return on Assets by 11.7 basis points for public sector banks (PSBs). For this, we have used the concept of beta weight (beta coefficient = $\beta \times (\sigma x/\sigma y)$. For GNPA, the beta coefficient is – 0.85314. It implies that for a 1 standard deviation increase in Gross Non-Performing Assets, the Return on Assets (ROA) of Public Sector Banks on average decreases by 0.85 standard deviation for PSBs.

The variable CASA has a positive and significant relationship with ROA in case of public sector banks (PSBs). We have also found that in terms of economic significance, a one standard deviation increase in CASA ratio (ratio of deposits in current and saving accounts to total deposits) can increase ROA of PSBs on average by 0.54 standard deviation. Thus, our results obtained in model 1 regression confirm that that banks having access to low cost CASA deposits and who are able to maintain higher capital adequacy ratio can sustain financial distress without a dent in the profits.

However, we don't find any significant impact of cost to income ratio (CostInc) and interest income to working funds (IntInc/WF) on profitability.

We have examined whether GoI capital infusion results in increase in the profitability of PSBs. As can be seen, the variable Capital infused to Net-worth (Cap/NW) has an insignificant impact on ROA of PSBs. Therefore, Capital infusion has enabled the PSBs to preserve capital but has not resulted into their profitability.

Model 2 exhibits the relationship between NIM and various independent variables. The Net Interest Margin for a bank is the difference between interest paid and interest received adjusted relative to the amount of interest generating assets. As can be seen GNPA has negative significant impact on the NIM of all the banks indicating that the problem of NPAs exerts pressure on the interest margins of PSBs as the interest payment is not received in an NPA account.

The CASA variable too has positive significant effect on NIM for all the PSBs. The positive effect is an indication that higher CASA implies access to low cost deposits which in turn leads to lower cost of funds and higher profits for the banks.

The Credit/Deposits ratio has a positive significant effect on the NIM of the PSBs. The results obtained are in line with the results of the study which stated that deposits have positive impact on the profits of commercial banks.

The model also brings out that Fee Income to Total Income ratio does not have any significant impact on the interest margins of the Public Sector Banks.

The variable Cap/NW has positive impact on the Net Interest Margins of PSBs. However the statistical result provides moderate level of significance reiterating that Capital Infusion by GoI in PSBs has not translated much into the profitability of PSBs.

It is important to note that the F and Wald Chi-square statistics provides indication about good overall fitness of the models.

In the same manner, one can use panel regression to determine market risk factors as well. Rosenberg and Schuermann's (2006) paper explains the use of such multivariate model to create market risk loss scenarios. In their regression model, dependent variable was: Annual trading revenues/(trading assets and liabilities). The independent regression factors were: equity return, equity volatility, change in interest rate, interest rate volatility, Foreign exchange return, Foreign exchange volatility and change in the slope of the yield curve. The regression model through statistical test confirms that foreign exchange returns, interest rate volatility, equity volatility and the change in slope of the yield curve (slope = difference between 10 year and 3 month treasury rate) positively influence the proportion trading revenues to trading assets and liabilities of banks.

Heteroskedasticity and Multicollinearity Tests

While finalizing the regression models, one should also check whether the presence of multicollinearity and heteroskedasticity are damaging the regression estimates. There is a Breusch-Pagan/Cook-Weisberg Test for Heteroskedasticity check to detect its presence. The null hypothesis in this test is = H_0: constant variance. A large chi-square would indicate rejection of the null hypothesis and presence of heteroskedaticity. This can be run in STATA. One can also use Jarque-Bera test to check the normality of the residual series.

To detect heteroskedasticity, we have performed Cook Weisberg test in STATA. This we have done on estimating factors that determine bank performance (measured by return on assets: ROA). We first run the regression in STATA:

Table 7.16 Regression Results on Bank Variables

. reg roa ln_totass costinc casa capnw gnpa

Source |	SS	df	MS	Number of obs = 189
-------------+----------------------------				F(5, 183) = 139.42
Model | .005218752	5	0.00104375		Prob > F = 0.0000
Residual | .001369979	183 7.4862e-06			R-squared = 0.7921
-------------+----------------------------				Adj R-squared = 0.7864
Total | .006588731	188 .000035046			Root MSE = .00274

roa |	Coef.	Std. Err.	t	P > |t|	[95% Conf. Interval]	
ln_totass |	−0.0006835	0.0002864	−2.39	0.018	−0.0012486	−0.0001185
costinc |	−0.0183999	0.0030158	−6.10	0.000	−0.0243502	−0.0124496
casa |	0.0196534	0.0031484	6.24	0.000	0.0134415	0.0258653
capnw |	−0.0073178	0.0029061	−2.52	0.013	−0.0130516	−0.001584
gnpa |	−0.1039077	0.0054714	−18.99	0.000	−0.1147029	−0.0931125
_cons |	0.0221188	0.0039237	5.64	0.000	0.0143772	0.0298603

Note: roa: return on assets; ln_totass: log of total assets; costinc = cost to income ratio; casa: bank CASA ratio; capnw = government infused capital to total net worth; gnpa: gross non-performing assets to total advances & _cons: intercept.

After running the regression, we perform heteroskedasticity test by running the following simple command in STATA:

```
. hettest

Breusch-Pagan / Cook-Weisberg test for
  heteroskedasticity
  Ho: Constant variance
  Variables: fitted values of roa

  chi²(1)  = 56.75
  Prob > chi² = 0.0000
```

Clearly, the null hypothesis of constant variance is rejected due to high chi2 and low p-value. Thus, it detects the presence of heteroskedasticity.

To remove the effects, a heteroskedaticity robust standard error can be generated using 'robust' command in STATA. Heteroskedasticity problem can be checked through increasing the sample size or grouping the observations based on common characteristics (using dummy variables or categorical variables). That is why in regression models presented in Table 7.15, we present heteroskedasticity robust standard errors.

For multicollinearity check, one should estimate pairwise correlation amongst the independent variables. If correlation is significant and the coefficient value exceeds 0.70, it would detect multicollinearity will be problematic in the regression model. The presence of multicollinearity inflates the variance (or standard error) and reduces the estimated t-value. It is also recommended to run Variance Inflation Factor test (VIF) to check whether multicollinearity is damaging the model estimates. It actually quantifies the extent of correlation between on predictor and the other factors in the regression model.

$$\mathrm{Var}(\hat{\beta}_j) = \frac{\sigma^2}{\sum x_j^2}\left(\frac{1}{1-R_j^2}\right) \qquad \text{Eq. 7.21}$$

where R = correlation;

$$\text{Note that: } VIF = \frac{1}{1-R_j^2} \qquad \text{Eq. 7.21a}$$

Thus, we can write that:

$$\text{Var}(\hat{\beta}_j) = \frac{\sigma^2}{\sum x_j^2} \times VIF \qquad \text{Eq. 7.21b}$$

Thus, higher the correlation between factors, higher the VIF and greater will be the variance of estimated regression coefficient. This will reduce the value of t-statistic and hence significance of the variable will drastically come down. This defines the problem of multicollinearity.

VIF and tolerance tests (inverse of VIF) are popularly used for diagnosing mullticollinearity. The higher the VIF (say it exceeds 10), the more the standard error is inflated. If regression model suffers from multicollinearity, overall R-square will be good but the significance of individual factor will be low since it is already correlated with other factors. Hence the risk analyst will not be able to detect whether that factor significantly contribute to the dependent variable. It can be estimated in STATA by typing command: vif after running a regression. Thus, a high R-square nut significant *t* ratios are indication of multicollinearity issue in a regression model. In order to resolve the multicollinearity issue in risk modelling, it is better to use ratios rather than absolute values of the parameters in the regression model. Scaling or dropping the correlated factors and increasing the sample size can reduce the effect of multi-collinearity problem. It is worthwhile to mention that the two regression models presented in Table 7.15 that relate bank performance with cost, risk and capital factors are free from multicollinearity. After running the regressions, we have checked that the mean VIF was below 1.24. Moreover, none of the joint correlation coefficients between the regression factors where above 0.40 and statistically significant. Both multicollinearity and heteroscedasticity issues are elaborated in Willams (2015a,b). The detailed test statistics and how to handle these econometric problems are detailed in Gujarati, Porter and Gunasekar (2017).

Summary

This chapter discussed the several regression methods available to a risk manager to develop risk prediction models. Various multivariate regression techniques to examine impact of different factors on risk outcomes have been demonstrated with hands on examples. The model diagnostic checks and their relevance in risk assessment have been elaborated in details. Logistic regression model is used to develop statistical scorecards to predict default risk. General regression models are used to forecast loan recovery or losses. Panel regression models can be used to link risk with return. It can also be used to predict credit losses as well as to link various market risk factors with treasury losses. We have also demonstrated how multivariate models can be presented properly and have shown interpretation of key empirical results including crucial diagnostic tests like normality test, heteroskedasticity and multicollinearity checks.

Review Questions

1. If we estimate a regression and find: $E(Y/X) = 0.37 + 0.82X$, a 1% change in X (say default rates) is expected to lead to what percentage change in Y (say LGD). Given $X = 4\%$, what will be the value of Y?
2. Using regression analysis on historical loan losses, a bank has estimated the following:

   $X_C = 0.002 + 0.8\ X_L$, and $X_H = 0.003 + 1.8\ X_L$ where X_C = loss rate in the commercial sector, X_H = loss rate in the household sector, and X_L = loss rate for its entire loan portfolio.

   a) If the bank's total loan loss rates increase by 10%, what are the expected loss rate increases in the commercial and consumer sectors?
   b) In which sector should the bank limit its loans and why?
3. Do you think multiple regression is better than two-variable regression? Why?
4. Is it true that as the variance of Y (dependent) variable explained by the X (independent) variable becomes increasingly larger relative to the unexplained variance, the R-square value will be decreasingly lower too?

5. Is it true or false that if the error term is correlated with the regressors (predictor variables), the regression coefficient would be unbiased?
6. Is it a true statement that an increasingly large F value will be evidence in favour of rejecting the null hypothesis that the two (or more) explanatory variables have no effect on the dependent variable?
7. Do you think that if a regression model suffers from multicollinearity problem, the R^2 value may be high but regressor coefficients may be in significant? Give arguments.
8. Why panel regression should be used in risk modelling?
9. What is the basic difference between fixed effect model vs. random effect regression?
10. What is Hausman test? What it detects?
11. What is the basic difference between linear regression and logistic regression?
12. How logit model can be used to predict default risk?
13. Explain the use of multivariate regression in operational risk management?
14. What is unboundedness problem? How it can be solved?
15. What is maximum likelihood estimation (MLE)? Explain its application in risk management.
16. How MDA is run and what are the key test statistics?
17. In MDA analysis run in SPSS, if between group sum of squares = 190 and within groups sum of squares = 184 and degrees of freedom are respectively 1 (between groups) and 50 (within groups), the Canonical Correlation value would be:
    a) <0.25
    b) 0.25–0.50
    c) 0.50–0.75
    d) >0.75
18. A researcher is investigating the key factors that determine the likelihood of loan payment default for retail loans. A logistic regression exercise has been carried out on 1500 borrower data in STATA. The dependent variable (default) is a binary dummy variable that capture default incidents (default = 1 for defaults and default = 0 for non-defaults). Five independent variables (or factors) were used in the regression model: (i) debtinc-debt to income ratio (or burden) in %; (ii) employ-number of years in the job; (iii) creddebtinc-credit

card debt to income ratio; (iv) ed-educational qualification based on degrees; and (v) income-income in '000$. The logit regression result is presented below:

Iteration 0: log likelihood = – 984.63781
Iteration 1: log likelihood = −762.42
Iteration 2: log likelihood = – 730.99043
Iteration 3: log likelihood = – 727.06905
Iteration 4: log likelihood = – 726.98467
Iteration 5: log likelihood = – 726.98462

Logistic regression					Number of obs = 1500	
					LR chi^2 (5) = –	
					Prob > chi^2 = 0.0000	
Log likelihood = -726.98462					Pseudo R2 = –	
default |	**Coef.**	**Std. Err.**	**z**	**P>|z|**	**[95% Conf. Interval]**	
debtinc |	0.098881	0.0140687	7.03	0.000	0.0713068	0.1264552
employ |	−0.2061911	0.0169391	−12.17	0.000	−0.2393912	−0.1729911
creddebtinc |	23.24551	3.367636	6.90	0.000	16.64506	29.84595
ed |	−.0599041	.0613427	−0.98	0.329	−.1801336	.0603254
income |	.010086	.0016068	6.28	0.000	.0069368	.0132351
_cons |	−1.63233	.2055068	−7.94	0.000	−2.035115	−1.229544

a) Find out the LR chi^2 of the Logit model
b) Estimate the Pseudo R2
c) Which regression factors are statistically significant? And why?
d) How will you interpret the regression coefficients?
e) What kind of optimization method is used? And why?
f) Now, using the above regression table, predict the dependent variable for a borrower with factors: debtinc = 24.2, employ = 13, creddebtinc = 0.1302, ed = 2 and income = 62; what will be its expected probability of default?
g) Why you should perform a Hosmer Lemeshow Test? What is the STATA command for this test?

19. In MDA analysis, the equality of variance–covariance matrices in the groups is tested through
 a) Mahalanobis's D
 b) Box's M

c) Wilk's Lambda
d) Baye's probability

20. In a logistic regression result, the obtained LL(α, β) = −100 and LL(α) = −200; the obtained McFadden's Pseudo R-square would be:
a) 50%
b) 75%
c) 100%
d) >100%

References

Baltagi, B. H. (2008). 'Econometric Analysis of Panel Data', Wiley.
Gujarati, D., D. Porter, and S. Gunasekar (2017). Basic Econometrics, 5th Edition, McGraw Hill Education.
Greene, W. H. (2008). Econometric Analysis, 6th Edition, NJ, Prentice Hall, p. 183.
Hausman, J. A. (1978). 'Specification tests in econometrics', *Econometrica*, Vol. 46, pp. 1251–1271.
Hendry, D. F., and B. Nielsen (2007). 'Econometric Modeling-A Likelihood Approach', Princeton Paperbacks, Chapter 4, The Logit Model (pp.47–65).
Hsiao, C. (1986). Analysis of Panel Data, Cambridge University Press.
Nagar, A. L., and R. K. Das (1983). 'Basic Statistics', 2nd Edition, Oxford University Press.
Reyna, O. T. (2007). 'Panel Data Analysis Fixed and Random Effects using STATA', Presentation Material, Princeton University, December.
Rosenberg, S. (2006). A General Approach to Integrated Risk Management with Skewed, Fat-tailed Risks, *Journal of Financial Economics*, Vol 79, Issue 3, 569–614.
Schmidheiny, K. (2015). 'Panel Data: Fixed and Random Effects'. Short Guides to Microeconometrics, Kurt Schmidheiny, University of Basel. URL: https://www.schmidheiny.name/teaching/panel2up.pdf
Stock, J. H., and M. W. Watson (2003). 'Introduction to Econometrics', 3rd Edition, Pearson Addison-Wesley, Chapter 10, pp. 289–290.
Walpole, R. E., R. H. Myers, S. L. Myers, and K. Ye (2012). 'Probability and Statistics for Engineers and Scientists', 9th Edition, Prentice Hall.
Willams, R. (2015a). Multicollinearity, URL: https://www3.nd.edu/~rwilliam/stats2/l11.pdf
Willams, R. (2015b). Heteroskedasticity, URL: https://www3.nd.edu/~rwilliam/stats2/l25.pdf
Wooldridge, J. M. (2010). 'Econometric Analysis of Cross Section and Panel Data'. MIT Press. Chapter 10.

8

Monte Carlo Simulation Techniques and Value at Risk

In financial mathematics and financial risk management, value at risk (VaR) is a novel measure of the risk of loss on a specific portfolio of financial assets. For a given portfolio, probability, and time horizon, VaR is defined as a threshold value such that the probability that the mark-to-market loss on the portfolio over the given time horizon does not exceed this value (assuming normal markets and no trading in the portfolio).

The value at risk (VaR) metric uses a set of statistical loss distributions to determine the required risk capital at any confidence interval. It is based on probabilistic assessment of potential future losses and is, therefore, potentially more forward looking. VaR summarizes in a single number the downside risk of an institution, under normal conditions, from financial market movements. Definition: VaR is the maximum loss over a target horizon such that there is a low, pre-specified probability that the actual loss will be larger.

For example, if a portfolio of stocks has a one-day 5% VaR of $1 million, there is a 5% probability that the portfolio will fall in value by more than $1 million over a one day period, assuming that markets are normal and there is no trading. Informally, a loss of $1 million or more on this portfolio is expected on 1 day in 20. A loss which exceeds the VaR threshold is termed a 'VaR break'. It has lot implications in measuring market risk. The VaR of a normally distributed portfolio VaR has five main uses in finance: (a) risk management, (b) risk measurement, (c) financial control, (d) financial reporting, and (e) computing regulatory capital. However, it does not measure the worst possible loss, because that is not calculable.

The VaR models seek to measure the maximum loss (of value) on a given asset or liability over a given time period at a given confidence interval (e.g. 95%, 99%, 99.9% etc.). For example, suppose the market price

(P) of a tradable equity today is \$80, and the estimated daily standard deviation (SD) of the value is \$10. Assume that the trader is concerned with the value loss on a bad day that occurs once in every 100 days, and the daily asset value is normally distributed around the current equity value of \$80. Statistically speaking, the one bad day has a one percent probability of occurring tomorrow. We know that in a normal distribution, roughly 98% of observations lie between +2.33 and −2.33 SDs from the mean. Because standard deviation is assumed to be \$10, there is a 1% chance that the value of the equity will fall to \$56.7 (= 80 − 10 × 2.33). Alternatively, there is a 99% probability that the equity holder will lose less than \$23.3 in value. The amount \$23.3 can be viewed as the VaR on the at 99% confidence interval. Thus, the VaR measure gives the risk manager to an estimate of the maximum possible loss, up to a given confidence level (here 99%). The key inputs in VaR computation of a marketable instrument are its current market value and the volatility of that market value.

Types of VaR Techniques

There are generally three types of VaR techniques:

1. Simple Historical Simulation (HS) VaR, 2. Variance–Covariance VaR, and 3. Monte Carlo Simulation (MCS).

1. Simple Historical Simulation (HS) VaR—Historical simulation (HS) consists of going back in time and applying current weights to a time series of historical returns. The main goal is to predict the future changes in current exposure, from actual distribution of past returns. It assumes past returns are reliable guides to actual future changes in prices. However, the question we ask is that if future returns are just as they were in the past, how would the current portfolio value be affected?

Steps in HS

1. Measure current portfolio value or current exposure in rupees (current weights).

2. Measure returns for the past 250 or 500 trading days. For bonds, use model prices.
3. Multiply all past returns by current portfolio value, i.e. (1) × (2) and add resultant losses or profits across all days.
4. Rank days from worst total losses to highest profits.
5. Mark off portfolio VaR as the 1% or 5% worst sample loss.

Historical simulation does not assume normality or serial independence. HS presumes that past returns are repeated in the future. VaR for different percentiles (e.g. 95% and 99%) are not constant multiples of each other, since we no longer assume that these capture shocks which are given multiples of SDs. This is a very simpler method for computing VaR, and hence, it is widely used by banks. However, when we assume that history repeats itself, we depend too much on historical data. Our sample may not contain large negative (or positive) shocks, while the future may be very different. Even if we are willing to treat past returns as future scenarios, all events may not be equally likely. Shocks from the recent past may be more probable than those from the distant past. However, since the basic model is so simple, these adjustments are easy to make. This is the major limitation of HS-based VaR calculation that may underestimate actual risk. Moreover, HS is not based on parameters like SD, VaR estimates cannot be linked across confidence levels.

2. Variance–Covariance VaR—It computes portfolio losses with individual volatilities and return correlations. It is a probabilistic measure of risk because shocks are drawn from the normal distribution, for different confidence levels.

Steps in VCVaR

1. Measure current portfolio value or current exposure in rupees (current weights).
2. Calculate returns for the past 250 or 500 days, i.e. convert past price data (S_t) into return data $\left(R_t = \dfrac{S_t - S_{t-1}}{S_{t-1}}\right)$.
3. Calculate SD of each return set, as a measure of volatility.

4. Express chosen confidence level as multiple of SD (NORMSINV in Excel). For 95% confidence level, the multiplier would be normsinv (95%) = 1.645.
5. Multiply each current exposure by confidence level to get daily VaR.
6. Calculate correlations between return datasets to find out daily portfolio VaR.
7. Finally, use the square root rule to convert daily VaR into T-day VaR.

$$10-\text{day VaR}_{99\%} = \sqrt{10} \times \text{Daily VaR}_{99\%}$$

In the variance–covariance approach, T-day VaR can be estimated by multiplying daily VaR by the square root of T.

The Variance–covariance method depends on parameters like SDs and correlations and the assumption of normally distributed returns. It computes portfolio losses with individual volatilities and return correlations. The variance–covariance matrix converts position volatilities into portfolio volatility.

3. MCS—Similar to HS but uses random numbers, from fitted distributions, to simulate losses. It estimates distributions and parameters for returns or losses, from historical data. If historical loss data are not available or are scarce, estimate distributions of underlying risk factors.

Steps in MCS

In MCS, many random numbers are generated to get the simulated returns/losses/shocks, from the distributions. Then current portfolio is revalued with the random numbers. Finally, portfolio Profit or Loss (P/L) is found and sorted, as before, to get VaR. One can use the Palisade bestfit™ to find out appropriate distribution and @RISK™ to run simulations using the best identified distribution.

MCS-based VaR is a more sophisticated approach than both HS VaR and VCVaR methods. It neither assumes a normal distribution for security returns and portfolio returns, nor does that history repeat itself. Instead, it suggests that future scenarios are based on past trends but are not identical to past returns.

MCS has some advantages as it is very useful in scenario analysis with scarce data. It can compute numbers for fat tail (non-normal) distributions. However, it is not intuitive as HS.

MCS has lot of business applications. Using the pattern of price and sales distribution, the CEO can use MCS to get insight about possible profits in a business.

Value at Risk as a Measure of Market Risk

Market risk capital is measured by VaR, which can be interpreted as the maximum loss under normal market conditions, as well as stress scenarios focusing on losses under extreme market conditions. VaR is the maximum loss over a target horizon such that there is a low, pre-specified probability that the actual loss will be larger. VaR gives us a number, in terms of money, which can be aggregated across risks and positions. Such risk measures are part of the determination of the overall limits for interest-rate and exchange-rate exposure. However, it does not measure the worst possible loss because that is not calculable.

Under market risk, VaR is a single measure which summarizes the downside potential risk of loss of a bank. For instance, a 99% daily VaR for a bond portfolio is Rs. 10,000 which means that there is a 99% chance of losing at most Rs. 10,000 over the next day. Alternatively, there is a 1% chance that actual loss may exceed Rs. 10,000 between today and tomorrow.

For a 10-day holding period, the VaR would be

$$10 - \text{day VaR} = \text{Daily VaR} \times \sqrt{10} \qquad \text{Eq. 8.1}$$

The choice of pre-specified probability at the tail (termed as α) is left to the organization and is linked to its risk appetite. A bank which has a higher risk appetite, would set higher value of α in order to obtain a conservative estimate of VaR. The market risk VaR estimation has been further explained in Dowd (2005) and in Jorion (2015). The Basel regulatory approach has been elaborated in BIS (2016).

In portfolio analysis, MCS is used to estimate the return distribution for each instrument in the portfolio. For example, of Log logistic function is best fitting the market returns, MCS assumes that future shocks should follow the same traits. This can be identified in statistical package like Bestfit or in @Risk. The computer-generated pattern that produces the closest match with the graph of historical returns is the chosen distribution for the sample data. If this distribution is the best proxy for historical trend, the simulated shocks are also generated based on the loglogistic distribution. MCS generates the large number of random shocks that helps the market risk manager to estimate future losses.

The MCS process is considered superior to both variance–covariance and HS techniques. This is because MCS considers more scenarios and consider best fitted distributions to generate larger shocks which cannot predicted neither by variance covariance model nor by HS. For example, assuming that there are 250 trading days per year, an MCS exercise with 10000 shocks generates forty years' (= 10000/250) worth of relevant scenarios, from limited historical data. This is the main advantage of MCS and statistically more superior than the simple historical-based VaR models.

VaR for Interest Rate Instruments

VaR calculation allows credit institutions to estimate potential losses from interest rate instruments. VaR expresses the maximum loss of the interest rate book's economic value with a specified probability (confidence level) during a given holding period. Losses of economic value, defined as a negative difference of future economic value from current economic value, are induced by changes in maturity-specific market interest rates. The VaR calculations for interest rate instruments have been elaborated in Jorion (2009, 2015) and Fabozzi (2017). The detailed regulatory guidelines for capital computations are given in RBI (2010).

Stressed VaR

Stress tests are designed to estimate potential economic losses in abnormal markets. Regular stress testing is increasing viewed as indispensable by risk managers and regulators as it enhances transparency by exploring a range of potential low probability events when VaR bands are dramatically exceeded. While VaR measures potential risks under normal market conditions, stress tests are designed to capture the risks (of bankruptcy or insolvency) in highly volatile or abnormal markets. Stress testing combined with VaR gives a more comprehensive picture of risk. The Basel Committee has recently included stress VaR in Pillar I capital charges for Internal Measurement Approach (IMA). RBI has conducted a series of stress tests for bank portfolios, in its Financial Stability Reports. Stress test tells to the top management: How much could the bank lose if a stress scenario occurs? The liquidity risk related to large market crashes, and the interactions with interest rate or credit risk, can be captured better by specific stress tests.

Credit VaR (C-VaR) for Loan Portfolio

Credit VaR is the worst possible loss due to borrower default over a given time period with a given probability. Normally, the time period is 1 year and the probability is known as the confidence interval. The C-VaR is the minimum loss of the next year if the worst 0.03% event occurs. In another words, VaR measures maximum possible loss over an above average loss.

Large banks in India normally allocate highest percentage of their regulatory capital to credit risks (70–85%), followed by operational risk (10–20%), and market risk (5–10%).

CreditMetrics™ was introduced in 1997 by J.P. Morgan and its co-sponsors (Bank of America, KMV Corporation, Union Bank of Switzerland, and others) as a VaR framework to apply to the valuation of non-tradable loan or privately placed bonds. The model generally seeks to determine year, how much the bank will lose on its loans and loan portfolio? Because the loans are not publicly traded, neither the loan's market value nor the volatility of its value over the horizon of interest are available. However, using (a) available data on a borrower's credit rating, (b) the probability that the rating will change over the next year (the rating Transition Matrix), (c) recovery rates on defaulted loans, and (d)the credit spreads and yields in the bond market, it is possible to estimate the market value of loan and its volatility and hence VaR. To calculate VaR of a loan portfolio, we need to calculate default correlations among counter-parties. The choice of transition matrix has material impact on the VaR calculations. Country-specific rating transition matrix is, therefore, a necessity. The effect of rating up-grades and down-grades is to impact the required credit risk spreads or premiums on the loan's remaining cash flows and, thus, the implied market (present) value of the loan.

$$Market\ Value = c + \frac{c}{(1+r_1+s_1)} + \frac{c}{(1+r_2+s_2)} + \ldots + \frac{c}{(1+r_i+s_i)} \quad \text{Eq. 8.2}$$

where c = coupon rate, r_i = risk-free rates (so-called forward zero rates) on zero coupon treasury bond expected to exist one year into the future; s_i = the annual credit spread on zero coupon loans of a particular rating class of 1 year, 2 year, and up to nth year of maturities derived from observed spread in the corporate bond market over treasuries.

Based on Equation 8.2, the market value of bond/loan will change according to credit rating. Credit spread will be lower if bond rating is high, and in those cases, bond market value will be higher on the right-hand side. However, if rating down-grade takes place, the value will fall due to higher spread and it will move to the left-hand side direction. For example, if the value is $100 at BBB rating, it becomes $108.64 when the rating of

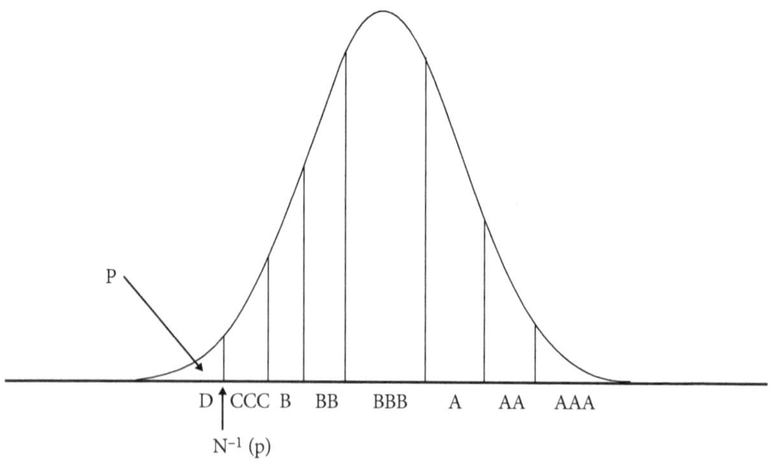

Figure 8.1 Market Value Distribution Depending Upon Credit Rating

the bond is upgraded to A. But the value erodes and reduces to $83.64 if the rating downgrades to CCC. We have assumed 6% annual interest rate and used forwards rates using spreads (Suanders and Cornett, 2011). The VaR is estimated using deviations of values from its mean at a threshold say $N^{-1}(p)$ which may be 1% (that means VaR confidence is 99%).

$$\begin{aligned}\text{Thus, VaR} &= P \times N^{-1}(99\%) \times \sigma,\\ &= P \times 2.33 \times \sigma,\end{aligned}$$

where P = market value of the position and σ = volatility of loan value over the horizon of one year.

The value of a loan has a fixed up-side and a long down-side i.e. the value of the loan is not symmetrically distributed. Thus CreditMetrics™ produces two VaR measures:

1) Based on normal distribution
2) Based on actual distribution

The VaR based on normality assumption will underestimate the actual VaR of the loan because of skewness. Using the CreditMetrics™ approach (Morgan, 1997; Risk Metrics Group, 2007), every loan is likely to have different VaR and, thus, a different implied economic capital (EC) in contrast to a uniform capital standard of 8% by BIS. This methodology has also been elaborated in Suanders and Allen (2002), Boris et al. (2015), and Saunders and Corneet (2011).

In MCS-based credit VaR models, log-normal and beta distributions are the two common type of distributions are generally used in estimating Credit VaR through MCS. The year-wise write-off data may be used as loss series to obtain VaR.

Credit Suisse financial products (CSF) had developed credit risk + model in October 1997. It applies simulation techniques from actuarial mathematics to compute the probabilities for portfolio loss events. It uses probability of default and loss given default distributions to obtain convoluted simulated loss. The method is similar to loss distribution approach for measuring operational VaR. This has been discussed in the next section. The Credit VaR and Economic Capital approach has been further explained in Marrison (2002) and Matten (2003).

Operational Risk VaR: Loss Distribution Approach

Measuring operational risk is a useful tool for risk-focused management reflecting inherent risk of business lines. It is an integral part of bank's overall optimal capital allocation process. Operational VaR offers a basis for risk managers to provide a consistent and integrated approach to the management of operational and other risks, leading to greater transparency and more informed management decisions.

Using probabilistic scenario-based MCS method enables the risk analyst to obtain the aggregate loss distribution. It is an open form solutions in which an algorithm is cleverly implemented in a computer and it does the job.

Using simulation, we can produce different scenarios for frequency and severity of losses by generating random numbers using corresponding type of distributions (identified using actual loss data).

The aggregation of frequency of events and severity of loss issue are straightforward: for the different scenarios, each potential loss is generated through a simulation that uses the random numbers from the identified frequency distribution. This in turn is used to generate corresponding severity of losses from the identified severity of loss distribution. The losses so generated are then aggregated to generate the aggregate loss distribution.

Data and Loss Events

To run simulation, we first identified the probability distributions of model drivers. To identify the probability distribution(s) of the model's driver(s), it is proper to use historical data for the particular variable. Globally, banks collect data from seven loss events being identified by the bank. They are LE1: internal fraud; LE2: external fraud; LE3: employment practices and work place safety; LE4: client, products, and business practices, legal britches, illegal practices, etc.; LE5: accident, fire, burglary, damage to physical assets, etc.; LE6: business disruption and system failure; and LE7: transaction error in execution, delivery, and process management. All these events are mapped with business lines as suggested by guidelines issued by the Basel Committee (BCBS) and prudential guidelines for operational risk drivers issued by various central banks.

Having obtained historical data, the goal is to match a probability distribution to the data.

Methodology

Identifying Probability Distributions of the Model's Drivers

To identify the probability distribution(s) of the model's driver(s), it is proper to use historical data for the particular variable.

Having obtained historical data, the goal is to match a probability distribution to the data.

Exploring various distributions, we evaluate the fit of the distribution based on some commonly used goodness-of-fit tests, such as

Chi-Square Test

Chi-square statistic measures how well the expected frequency of the fitted distribution compares with the frequency of a histogram of the observed data.

It is most useful for fitting distributions to discrete data.

Kolmogorov–Smirnov Test (K–S)

K–S statistic is only concerned with the maximum vertical (absolute) distance between the cumulative distribution function of the fitted distribution and the cumulative distribution of the data. The data have to be ranked in ascending order.

Anderson–Darling (A–D) Test

A–D statistic is a sophisticated version of the K–S statistic.

It is generally more useful measure of fit than the K–S statistic especially where it is important to place equal emphasis on fitting a distribution at the tails as well as the main body.

P–P & Q–Q Plot

Finally, one should also check Percentile–Percentile Plot (or P–P plot) and Quantile–Quantile plot (Q–Q plot). These are graphical representation of fitness of a distribution. P–P is a plot of the cumulative frequency of the fitted curve $F(x)$ against the actual cumulative frequency $F_n(x) = i/n$ where i = rank. The better the fit, the closer this plot resembles a straight diagonal line. It is a very useful test for fitting continuous data. This implies fitted distribution percentile, and actual series percentiles match properly. This is important for checking the fitness of body of a distribution. It helps a risk manager to have idea about loss provisioning and predict regular 75% range of losses. The Q–Q plot can be useful if one is interested in closely matching cumulative percentiles, and it will show significant differences between the tails of the two distributions. For this, observations need to be ranked in descending order. Then we need to find the fitted cumulative distribution function and the respective quantiles against the actual (or empirical) one through a plotting formula such as: $(n - k + 0.5)/n$, where n = number of data points and k = rank of the data point (where highest rank = 1).

Q–Q plot is very popular test in risk modelling to identify and fit non-normal loss distributions. Such loss fitting is crucial for estimation of operational risk capital using VaR technique. These fitting tests can be carried out in Excel and also in Palisade Bestfit and @Risk software. The concept has been already discussed in Chapter 4.

Figure 8.2 explains the utility of PP plot to identify right kind of distribution. The figures reported in the Panel A and Panel B are based on data series of legal liability losses of a French bank. The mean loss is considerably larger than the median, which is reflected in a positive skew = 2.8064. Second, the losses are very fat tailed, with a kurtosis in excess of 15. This is an example of fat-tailed distribution which should be captured through a right kind of distribution like exponential

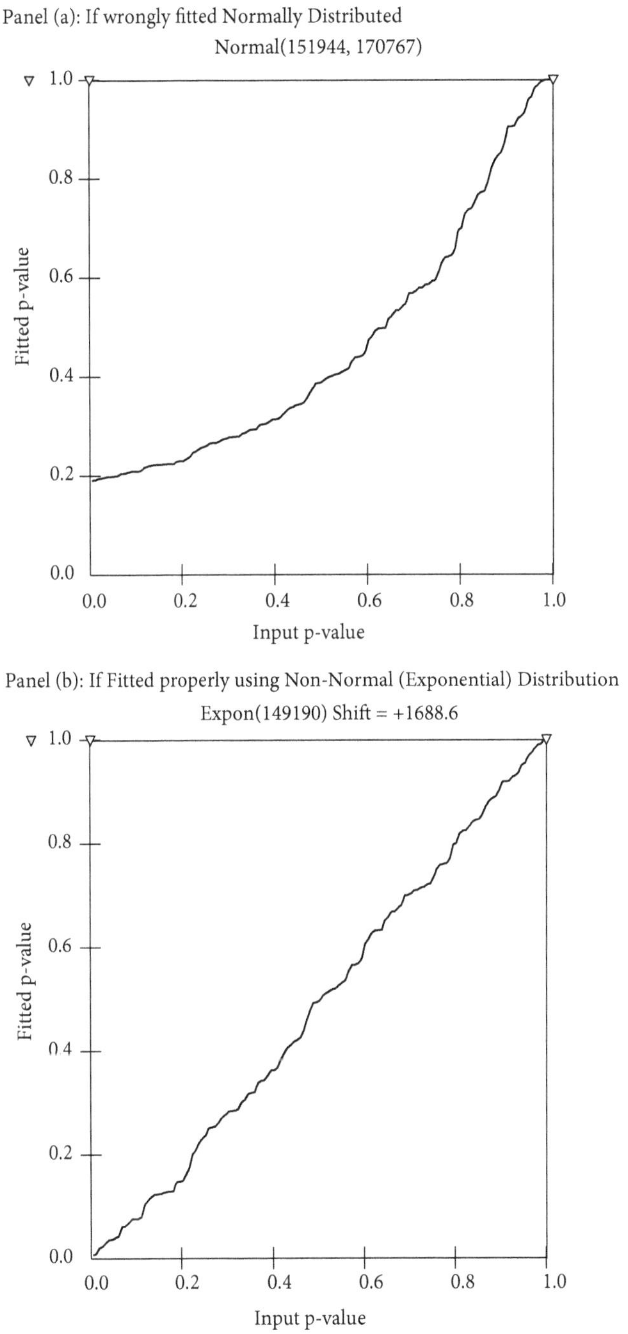

Figure 8.2 Probability–Probability Plot for a Non-Normal Loss Series
Panel A: If wrongly fitted Normally Distributed
Panel B: If Fitted properly using Non-Normal (Exponential) Distribution

distribution. In Panel A of Figure 8.2, it was forcefully fitted normally distributed, and hence, PP plot deviates a lot from the diagonal line. However, when it was fitted with exponential distribution which takes care of such fat tail kind of distribution, the PP plot becomes closer to the diagonal line. This is quite evident in the above figure. Similarly, QQ plot also will properly capture the tail portion. The operational loss distribution fitting approaches are further detailed in Lewis (2004).

Monte Carlo Method

Perhaps the simplest and often most direct approach is MCS.

The Monte Carlo method involves the following steps:

Step 1: Estimating a frequency distribution

First, frequency of loss probability model is identified (Poisson = mean; Binomial = mean and SD to obtain p). The most commonly used distribution is Poisson. However, if we find variance is higher than the mean, then negative binomial or geometric discrete distributions are used. Figure 8.3 plots the frequency distribution from the data of number of discrete events captured over months or quarters.

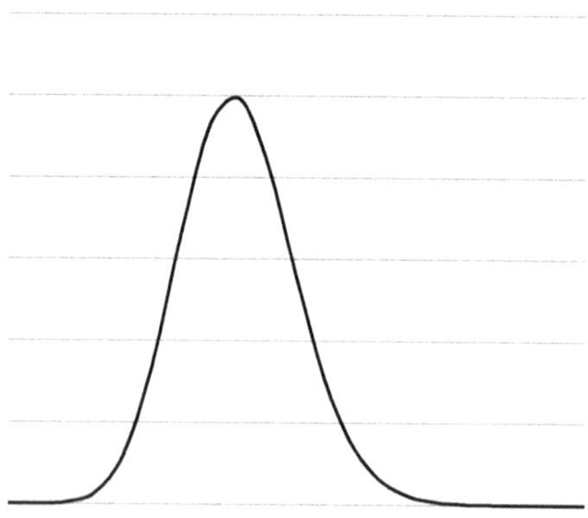

Figure 8.3 Frequency Distribution

Source: Author's own illustration

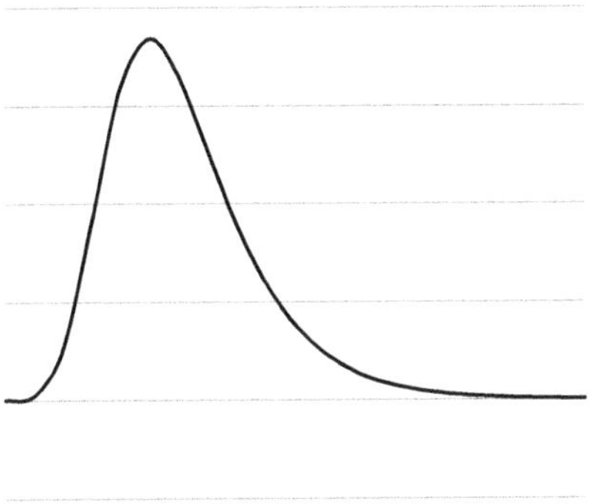

Figure 8.4 Severity Distribution
Source: Author's own illustration

Step 2: Estimating a severity distribution
Choose a best fitted severity of loss (say Weibull/Frechet/Gumbel/Pareto/Exponential) using location (alpha) & shape parameters (beta)) obtained from fitting tests (using Bestfit or @Risk). Figure 8.4 presents such continuous distribution which has been identified by plotting the loss values.

Step 3: Running a statistical simulation to produce a loss distribution
In the third step, both the frequency and severity are combined using MCS. This way, MCS technique can be used for estimating the aggregate loss distribution. Within the realm of simulation there exist some efficient methods, such as Latin Hypercube, in which random numbers are generated according to the frequency implied by the shape of the probability distribution, i.e. more random numbers are generated at the regions of the distribution where there exists more probability, hence random numbers are not 'wasted' and are more representative.

Step 4: Estimate VaR from convoluted and simulated distribution
The number of losses and individual loss amounts are simulated and then the corresponding aggregate loss is calculated. Repeat many times (at least 5,000 iterations) to obtain an empirical aggregate loss distribution and then rank the simulated observations. The convoluted aggregate loss distribution series plot has been presented in Figure 8.5. VaR is calculated as the 99.9 percentile from the loss distribution.

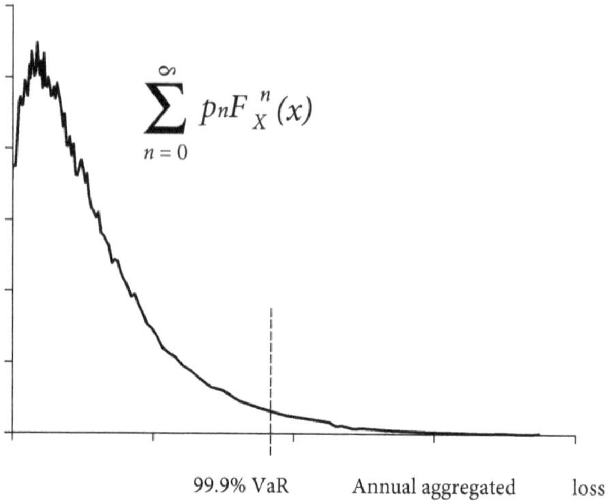

Figure 8.5 Convoluted Aggregate Loss Distribution
Source: Author's own illustration

Based on the above concept, we now practically demonstrate the VaR calculation. To compute the Operational VaR, we simply rank the simulated aggregate external fraud losses in descending order. After ranking the loss figures, we obtain the VaR percentiles of aggregate loss distribution to compute the operational risk capital. This is also termed as economic capital.

Exercise-Operational Risk VaR Method

We demonstrate the MCS-based Op-VaR convolution method with an example. We use data of 19 quarters of external fraud incidents and their loss figures of a mid-sized public sector bank in India. The tabulated data are presented in Table 8.1.

The loss data have two components: frequency of events and severity (gross loss). Using best fit, we identify that the external fraud events follow geometric distribution, and the gross loss follows lognormal distribution.

We give the following seed input in @Risk:

Frequency: = RiskGeomet(0.04914); selected based on Chi^2 test and P–P plot.

Severity: RiskLognorm(10.791, 96.986, RiskShift(−0.0069796)); selected based on KS test and P–P and Q–Q plot.

Table 8.1 Operational Loss Data Analysis

Date	Jun-14	Sep-14	Dec-14	Mar-15	Jun-15	Sep-15	Dec-15	Mar-16	Jun-16	Sep-16	Dec-16	Mar-17
Frequency	1	6	3	6	7	20	113	44	1	7	8	6
Gross loss (Rs. Lakh)	0.36	33.59	2.46	52.22	1.02	1.15	9.42	0.70	0.05	0.68	0.28	1.37
	Jun-17	**Sep-17**	**Dec-17**	**Mar-18**	**Jun-18**	**Sep-18**	**Dec-18**	**Mar-19**				
Frequency	16	12	11	65	41	13	2	5				
Gross loss (Rs. Lakh)	4.86	3.17	0.68	0.12	0.32	3.29	0.00	17.33				

Source: Author's own loss study

To derive the simulated, convoluted operational losses, we need to create an output function in Excel.

In output column cell, we write the following function:

= RiskOutput() + RiskCompound(D2,E2)

Next, we go to setting of @Risk and choose 10,000 iterations for MCS. The risk compound function is simply aggregating the frequencies with severity values. It is like first use geometric distribution to predict number of frauds in the next month and says it predicts six events. Next, using lognormal distribution, @Risk predicts six gross loss values. This is being repeated 10,000 times and the aggregate loss value series are generated in this process. The @Risk simulation steps are elaborated in Nersesian (2011).

Despite simulation of 10,000 probabilistic scenarios, we calculate 99.9% VaR using percentile function. This can also be done by ranking the convoluted losses and then pick up the 10th largest loss amount to derive 99.9% VaR estimate. The simulated VaR number is Rs. 453 million. That means the bank will have to internally keep at least Rs. 181.23 crore as capital in a year as a protection against external frauds.

VaR Back Testing

Back testing is fundamental in the internal models approval by regulators. It is equally true for market risk as well. It is essential to verify the accuracy of VaR threshold and check both type I and type II errors. There may be trade-off between the two types of errors. A right balance between the two would give risk management department to effectively control risk. A back testing enables the bank to keep right level of limits to prevent future loss. At present, most of the banks back test their portfolio VaR at the 99% confidence interval. This is as per the Basel guidelines for market risk capital. While regulatory capital must be held at the 99% confidence level, daily market VaR should also be back tested at a lower confidence level (e.g. 95%), for proper model validation. The reason is that the VaR estimate could be too high at the 99% confidence level (c.l.), and actual losses under normal conditions may not be large enough to breach such a threshold. The model should be allowed to fail, at the experimental stage itself, before it is used in practice for capital estimation and setting risk limits. For instance, at the 95% c.l., 14 violations are expected per year (as opposed to only 4 at the 99% c.l.). A model may not fail at the 99% c.l. but be deemed unsatisfactory at the 95% confidence level. This way VaR limits can be fixed.

Summary

In this chapter, we discussed VaR and simulation techniques to analyse loss data. We have described MCS techniques to assess credit, market, and operational losses. Steps in identifying proper frequency as well as severity distributions and fitting them for loss prediction have been elaborated with numerous examples. VaR is a prudent indicator of risk to understand portfolio risk position. It tells the risk manager from which segment the risk arises, how it affects portfolio losses and how to mitigate such outcomes. On this basis, a more refined trading or lending strategies can be undertaken. Globally, VaR has been widely applied for internal estimate of capital charges. VaR has emerged as a natural measure for Economic (or internal) capital since it provides the flexibility to choose own portfolio valuation and devise loss prediction models. Moreover, VaR-based limits can be set to preserve scarce capital.

Review Questions

1. What is VaR? Why this technique is important?
2. How VCVaR is computed?
3. What are the simulation approaches?
4. What is the difference between loss frequency and loss scenario?
5. How credit VaR differs from market VaR?
6. How operational VaR analysis is different from market VaR?
7. What is loss convolution? How it can be done?
8. What is the role of VaR-based limits in managing risk?
9. Why MCS is better than HS?
10. What is the difference between loss variance and VaR?

Table 8.2 Loss Statistics

Mean	£151,944.04		GOF	
Median	£103,522.90	Chi^2 statistics		
Standard deviation	£170,767.06		Normal	Exponential
Skew	2.84	Test value	83.79	10.24
Kurtosis	12.81	P-value	0.000	0.595

11. Is there any difference between market risk VaR and operational risk VaR?
12. How VaR limits can be set?
13. Why the normal probability distribution not necessarily a good choice for predicting severity of losses? Under what circumstances would you envisage using the normal distribution? Now check the statistical characteristics of losses of a bank and tell whether the data come from a normal distribution? Check the Chi^2 statistic comment whether Exponential distribution is a good fit for this data?
14. How we can run MCS from after identifying the loss distribution?
15. What is the difference between P-P plot and Q-Q plot? How it helps the risk manager?

References

BIS (2016). 'Minimum Capital Requirements for Market Risk, Basel Committee on Banking Supervision', January.

Boris, K., W. Ivana, and S. Anna (2015). 'Quantification of Credit Risk with the Use of Credit Metrics', *Procedia Economics and Finance*, Vol. 26, pp. 311–316.

Dowd, K. (2005). 'Measuring Market Risk', 2nd Edition, John Wiley and Sons, Chichester, England.

Fabozzi, F. J. (2017). 'The Handbook of Fixed Income Securities', 8th Edition, McGraw Hill Education, New York.

Jorion, P. (2009). 'Value at Risk: The New Benchmark for Managing Financial Risk', 3rd Edition, Tata McGraw Hill Education Pvt. Ltd., India.

Jorion, P. (2015). 'Financial Risk Manager Handbook', 6th Edition, John Wiley and Sons, New Delhi.

Morgan, J. P. (1997). 'Introduction to CreditMetrics', 2 April, New York. URL: http://homepages.rpi.edu/~guptaa/MGMT4370.09/Data/CreditMetricsIntro.pdf.

Lewis, N. D. (2004). 'Operational Risk-Applied Statistical Methods for Risk Management', Wiley Finance, USA.

Marrison, C. (2002). 'The Fundamentals of Risk Measurement', Chapter 6, 10, Tata McGraw-Hill, USA.

Matten, C. (2003) 'Managing Bank Capital', 2nd Edition, Chapters 10 and 11, John Wiley & Sons Ltd, USA.

Nersesian, R. L. (2011). '@Risk Bank Credit and Financial Analysis', Palisade, UK.

RBI (2010). 'Prudential Guidelines on Capital Adequacy—Implementation of Internal Models Approach to Market Risk', DBOD No. BP.BC.86/21.06.001(A)/ 2009-10.

Risk Metrics Group (2007). 'Credit Metrics' Technical Document. URL: https://www.msci.com/documents/10199/93396227-d449-4229-9143-24a94dab122f.

Saunders, A., and L. Allen (2002). 'Credit Risk Measurement-New Approaches to Value at Risk and Other Paradigms', 2nd Edition, John Wiley & Sons, Inc, USA.

Saunders, A., and M. M. Cornett (2011). 'Financial Institutions Management-A Risk Management Approach', 7th Edition, McGraw Hill, USA.

9

Statistical Tools for Model Validation and Back Testing

It is of paramount interest to a bank to know the risks in its business. Risk Models allow a bank to systematically measure risks and to manage them consistently across the entire business. The supervisor seeks to encourage reporting banks to continuously develop and use better risk management techniques in monitoring and managing their risks and ensure that they in place a rigorous process for determining the adequacy of their capital to support all risks to which they are exposed. Model validation has been a key task for risk focused management for internal management of risk across various business lines. Reliable rating systems require efficient validation strategies.

Model validation is possibly the most important step in the model building sequence. It checks the predictive power of risk models. It is part of the regulatory structure that these risk models be validated both internally (Bank will do that using internal data) and externally (regulator will review). It mainly assesses the critical steps, data input quality, and discriminatory power of the models in predicts default or loss.

Calibration is the validation of specific measurement techniques like risk models. At the simplest level, calibration is a comparison between measurements—one of known magnitude or correctness made or set with one device and another measurement made in as similar a way as possible with a second device. For example, comparing rating model's prediction about PD and mapping the prediction using historical default experiences. Similarly, it is like comparing Bank's internal rating with external rating and their outcomes.

The quantitative validation mainly checks the discriminatory power or separation power or predictive power of rating models. The term discriminatory power refers to the fundamental ability of a rating system to differentiate between good (solvent or standard) and bad (defaulted or NPA) cases. The term is often used as a synonym for classification accuracy.

Various statistical techniques like Gini coefficient (or accuracy ratio), information value (IV), Pietra index, Kolmogorov and Smirnov (KS) test, Wilk's Lambda, receiver operating characteristics, percentile—percentile graph, etc. are used to measure the quality of predictor models used mainly in the management of credit, market, and operational risk. For multivariate models like logistic regression, Hosmer–Lemeshow test is used for testing the model validity.

Power Curve

The rating-wise distribution of borrowers rated by different RAM models has been described in Table 9.1. It gives us idea about the loan pool position in a Financial Year that is internally rated by a leading public sector bank. One can notice that the default rate monotonically increases as we move down to the rating scale. In terms of percentage share, there is a higher concentration of borrowers in rating segment A and BBB.

Table 9.1 Corporate Loan Pool: Rating-Wise Asset Distribution Rated by Internal Risk Assessment Model (RAM) of a Bank

Borrower Rating	Mean Score	Total Number of Borrowers	% Share in Total Number	Number of Defaults	Default Rate
AAA	8.672	6	0.28%	0	0.00%
AA	8.062	161	7.55%	0	0.00%
A	7.265	927	43.46%	1	0.11%
BBB	6.439	748	35.07%	3	0.40%
BB	5.543	187	8.77%	6	3.21%
B	4.731	89	4.17%	10	11.24%
CCC	3.963	15	0.70%	2	13.33%
Total	6.760	2133	100%	22	1.03%

Note: Author's own study

At a next level, we have used power curve or receiver operating characteristic (ROC) curve to check classification power of RAM models. First, we do it for all models rated by RAM.

In a ROC curve, the true positive rate (sensitivity) is plotted in function of the lase positive rate (100 specificity) for different cut-off points of the rating scale (here Borrower Grades AAA, AA, A, … ,CCC). ROC curve is a standard statistical tool used for diagnostic test evaluation of a rating model. The ROC figure for all models that puts together is presented in Figure 9.1.

The area under ROC curve (AUC) is a measure of how well the ratings can distinguish between defaulted (NPA) and solvent (or standard or good) accounts. The steeper the curve, the greater the area above diagonal 45^0 line and the better the predictive power of the model.

The ROC figure plots sensitivity vs. one specificity—the greater the area above diagonal 45^0 line, the better the predictive power of the model. The ROC curve is concave and lifted upward. However, the distances between B and CCC (check from the bottom portion of the smooth concave

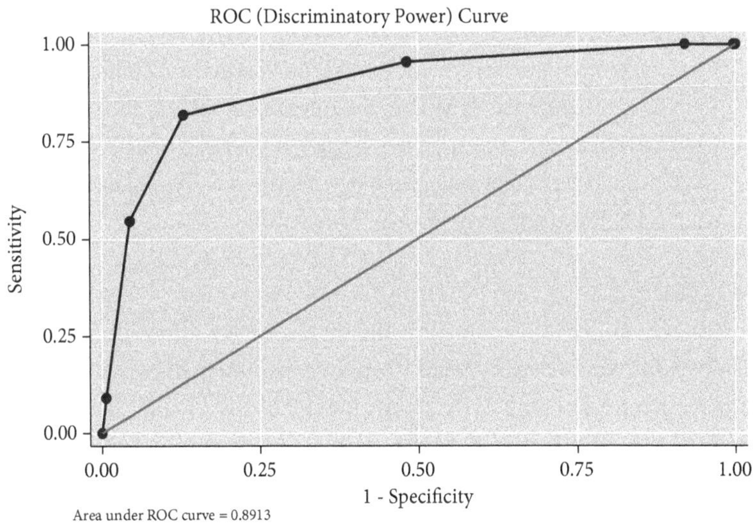

Note: The above chart has been generated in STATA

Figure 9.1 Discriminatory Power of the Internal Rating Model through ROC Curve

Note: The above figure has been generated in STATA

Table 9.2 Distribution of Defaulted vs. Rated Accounts

Account Status in T + 1 Period: (DDEF)	**AAA**	**AA**	**A**	**BBB**	**BB**	**B**	**CCC**	**Total**
0 (Good)	6	161	926	745	181	79	13	2111
Relative share of Good	0.28%	7.63%	43.87%	35.29%	8.57%	3.74%	0.62%	100.00%
1 (Bad)	0	0	1	3	6	10	2	22
Relative share of Bad	0.00%	0.00%	4.55%	13.64%	27.27%	45.45%	9.09%	100.00%

curve) and between AAA and AA (check from the top) are relatively less. Accuracy is measured by the area under the ROC curve. The greater the area, the better the discriminatory power.

The above figure is constructed at various rating based cut-off points using the following Table 9.2:

- ROC is plotted using NPA classification statistics obtained from the model's prediction.
  - Count % correction prediction (True Positive and True Negative)
  - Check Sensitivity-True Positive rates or hit rates: TP/(TP + FN)
  - Also check Specificity-True Negatives: TN/(TN + FP)
  - Count Type I error rate: False +ve: FP rate= & Type II error: False –ve: FN Rate (also termed as 1 – specificity)

Note that true positive (TP) is true defaults (TD).

The area under ROC curve is estimated as 0.8913. The Gini coefficient can be approximately estimated from the area under ROC. The relationship between Gini and AUROC can be established using the following equation:

$$2 \times \text{AUROC} - 1 = \text{Gini} \qquad \text{Eq. 9.1}$$

$$\Rightarrow \text{Gini} = 2 \times 0.8913 - 1$$

Therefore, Gini = 0.7826

This is also the Accuracy Ratio (AR) of the model. Gini or Accuracy ratio is a global measure of assessing the discriminatory power of a rating system. The greater the value of Gini index, the higher the rating model's quality. These are approved by BCBS in performing model validation (see BCBS 2005, working paper no. 14). The Accuracy ratio is quite high compared to internationally established benchmarks used in rating model validation. Note that the CRISIL default study publishes AR number of 0.70 as a good criteria. Hence, the RAM model in overall has good discriminatory power. Accuracy ratio of Gini coefficient is the most used indices in practice for validation of scoring models. It is popularly used by European banks.

On the basis of the resulting sample from bank's internal data, we have further performed various analyses to check the rating procedure's discriminatory power. The overall discriminatory power of the RAM model used by the bank to sanction various commercial loans has been reviewed ex post using data on defaulted and non-defaulted cases.

Kolmogorov–Sminrov (K–S) Test

Kolmogorov–Smirnov (K–S) statistic has been extensively used for the model validation of credit rating models. It is most widely used in North America. The K–S value can range between 0 and 100, with value closure to 100 implying higher capability of the rating model in predicting defaults or separating the two populations. In general, the higher the K-S, the better the model power.

We have assessed the rating prediction done in T time period and checked the NPA status of the accounts in the following year T + 1. We have used dummy variable DDEF to capture the information and used default dummy DDF = 1 if account becomes NPA and DDEF = 0 if it remains good or solvent with an interval of 1 year through rating migration analysis. The rating validation data for all loans rated by RAM model for commercial loans are summarized in Table 9.3:

One can notice that the default rate (i.e. proportion of bad cases) steadily increases as we move down to the rating scale from AAA to CCC. The odd ratio in favour of good also sharply comes down. Therefore,

Table 9.3 RAM Rating Validation Data for Year T + 1

Rating	Score Upper Bound	Score Mid-point	Number of Borrowers at Start	Number of Defaults during Year	Number of Good Accounts	Odd Ratio (Good vs. Bad)	Default Rate
AAA	10	9.25	6	0	6	--	0.00%
AA	8.5	8	161	0	161	--	2.17%
A	7.5	7	927	1	926	926	1.79%
BBB	6.5	6.125	748	3	745	248.33333	2.72%
BB	5.75	5.375	187	6	181	30.166667	2.89%
B	5	4.625	89	10	79	7.9	4.10%
CCC	4.25	2.125	15	2	13	6.5	4.00%
Total			2133	22	2111	95.954545	2.80%

the RAM rating system is obviously able to classify cases by default probability.

For KS test, we check the frequency distribution of good and bad cases to develop statistical indicators to assess the discriminatory power of the RAM model. Using their frequency distribution, we plot the curve of density functions to check the separation power of the model. We also calculate the Kolmogorov–Sminrov (K–S) value which is simply the maximum difference between two columns: cumulative % defaults vs. cumulative % good. The density functions are reported in Table 9.4.

Figure 9.2 reports the separation power of the RAM models. It is constructed based on the density functions of good and bad cases.

It is quite evident from Figure 9.2 is that RAM model has good separation power. Note that the percentage of defaulted customers classified as non-defaulted is denoted by alpha and is statistically termed as type I error rate. The model validation aspects and their relevance in IFRS 9 ECL has been demonstrated in Bellini (2019). The internal model validation tests for regulatory requirements are discussed in Medema, Koning and Lensink (2009), Morrison (2003), Rezac and Rezac (2011).

Information Value (IV)

Information value is a statistical check to test the validity of model parameters. Using the borrower level rating data on Education Loan of Bank, we use IV test to check whether course employability can be considered as an important factor in predicting default risk in Education Loan. For this, weight of evidence (WOE) and information value (IV) metric have been computed. The results show that course category can significantly differentiate good borrower from their bad counterparts. This confirms the fact that course category is an important factor in determining creditworthiness of educational loan borrower. The results are summarized in Table 9.5.

The formulas used for calculation of WOE and IV are given here.

$$WOE = \left[\ln\left(\frac{Distr\ Good}{Distr\ Bad}\right)\right] \times 100 \qquad \text{Eq. 9.2}$$

Table 9.4 Density Functions Good vs. Bad and K-S Value

Rating	No. of Good Cases	No. of Bad Cases	Total	Proportion per Rating Class	Density Function for Good Cases	Density Function for Bad Cases	Cumulative %Defaults	Cum. %Good	Difference in Cum.
AAA	6	0	6	0.28%	0.28%	0.00%	100.00%	100.00%	0.00
AA	161	0	161	7.55%	7.63%	0.00%	100.00%	99.72%	0.28
A	926	1	927	43.46%	43.87%	4.55%	100.00%	92.09%	7.91
BBB	745	3	748	35.07%	35.29%	13.64%	95.45%	48.22%	47.23
BB	181	6	187	8.77%	8.57%	27.27%	81.82%	12.93%	**68.89**
B	79	10	89	4.17%	3.74%	45.45%	54.55%	4.36%	50.19
CCC	13	2	15	0.70%	0.62%	9.09%	9.09%	0.62%	8.48
Total	2111	22	2133	100.00%	100.00%	100.00%	0.00%	0.00%	

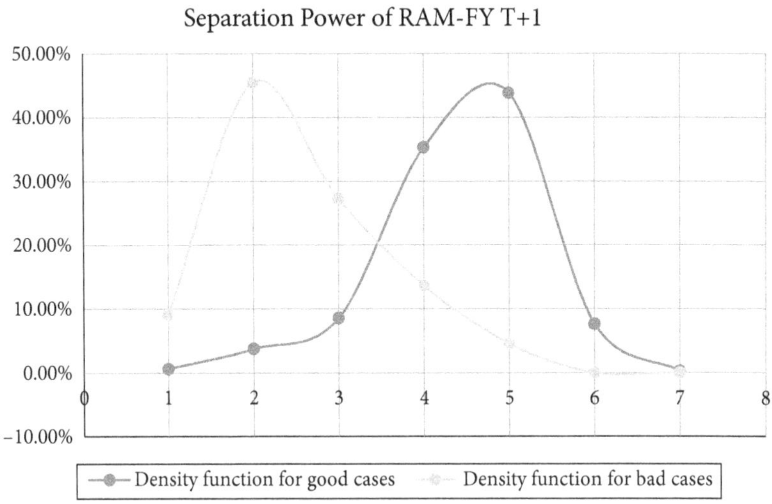

Figure 9.2 Separation Power through KS Test
Source: Author's computation

$$IV = \sum_{i=1}^{n} (Distr\ Good_i - Distr\ Bad_i) \times \ln\left(\frac{Distr\ Good}{Distr\ Bad}\right) \qquad \text{Eq. 9.3}$$

The IV threshold levels are given below:

Thus, the findings reported in the Table 9.5a confirm that course stream is a very strong factor for account becoming NPA as the course stream is directly linked to the employability. Therefore, the IV test helps the analyst to discover that course category can be an important factor to be included in the credit rating model of the bank.

The WOE and IV tests are important to convert a logit regression model to a scorecard and to assign weights.

Following scaling factor is popularly used to convert logit regression model to a scorecard:

$$Score = \ln(odds \times factor + offset$$
$$= -\left(\sum_{j,i=1}^{k,n}\left(woe_j \times \beta_i\right) + \alpha / n) \times factor + \frac{offset}{n}\right) \qquad \text{Eq. 9.4}$$

Table 9.5 Weight of Evidence and Information Value Check

Stream	Count	Tot Distr	Goods	Distr Good	Bads	Distr Bad	Bad Rate	WOE	Range
Agriculture Sciences	677	1.88%	653	1.98%	24	0.76%	3.55%	95.492	0.011648
Chartered Accountancy	13	0.04%	12.99	0.04%	0.00001	0.00%	0.00%	1172.927	0.00463
Diploma Courses	1040	2.88%	915	2.78%	125	3.97%	12.02%	−35.799	0.004282
Engineering	26980	74.79%	24710	75.04%	2270	72.18%	8.41%	3.883	0.00111
Law	36	0.10%	34	0.10%	2	0.06%	5.56%	48.4613	0.000192
Management	1090	3.02%	923	2.80%	167	5.31%	15.32%	−63.896	0.01602
Medical	1281	3.55%	1249	3.79%	32	1.02%	2.50%	131.576	0.036516
Nursing	1430	3.96%	1354	4.11%	76	2.42%	5.31%	53.1484	0.009009
Others	3529	9.78%	3080	9.35%	449	14.28%	12.72%	−42.294	0.020824
Total	36076	100.00%	32931	100.00%	3145	100.00%	8.72%		**0.104232**

Source: Author's own study based on Education loan data of a large public sector bank.
Note: Tot Distr: Total distribution (i.e. relative proportion); Goods: Number of solvent accounts; Dist Good: Relative proportion of solvent (good) accounts; Bads: count of delinquent or defaulted accounts; Distr Bad: Relative proportion of bad accounts; Bad Rate: default rate.

Table 9.5a IV Ranges

Range:	Precision
<0.02	Unpredictive
0.02-0.1	Weak
0.1-0.3	Medium
0.3+	Strong

Source: Naeem Sidiqi

Note that

$$Offset = Score - \{Factor \times \ln(Odds)\} \quad \text{Eq. 9.4a}$$

$$Factor = \frac{pdo}{\ln(2)} \quad \text{Eq. 9.4b}$$

$$pdo = Factor \times \ln(2) \quad \text{Eq. 9.4c}$$

where
WOE = weight of evidence for each grouped attribute
β = regression coefficient for each characteristic
α = intercept term from logistic regression
n = number of characteristics
k = number of groups (of attributes) in each characteristic
pdo = 'points to double the odds'.
For example, if a scorecard was being scaled where the bank wants odds of 50:1 at 600 points for the customer with the highest creditworthiness (say AAA) and desired the odds to double every 20 points (i.e. $pdo = 20$), then the factor and offset would be

$$Factor = \frac{20}{\ln(2)} = 28.8539$$

$$Offset = 600 - \{28.8539 \times \ln(50)\}$$

$$= 487.123$$

Similarly, each score corresponding to each set of odds (or each attribute) can be calculated as follows:

$$Score = 487.123 + 28.8539\ \ln(odds)$$

The scorecard development from logistic regression using odd ratios explained in detail in Naeem Siddiqui (2006).

Hosmer–Lemeshow (HL) test

The Hosmer–Lemeshow (HL) test for logistic regression is widely used to answer the question: 'How well does my model fit the data?' Hosmer and Lemeshow (2000) proposed a statistic that they show, through simulation, is distributed as chi square when there is no replication in any of the subpopulations. This test is available only for binary response models. First, the observations are sorted in increasing order of their estimated event probability. Note that the number of groups, g, can be smaller than 10 if there are fewer than 10 patterns of explanatory variables. There must be at least three groups in order for the Hosmer–Lemeshow statistic to be computed.

The Hosmer–Lemeshow goodness-of-fit statistic is obtained by calculating the Pearson chi-square statistic from the $2 \times g$ by table of observed and expected frequencies, where g is the number of groups. The statistic is written as follows:

$$\chi^2_{HL} = \sum_{i=1}^{g} \frac{(O_i - E_i)^2}{E_i}$$

Or,

$$\chi^2_{\mathrm{HL}} = \sum_{i=1}^{g} \frac{\left(O_i - N_i\bar{\pi}_i\right)^2}{N_i\bar{\pi}_i\left(1-\bar{\pi}_i\right)} \qquad \text{Eq. 9.5}$$

where N_i is the total frequency of subjects in the ith group, O_i is the total frequency of event outcomes in the ith group, and $\bar{\pi}_i$ is the average estimated predicted probability of an event outcome for the *i*th group. Symbol *g* denotes the number of groups.

Goodness-of-Fit Test

Pseudo R2 is a measure of predictive power, that is, how well you can predict the dependent variable based on the independent variables. That may be an important concern, but it does not really address the question of whether the model is consistent with the data. By contrast, goodness-of-fit (GOF) tests help you decide whether your model is correctly specified. They produce a *p*-value—if it is low (say, below.05), you reject the model as the fit is bad. If it is high, then your model passes the test. The 'estat gof,group(10) command' in STATA after running logistic regression produces a chi-square statistics with a degree of freedom (df) and yields a *p*-value on which basis we check whether the model fit is satisfactory (a high p-value > 0.10 means fit is satisfactory).

Steps in HL Test

The Hosmer and Lemeshow (HL) test actually measures the association between actual events and predicted probability. In other words, it is a measure of how close the predicted probabilities are to the actual rate of events.

In HL test, null hypothesis states that sample of observed events and non-events supports the claim about the predicted events and non-events. In other words, the model fits data well.

Post-logistic regression estimation, HL test procedure steps are as under

1) Calculate estimated probability of events by using logistic regression method
2) Split data into 10 sections based on ascending order of probability
3) Calculate number of actual events and non-events in each section

Table 9.6 Computation Process of HL Statistic from Predicted EPD Bins

	Observed				Expected		
	1	0	Pred Prob=1	Pred Prob=0	1	0	HL Statistic
1	362	219	0.59141	0.40859	343.61	237.39	2.41
2	186	273	0.49833	0.50167	228.73	230.27	15.91
3	175	217	0.37505	0.62495	147.02	244.98	8.52
4	69	180	0.29171	0.70829	72.64	176.36	0.26
5	167	475	0.27109	0.72891	174.04	467.96	0.39
6	191	594	0.20334	0.79666	159.62	625.38	7.74
8	98	930	0.1336	0.8664	137.34	890.66	13.01
10	68	486	0.0957	0.9043	53.02	500.98	4.68

4) Calculate Predicted Probability = 1 by averaging probability in each section
5) Calculate Predicted Probability = 0 by subtracting Predicted Probability = 1 from 1
6) Calculate expected frequency (E) by multiplying number of cases by Predicted Probability = 1
7) Calculate chi-square statistics taking frequency of observed (O) and predicted events and non-events

Note that the general thumb rule for Chi-square test is that if p-value > 0.05, the model fits well with the data.

We obtain the HL statistic by adding (O-E)^2/E for all 10 class intervals. Note that the class intervals are the decile values based on the ranks of the predicted scores. The Hosmer–Lemeshow chi2 test statistic is obtained using summation: Σ(O-E)^2/E.

STATA Example

Let us consider machine output logistic regression exercise where Output = f(Age, Shift)

After running the logistic regression, we run

```
. estat gof,group(10) table
```

Table 9.7 HL Test Retail Model Validation Results
(Table Collapsed on Quantiles of Estimated Probabilities)

Group	Prob	Obs_1	Exp_1	Obs_0	Exp_0	Total
1	0.0013	0	0	2	2	2
2	0.0217	0	0	2	2	2
3	0.1664	0	0.1	2	1.9	2
4	0.3904	0	0.6	2	1.4	2
5	0.4904	1	0.9	1	1.1	2
6	0.7075	2	1.2	0	0.8	2
7	0.8398	2	1.5	0	0.5	2
8	0.9244	2	1.8	0	0.2	2
9	0.9603	1	1.9	1	0.1	2
10	0.9952	2	2	0	0	2

Number of observations = 20
Number of groups = 10
Hosmer–Lemeshow chi2(8) = 8.67
Prob > chi^2 = 0.3707
Note: the degree of freedom (df) is 8.

Logistic model for Machine_Output, goodness-of-fit test
Clearly, this is a good fit.

In the same manner, we can now perform the validation of our earlier developed retail PD model personal loans using logistic regression. After estimation of logit model in STATA we write the following command to perform HL test. The HL test result has been presented in Table 9.7.

```
estat gof,group(10) table
```

It gives us following results output (Table 9.8)

Note that HL weights are computed using (O-E)^2/E for both 1 and expected 1 and 0 and expected 0 at each decile class. If we add all weights, we obtain the HL statistic = sum((O-E)^2/E)=7.81.

Since obtained HL stat follows a Chi^2 distribution and through CHi^2, we check:

H0: there is no difference between observed and predicted observations

Table 9.8 Logistic Model for Default, Goodness-of-Fit Test (Table Collapsed on Quantiles of Estimated Probabilities)

Group	Prob	Obs_1	Exp_1	Obs_0	Exp_0	Total |
1	0.0159	0	0.7	150	149.3	150 |
2	0.0808	6	7.0	144	143.0	150 |
3	0.1615	18	18.4	132	131.6	150 |
4	0.2431	33	30.5	117	119.5	150 |
5	0.3230	41	42.6	109	107.4	150 |
6	0.4149	60	54.9	90	95.1	150 |
7	0.4990	69	68.5	81	81.5	150 |
8	0.6272	79	83.9	71	66.1	150 |
9	0.7981	101	105.7	49	44.3	150 |
10	1.0000	141	135.9	9	14.1	150 |

Number of observations = 1500
Number of groups = 10
Hosmer–Lemeshow chi2(8) = 5.33
Prob > chi^2 = 0.7219

Ha: There is a difference.

Since the error in all deciles is less and hence low HL stat and since Prob > chi2 = 0.4518 and is greater than 10%, we cannot reject the null hypothesis and hence the model fits well with the data.

The Hosmer–Lemeshow goodness-of-fit test is based on dividing the sample up according to their predicted probabilities, or risks.

Besides, HL test, we have also generated ROC plot by comparing predicted PD from logit model with actual default (dummy DDEF = 1).

ROC Curve Generated from Retail Logit PD Model

Note that the ROC curve is above 45 degree diagonal line. The area under ROC curve is 0.8433 as depicted in Figure 9.3. This confirms that our retail PD model based on logistic regression (reported in Table 7.12 in Chapter 7) fits well. After logit regression, we type 'lroc' command in STATA for drawing the ROC curve.

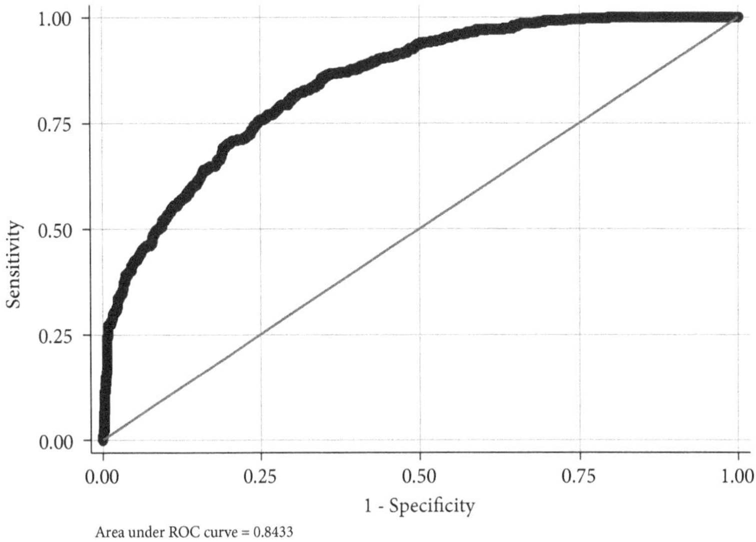

Figure 9.3 Model Accuracy

Kendall's Tau: Kendall's (1955) rank correlation is a non-parametric method to evaluate the degree of similarity between two sets of ranks given to a same set of objects.

It is a non-parametric correlation analysis which can be used to compare internal RAM rating with external ratings. This way, the bank can also benchmark its rating standing with external agency rating.

In logistic regression, we find a goodness-of-fit statistic with a p-value displayed along with it. The null hypothesis is that the model is fit. If the p-value is less than 0.05 and the null hypothesis is rejected, it means that the model is not fit.

Mean-Square Error (MSE): It is used to estimate the forecast error.

$$MSE = \frac{\Sigma\left(r_i - \hat{r}_i\right)^2}{n-1} \qquad \text{Eq. 9.6}$$

where r_i is the actual or observed series and $\hat{r}_i$ is the fitted or forecasted series, and n is the number of observations.

A lower MSE signifies better predictive power of the model. A forecast error within one standard error of the actual value is acceptable.

Mean-square error method is used to back test market VaR models. The actual losses (r_i) are compared with the estimated VaR ($\hat{r}_i$).

Akaike Information Criterion

This statistical method is used to check the out of sample predictor error in model forecasting. Akaike Information Criterion (AIC) estimates the relative amount of information is lost by the model. The Lower the value of AIC, the better the quality of the model. It has popular application in comparative evaluation of among time series forecasting models as well. AIC gives estimates of information lost when a specific model is used. It balances between the goodness of fit and the complexity of the model. Mathematically, the AIC is calculated using the following equation:

$$AIC = -2 \times \frac{l}{m} + 2 \times \frac{k}{n} \quad \text{Eq. 9.7}$$

where

N = number of observations; k = number of estimated parameters (e.g. regressors including intercept); and l = the log likelihood function (assuming normally distributed errors).

$$l = -\frac{n}{2}\left(\left(1 + \ln(2\pi) + \ln\left(\frac{1}{n}\sum_{i=1}^{n}\left(y_i - \widehat{y_i}\right)^2\right)\right)\right) \quad \text{Eq. 9.8}$$

where y_i is the observed dependent variable and $\widehat{y_i}$ is the fitted dependent variable. The second part in the above l equation is also termed as residual sum of squares (RSS).

In a simpler form AIC is also expressed as

$$AIC = \ln\left(\sigma^2\right) + 2 \times \frac{k}{n} \quad \text{Eq. 9.9}$$

where σ^2 is the residual variance (or RSS) and k is the total number of parameters.

A lower AIC value assures a good balance between goodness of fit and complexity.

Bayesian Information Criterion (BIC) or Schwarz Criterion

It is a non-parametric criterion used for selection among a finite set of predictive models. It is a likelihood function and is closely related to AIC. It is also used to compare predictive power of forecasting models. The test statistic was developed by the statistician Gideon Schwarz. BIC and AIC are closely related; however, we can rely more on BIC when too many factors are included in a model to increase the goodness of fit of the model. In such cases, BIC penalizes more and gives more conservative view on the model accuracy.

Mathematically, BIC is estimated using the following equation:

$$BIC = -2 \times \frac{l}{m} + \frac{k \times \ln(n)}{n} \qquad \text{Eq. 9.10}$$

Like Akaike, the lower the value of BIC, the better the model fitness compared to alternatives. It imposes a greater penalty for additional factors. These additional validation test criteria and their applications in risk modelling are also mentioned in Vose (2008).

Summary

The ability of a financial institution to manage its risks and make informed decisions has become highly dependent on the quality and sophistication of its risk management framework and systems. An independent and objective validation of the predictive power and efficacy of valuation and risk models is an integral part of a robust risk management system. Reliable rating systems require efficient validation strategies. Various standard statistical tests (such as Kendall's Tau, Spearman rank correlation, power curve, Hosmer–Lemeshow test, KS test, information value, etc.) have been explained with examples to exhibit model validation and back-testing exercise. These tests enable an assessment of reliability of risk models. For example, Hosmer–Lemeshow test checks the overall fitness of the Logit model. It is a goodness-of-fit (GOF) tests help you to decide whether your model is correctly specified. Good statistical model governance framework in banks enhances internal decision-making abilities and regulatory reporting standards.

Review Questions

1. What is model validation? Why it is important in Banks?
2. What is Hosmer–Lemeshow Test? How it can be used in risk model validation?
3. What is the difference between AIC and BIC?
4. What is information value (IV)? How it can be interpreted?
5. What is power curve? How it can be read?
6. What is the difference between KS test and mean-square error test?
7. What is VaR back testing?
8. What is GOF test?
9. How to interpret HL chi^2 test results?
10. Why model validation and back testing are important?

References

BCBS (2005). 'Studies on the Validation of Internal Rating Systems', BIS working paper no. 14.

Bellini, T. (2019). 'IFRS 9 and CECL Credit Risk Modelling and Validation-A Practical Guide with Examples Worked in R and SAS', Chapter 2, Academic Press, Elsevier.

Hosmer, W., and S. Lemeshow (2000)., 'Applied Logistic Regression', Wiley, New York.

Kendall, M. G. (1955)., 'Rank Correlation Methods', 2nd Edition, Hafner Publishing Co., New York.

Medema, L., R. H. Koning, and R. Lensink (2009). 'A Practical Approach to Validating a PD Model', *Journal of Banking & Finance*, Vol. 33, pp. 701–708.

Morrison, S. J. (2003). 'Preparing for Basel II Modeling Requirements-Part 2: Model Validation', *The RMA Journal*, June, pp. 43–47.

Siddiqi, N. (2006). 'Credit Risk Scorecards-Developing and Implementing Intelligent Credit Scoring', John Wiley & Sons, Inc.

Rezac, M., and F. Rezac (2011). 'How to Measure Quality of Credit Scoring Models', *Czech Journal of Economics and Finance* (Finance a uver), Charles University Prague, Faculty of Social Sciences, Vol. 61, Issue 5, pp. 486–507, November.

Siddiqui, N. (2006). 'Credit Risk Scorecards: Developing and Implementing Intelligent Credit Scoring', New York: John Wiley & Sons.

Vose, D. (2008). 'Risk Analysis-A Quantitative Guide', 3rd Edition, Chapter 10, Wiley.

10

Time-Series Forecasting Techniques for Banking Variables

A time series is a set of observations on a variable measured at successive points of time. A time series that consists of single (scalar) observations recorded sequentially over equal time increments. Usually, the variable values are recorded over equal time intervals—yearly, quarterly, monthly, etc. A large proportion of economic data are in the form of time series, e.g. monthly movement of interest rate, stock price and returns, national income, agricultural income, yield on bonds, index of industrial production, wholesale price index, etc. It is essential for banks and FIs to understand the movement of macro-factors and their influence on banking variables.

In order to forecast the financial variables more accurately, one has to devise a scheme to describe the movement in a time series adequately. For this purpose, we need to decompose the time series into four components:

1. The *Trend* component represents the long-run smooth movement of the variable.
2. The *Cyclical* component represents oscillatory movement around the trend. It may be strictly periodic, that is to say, the same value of the variable is repeated after a fixed time series (agricultural production/BSE stock index for example), or it may be aperiodic. A cyclical movement is, therefore, characterized by up and down movements (like business cycle). This continues till it reaches the trough and again the upswing starts. So, one has to find out the period lag to capture cyclicality.
3. The *Seasonal* component is also oscillatory in character but is strictly confined to intra-year movement, hence, the name seasonal. For instance, the data on the market price of rice or monthly whole

sale price index (WPI—monthly) or monthly consumer price index (CPI—monthly) or monthly movement of stock index will show seasonal variations. However, any series recorded on the annual basis naturally eliminate any seasonal component.

These three components are known as the *systematic* components of a time series. One can develop better forecasting models through analysis of these components. It is essential to embed the systematic components to better predict the uncertainty. Many default forecasting as well as interest rate forecasting models are developed using time-series techniques. Bank can examine the effect of various macroeconomic scenarios on loan default rates or fresh slippage rate to estimate their loan provisioning as well as future capital requirements. In this chapter, we discuss various simple but effective time-series modelling techniques that would help the risk manager to assess future business risk.

Analysis of Trend: Polynomial Trend

The trend component of a time series reflects the long run movement. Usually, it is a rising or falling smooth curve. It is very advantageous for forecasting population growth trend etc. if we can represent the trend by a simple mathematical function.

The linear trend is a special case of polynomial trend. An nth degree polynomial trend can be written as follows:

$$Y_t = a_0 + a_1 t + a_2 t^2 + a_3 t^3 + \ldots + a_n t^n. \qquad \text{Eq. 10.1}$$

One can get a simplest linear trend if the equation is polynomial of degree 1 (means t).

The equation will be

$$Y_t = a_0 + a_1 t. \qquad \text{Eq. 10.2}$$

In this case, Y grows at a constant rate a_1, and a_0 is the intercept or the constant term. If $a_1 > 0$, it means the coefficient of first difference of Y_t

with respect to t is positive and it is actually the growth rate of Y is increasing over time.

Similarly, for a quadratic case, it is a polynomial of degree 2. The equation looks like the following:

$$Y_t = a_0 + a_1 t + a_2 t^2. \quad \text{Eq. 10.3}$$

However, here, the growth rate may be upward or it may be downward and it may also have turning points depending upon the size and sigh of the two coefficients (a_1 and a_2).

For a cubic equation, another term t^3 gets added.

Application of Trend Forecasting

A trend fitting can be done with simple OLS by regressing the log value of dependent variable over time. Suppose, a risk analyst wants to project gross non-performing percentage for entire scheduled commercial banks in India. NPA projection is helpful in understanding the credit risk position for the banking system. The polynomial trend regression method can be used to project the risk. Such forward-looking analysis would enable the analyst to foresee future risk of the banking industry and estimate provision or capital requirements.

In order to meet these objectives, the analyst collects the data from RBI's website. Table 10.1 summarizes the NPA percentage. There was a policy change since 1999 as the NPA definition underwent a change (from 180 days past due to 90 days). Therefore, we have truncated the data from 2003 to 2017. A trend projection was done for the year 2017–2018, and the forecasted value was compared with the actual GNPA% in FY 2018. This regression analysis was done using EVIEWS 10 package. However, trend regression can be run in Excel, STATA, SPSS, and also in R studio.

The data need to be arranged as shown in Table 10.1:

Using the above data, we try to fit a trend regression model. It has been found that quadratic equation 3 fits well with GNPA ratio as reported in the 4th column of the above table.

Table 10.1 Data for Non-Performing Assets for SCBs in India

Year	Gross Advances	Gross NPA	GNPA%	T
2002–2003	7780.43	687.17	8.83%	1
2003–2004	9020.26	648.12	7.19%	2
2004–2005	11526.82	593.73	5.15%	3
2005–2006	15513.78	510.97	3.29%	4
2006–2007	20125.1	504.86	2.51%	5
2007–2008	25078.85	563.09	2.25%	6
2008–2009	30382.54	683.28	2.25%	7
2009–2010	35449.65	846.98	2.39%	8
2010–2011	40120.79	979.00	2.44%	9
2011–2012	46655.44	1429.03	3.06%	10
2012–2013	59882.79	1940.74	3.24%	11
2013–2014	68757.48	2641.95	3.84%	12
2014–2015	75606.66	3233.45	4.28%	13
2015–2016	81673.45	6119.47	7.49%	14
2016–2017	85138.79	7917.91	9.30%	15
2017–2018			—	**16**

Source: RBI Data. Units in Rs. Billion.

We obtain the following fitted regression equation:

$$\text{GNPA\_Rato} = 0.107219 - 0.022409 \times T + 0.001416 \times (T)^2 \quad \text{Eq. 10.4}$$

$$(21.16^*)\ (-15.38^*)\ (15.99^*)$$

The values in the parentheses are the t-values, * denotes significance at 1% or better.

R-square = 0.955 and Adjusted R-square = 0.947

Next, using the quadratic trend equation estimates as given in Equation 10.4, we can predict GNPA ratio for the year 2017–2018. For this, we apply $T = 16$ and using the intercept and coefficients, we get predicted value of the dependent variable.

The predicted GNPA ratio for the year 2017–2018 is estimated as 11.12%. The actual reported value as given by RBI is 11.22%. Thus, the forecast error is very low = (11.22% − 11.12%) / 11.12% = 0.90%.

Any time series which contains no trend can be represented as consisting of two parts: AR Process (lag dependent variable itself) and MA Process (lag error dependence or serial correlation in the disturbance). Trend projections and modelings applications are further demonstrated in Profillidis and Botzoris (2019).

Time Series: AR and MA Process

A more advanced modelling framework would be fit the data through auto-regressive moving average (ARMA) process using Box and Jenkin's approach. In the univariate case (single series), a series is modelled only in terms of its own past values and some disturbance. The general expression is

$$y_t = f(y_{t-1}, y_{t-2}, \ldots, u_t) \qquad \text{Eq. 10.5}$$

To make the above equation, operational one must specify three things: the functional form f(), the number of lags, and a structure for the disturbance term. If, for example, one specified a linear function with one lag and a white noise disturbance, the result would be the first-order, auto-regressive AR(1) process:

$$y_t = \alpha + \phi y_{t-1} + w_t \qquad \text{Eq. 10.6}$$

The general AR (p) process is shown as follow:.

$$y_t = \alpha + \varnothing_1 y_{t-1} + \varnothing_2 y_{t-2} + \ldots + \varnothing_p y_{t-p} + w_t \qquad \text{Eq. 10.7}$$

When the disturbance is white noise (it means stationary, explained in detailed later) it is a pure AR (p) process. When w is not assumed to be white noise, the usual alternative specification is a moving average, MA(q) process.

Stationarity

A stationarity process has the following properties:

Expected value of each observation is the same, i.e. $E(y_t) = E(y_{t+n})$ for $n \neq 0$; the variances of each observation are the same, i.e. $V(y_t)=V(y_{t+n})$ for $n \neq 0$, and the covariance $C(y_t, y_{t+n})$ are invariant of any offset in time.

That is, mean, variance, and autocorrelation structure do not change over time. The process is also called white noise. Or it is a flat-looking series without a trend or periodic fluctuations. Or more precisely, the probability distribution of the process is time invariant.

Seasonality

A time series displays seasonality if it has periodic fluctuations over time. If it is identified properly, forecasting of the series becomes more accurate.

ARMA Model

Any time series which contains no trend can be represented as consisting of two parts:

A self-deterministic part—forecastable by AR (p) model which has been given in Equation 10.7 and a disturbance component (residuals from AR model) which is representable by MA(q):

$$y_t = \alpha + w_t + \theta_1 w_{t-1} + \theta_2 w_{t-2} + \ldots + \theta_q w_{t-q} \qquad \text{Eq. 10.8}$$

A combination model containing AR(p) and MA(q) is classified as an ARMA(p,q) model. For an ARMA(p,q) model, we have

$$\begin{aligned} y_t = \alpha + \varnothing_1 y_{t-1} + \varnothing_2 y_{t-2} + \ldots + \varnothing_p y_{t-p} \\ + w_t + w_{t-1} + \theta_2 w_{t-2} + \ldots + \theta_q w_{t-q} \end{aligned} \qquad \text{Eq. 10.9}$$

Or, it can be expressed using lag operator as follows:

$$\varnothing(L)\,y_t = \theta_p(L)\,w_t$$

where $\varnothing_p \neq 0$, $\theta_q \neq 0$ and $\sigma_w^2 > 0$.

Autoregressive Model

Under autoregressive (AR) time-series process, the current value of a variable (Y) depends upon only its past values observed in previous periods plus an error term. A time-series AR(2) model was run in EVIEWS package to project RBI balance sheet figure. The similar data and method were used in Jalan Committee Report (2019). The regression results are reported below:

Table 10.2 AR(2) Model

Dependent Variable: LRBI_BS
Method: Least Squares
Date: 09/05/19 Time: 17:49
Sample: 2001 2019
Included observations: 19

Variable	Coefficient	Std. Error	*t*-Statistic	Prob.
C	0.441885	0.249877	1.768406	0.0961
LRBI_BS(-1)	0.887877	0.241015	3.683912	0.0020
LRBI_BS(-2)	0.079990	0.236730	0.337896	0.7398
R-squared	0.988915	Mean dependent var		9.583160
Adjusted R-squared	0.987530	S.D. dependent var		0.758682
S.E. of regression	0.084722	Akaike info criterion		−1.954933
Sum squared resid	0.114846	Schwarz criterion		−1.805811
Log likelihood	21.57186	Hannan-Quinn criter.		−1.929695
F-statistic	713.7128	Durbin-Watson stat		2.085902
Prob(F-statistic)	0.000000			

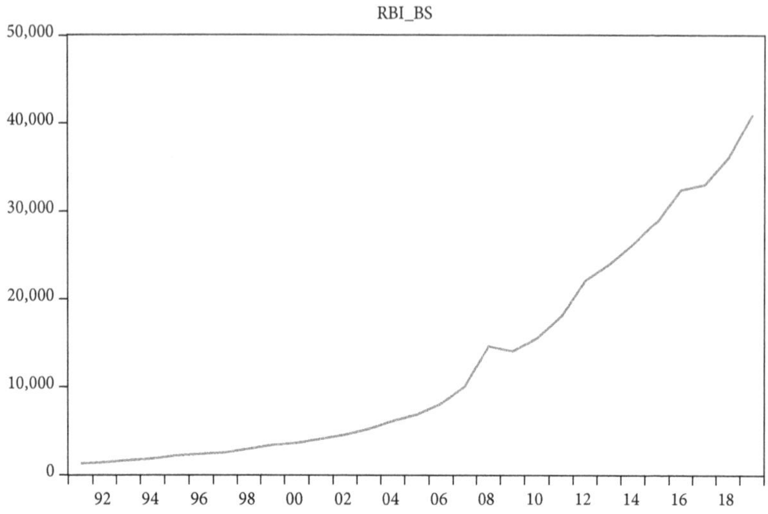

Figure 10.1 Series-RBI Balance Sheet

The dependent variable is natural log of balance sheet value of RBI and independent variables are lag-dependent variable. The AR(1) coefficient is statistically significant since ($p < 0.01$). The intercept is statistically significant at 10% level. The above regression model can be used to forecast future values of the balance sheet size of the Central Bank. The projected balance sheet has been reported in the RBI (2019) report page number 110.

The RBI balance sheet data have been plotted in Figure 10.1. Clearly the data have a time-series trend.

Note that a chow test was performed and a structural break was deducted for a longer data period (actually the time period was from 1991–1992 to 2018–2019). Due to the presence of structural break, a shortened time period from 2001 to 2019 was used in the regression analysis.

AR time-series model can also be used to predict forward-looking z index under the IFRS 9 ECL modelling approach. This has been demonstrated below.

Stationarity Condition

Stationarity is a desirable property for an estimated AR model. For this, we have to perform the residual unit root test.

Autocorrelation Function and Partial Autocorrelation Function

Autocorrelation function (ACF) gives us complete description of time-series process for different time lags. It checks internal association between observations at various lag intervals (k). ACF actually plots the autocorrelation of a time-series variable with respect to different time lags (k = 1, 2, ... n). Specifically, ACF is used to detect the presence of moving average process (seasonality and trend) in time-series data.

Unit Root Test

In order to illustrate the Dickey–Fuller unit root test to check non stationarity, let us consider an AR(1) process:

$$y_t = \mu + \rho y_{t-1} + u_t \qquad \text{Eq. 10.10}$$

Where μ and ρ are parameters and u_t is assumed to be white noise.

Note that y is considered to be stationary if—$1 < \rho < 1$. However, if f, y is called a non-stationary series (or a random walk with drift) since the lagged value will not converge. Adding the constant term μ is termed as random walk series with a drift.

If we subtract y_{t-1} from the above equation, we get

$$\Delta y_t = \mu + (\rho - 1) y_{t-1} + u_t \qquad \text{Eq. 10.11}$$

where $\gamma = \rho - 1$ and we obtain one tail hypothesis:

$$H_o : \gamma = 0$$

vs. alternate

$$H_1 : \gamma < 0$$

If the series becomes stationary after first difference, it is called differenced stationary process or integrated of order 1. Thus, to generalize, we can state that if a non-stationary series y_t has to be differenced d times before it becomes stationary, then it is said to be integrated of order d. Trend removal by differentiation to induce stationarity is an important step in AR-integrated moving average model (Box and Jenkins, 1976). It is important to identify the true nature of non-stationary series (trend, intercept etc.). A white noise process has constant mean $E(y_t) = \mu$ and variance $var(y_t) = \sigma^2$ and zero autocovariance except at lag zero.

$$E(y_t - E(y_t))(y_{t-s} - E(y_{t-s})) = \gamma_s \qquad \text{Eq. 10.12}$$

where = 0, 1, 2, ...

The above function is known as autocovariance function.

Dickey–Fuller test uses tau (τ) instead of t statistic to check non stationarity. The critical values at different level of significance are tabulated by Dickey and Fuller. The null hypothesis in ADF test is unit root is present (or non-stationarity). A higher value of tau and lower p value would reject the null and accept alternate, and the series would be identified as stationary. On the other hand, a lower tau value and higher p value ($p > 0.10$) would detect non-stationarity (or unit root) as we fail to reject the null hypothesis.

The above model can be further extended by combining AR(p) and MA(q) models and then we get augmented Dickey–Fuller (ADF) test statistic to check non stationarity. ADF approach controls for higher order correlation by adding lagged differenced terms.

Autoregressive Integrated Moving Average Model

Autoregressive integrated moving average (ARIMA) model is an integrated ARMA model. It is integrated because the model fitted to the differenced data and hence has to be integrated to provide a model for the original non-stationary data. ARIMA model can improve forecasting power as it incorporates trend, cyclicality, and seasonality.

The practical problem is to choose the most appropriate values for p, q (lag orders) that is to specify the ARIMA model. This problem is resolved by examining ADF test and through correlogram analysis—by checking ACF and PACF.

Note that, the term d is the number of times that the series is to be differenced to produce a stationary series. This is an important step in ARIMA specification.

If a series becomes stationary after first difference, it is called integrated of order or I(1) series. If it becomes stationary after 2nd difference, it is termed as I(2) and so on.

Concept about Autocorrelation Function (ACF): The ACF for equal k time lag helps us to identify moving average pattern in a time series. It gives us values of autocorrelation of a series with its time-lagged values. The ACF has the following form:

$$ACF = \frac{Cov\left(y_t, y_{t-k}\right)}{\sigma_{y_t}\sigma_{y_{t-k}}}$$

$$= \frac{\Sigma\left(y_t - \bar{y}\right)\left(y_{t-k} - \bar{y}\right)}{\Sigma\left(y_t - \bar{y}\right)^2}$$

$$= \frac{\gamma_k}{\gamma_0} \qquad \text{Eq. 10.13}$$

The above expression shows the autocorrelation between y_t and $y_{t\text{-}k}$.

If we plot these values along with confidence band in EVIEWS, it describes how well the current value of the series is correlated with its past values. By plotting ACF values against k lags provides help to the risk analyst to know what type of process is generated through the data series. Such correlation analysis through correlogram helps us in detecting MA process in time-series forecasting.

If ACF spikes help us to identify moving average (MA) pattern. If it drops to zero after the small number of lags, it is a sign of lower-order MA pattern. Note that seasonality of time-series variable is captured through MA lags.

Concept about Partial Autocorrelation Function: PACF helps us to distinguish between AR process of different orders solely based on correlogram analysis.

Like in AR(2) process,

$$y_t = \alpha + \theta_1 y_{t-1} + \theta_2 y_{t-2} + \varepsilon_t \qquad \text{Eq. 10.14}$$

The parameter θ_2 is the partial correlation between y_t and y_{t-2} with y_{t-1} is held constant.

$$\text{Hence, } r_{13.2} = \frac{r_{13} - r_{12}r_{23}}{\sqrt{1-r_{12}^2}\sqrt{1-r_{23}^2}} \qquad \text{Eq. 10.15}$$

We get $r_{12} = corr(y_t, y_{t-1}) = corr(y_{t-1}, y_{t-2}) = r_{23} = \rho_1$.
Similarly, $r_{13} = corr(y_t, y_{t-2}) = \rho_2$
Therefore, we can write

$$r_{13.2} = \frac{\rho_2 - \rho_1^2}{1-\rho_1^2} = \theta_2 \qquad \text{Eq. 10.15a}$$

It is like partial correlation analysis across lag structure. For example, $r_{13.2}$ measures the correlation between current period (y_t) and 3rd lag (y_{t-3}) with 2nd lag is held constant. Similarly, $r_{12.1}$ measures correlation between current period and 2nd lag when 1st lag of the variable is held unchanged. Thus, it basically detects the partial effects of lags.

The statistical package EVIEW calculates the PACFs at each lag interval.

ARIMA Model Identification

- Once *d* is determined, one can work with the stationary series and examine both its ACF and its PACF to determine the proper specification of *p* and *q*. These should be checked on the differenced series.
- Note that **spikes** in ACF are indicative of MA terms and the PACF can be used to specify AR terms.
- For AR term, one should check the PACF pattern and for MA term, ACF pattern.
- If the process is ARMA (*p*, *q*), the ACF will show spikes up to lag *q*, and then decay either directly or in an oscillatory manner. The PACF will show spikes up to lag *p* and then decay either directly or in an oscillatory manner.

Table 10.3 Model Specification through ACF and PACF Structure

Model	ACF pattern	PACF pattern
Pure Moving Average (MA) process	Spikes at lag 1-q then cut off (no. of non-zero points of ACF=MA order)	Geometrically decaying (Tail off)
Pure AR process	A geometrically decaying tail off (slow decay)	Spikes at lag 1-p then cut off (no. of non-zero PACF points=AR order)
ARIMA*	Spikes and decline (geometrically)	Spikes and decline (geometrically)

*Note: Mixed (ARMA) processes typically show exponential declines in both the ACF and the PACF.

If ACF decay in oscillatory manner, then there will be presence of seasonal effects (Seasonality is very common in monthly/weekly data).

Detecting Trend and Seasonality in a Series

- One can identify **trend** in a series using the ACF. If trend is present, ACF will slowly decay with an increase in time lags k.
- If you are looking at **seasonality**, you look at the autocorrelation function (ACF) pattern again, them there will be definitely seasonality (e.g. if there are high and low (particular spikes) in ACF pattern in the correlogram analysis.
- It is essential to determine the **order of the model** required to capture the dynamic features of the data. This can be identified graphically through plotting the data over time and plotting the ACF and PACF to determine the most appropriate specification.

Estimating the ARIMA Model-Box-Jenkins Approach

- Once the parameters p and q of the ARMA (p, q) process has been diagnosed, it is very useful to do the **Ljung and Box Q test** on the residuals.
- ARIMA model is estimated on difference stationary series using **least squares** or **maximum likelihood method**.

- If the ARMA (p, q) process has been reasonably accurately identified, the **residuals** should be **white noise**. This can be verified through Ljung Box Q test.
- Accordingly, the correlations up to any lag among the residuals should be zero (or insignificant spike, check whether $p > 0.10$).
- In general, there would be several candidate ARMA (p, q) models.
- **EVIEWS** provides several statistics that can be used as model selection criteria (e.g. R-square—the higher the better, Akaike Information—the lower the better and Scwartz Bayesian Criterion—lower values are better).

Forecasting with ARIMA Model

- Finally, the estimated model can be used to generate both static (one period ahead) and dynamic forecasts (two periods ahead).
- The forecasted values are then compared with actual series to validate the forecast error.
- Root-mean-square error, mean absolute error, and mean absolute percentage errors are checked to validate the forecasting models.

Key Steps in Building ARIMA Forecasting Model

- **Model Identification Stationarity** checks, identifying level of stationarity of the series (or order of integration) and AR and MA process specification

  Methods
  - **A. Correlogram analysis**: studying the ACF and PACF lag structure
  - Dickey–Fuller unit root Test
- **B. Model Estimation:** Having determined the orders of the ARIMA model, the model can be estimated in EVIEWS 10 or STATA 14 using differenced regression technique.
- C. **Diagnostic Checks:** Once the ARIMA model is specified and parameters are estimated, the adequacy of the models may be checked through Box-Pierce-Ljung-residual test (or white noise test of the residual)

- **D. Forecasting:** After diagnostic checks, the regression equation may be used to generate short-term (static) or long-term (dynamic) forecasts.

  A detailed discussions about various ARMA model specifications are given in Johnston and DiNardo (1997), Enders (2014), and Tsay (2014)

ARIMA Forecast Example

The following series represent quarterly time-series data on exchange rate (Rupee vs. Dollar) for time period 2003Q3 (i.e. September 2003) to 2018 Q2 (June 2018). The log-transformed series LEXCR has been used to fit the ARIMA model as well run necessary time-series tests.

First, we plot the time series data in a graph to understand the series. The line graph of log value of the series presented in Figure 10.2 clearly depicts non stationarity and presence of a time trend.

ACF and PACF for the original level series are shown in the correlogram in Figure 10.3.

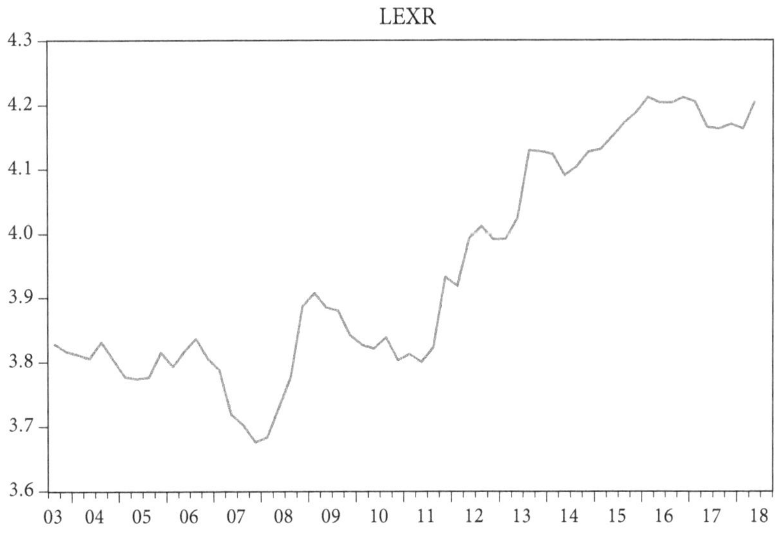

Figure 10.2 Time-Series Line Graph for Log of Exchange Rate

Sample: 2003Q3 2018Q3
Included observations: 60

<table>
<tr><th>Autocorrelation</th><th>Partial Correlation</th><th></th><th>AC</th><th>PAC</th><th>Q-Stat</th><th>Prob</th></tr>
<tr><td>. |*******</td><td>. |*******</td><td>1</td><td>0.956</td><td>0.956</td><td>57.671</td><td>0.000</td></tr>
<tr><td>. |*******</td><td>.*| . |</td><td>2</td><td>0.909</td><td>−0.066</td><td>110.67</td><td>0.000</td></tr>
<tr><td>. |******|</td><td>.*| . |</td><td>3</td><td>0.854</td><td>−0.115</td><td>158.26</td><td>0.000</td></tr>
<tr><td>. |******|</td><td>. | . |</td><td>4</td><td>0.801</td><td>0.005</td><td>200.88</td><td>0.000</td></tr>
<tr><td>. |***** |</td><td>. |*. |</td><td>5</td><td>0.759</td><td>0.102</td><td>239.83</td><td>0.000</td></tr>
<tr><td>. |***** |</td><td>.*| . |</td><td>6</td><td>0.708</td><td>−0.141</td><td>274.37</td><td>0.000</td></tr>
<tr><td>. |***** |</td><td>. | . |</td><td>7</td><td>0.664</td><td>0.039</td><td>305.33</td><td>0.000</td></tr>
<tr><td>. |**** |</td><td>. | . |</td><td>8</td><td>0.617</td><td>−0.040</td><td>332.60</td><td>0.000</td></tr>
<tr><td>. |**** |</td><td>. | . |</td><td>9</td><td>0.573</td><td>−0.003</td><td>356.54</td><td>0.000</td></tr>
<tr><td>. |**** |</td><td>.*| . |</td><td>10</td><td>0.526</td><td>−0.079</td><td>377.13</td><td>0.000</td></tr>
<tr><td>. |*** |</td><td>. | . |</td><td>11</td><td>0.480</td><td>0.010</td><td>394.64</td><td>0.000</td></tr>
<tr><td>. |*** |</td><td>. | . |</td><td>12</td><td>0.437</td><td>0.013</td><td>409.46</td><td>0.000</td></tr>
<tr><td>. |*** |</td><td>.*| . |</td><td>13</td><td>0.384</td><td>−0.151</td><td>421.12</td><td>0.000</td></tr>
<tr><td>. |** |</td><td>.*| . |</td><td>14</td><td>0.328</td><td>−0.082</td><td>429.80</td><td>0.000</td></tr>
<tr><td>. |** |</td><td>.*| . |</td><td>15</td><td>0.262</td><td>−0.107</td><td>435.49</td><td>0.000</td></tr>
<tr><td>. |*. |</td><td>. | . |</td><td>16</td><td>0.198</td><td>−0.047</td><td>438.79</td><td>0.000</td></tr>
<tr><td>. |*. |</td><td>. | . |</td><td>17</td><td>0.137</td><td>−0.018</td><td>440.42</td><td>0.000</td></tr>
<tr><td>. | . |</td><td>.*| . |</td><td>18</td><td>0.069</td><td>−0.149</td><td>440.85</td><td>0.000</td></tr>
<tr><td>. | . |</td><td>. | . |</td><td>19</td><td>0.004</td><td>−0.058</td><td>440.85</td><td>0.000</td></tr>
<tr><td>. | . |</td><td>.*| . |</td><td>20</td><td>−0.065</td><td>−0.086</td><td>441.24</td><td>0.000</td></tr>
<tr><td>.*| . |</td><td>. |*. |</td><td>21</td><td>−0.113</td><td>0.188</td><td>442.46</td><td>0.000</td></tr>
<tr><td>.*| . |</td><td>. | . |</td><td>22</td><td>−0.151</td><td>0.037</td><td>444.69</td><td>0.000</td></tr>
<tr><td>.*| . |</td><td>. | . |</td><td>23</td><td>−0.182</td><td>0.010</td><td>448.01</td><td>0.000</td></tr>
<tr><td>**| . |</td><td>.*| . |</td><td>24</td><td>−0.214</td><td>−0.102</td><td>452.74</td><td>0.000</td></tr>
<tr><td>**| . |</td><td>. | . |</td><td>25</td><td>−0.249</td><td>0.000</td><td>459.33</td><td>0.000</td></tr>
<tr><td>**| . |</td><td>. |*. |</td><td>26</td><td>−0.269</td><td>0.136</td><td>467.28</td><td>0.000</td></tr>
<tr><td>**| . |</td><td>.*| . |</td><td>27</td><td>−0.298</td><td>−0.106</td><td>477.30</td><td>0.000</td></tr>
<tr><td>**| . |</td><td>. |*. |</td><td>28</td><td>−0.311</td><td>0.143</td><td>488.52</td><td>0.000</td></tr>
</table>

Figure 10.3 Correlogram Analysis-Level Series

Through correlogram inspection, we detect that there is a significant spike present in both ACF and PACF. Hence it is a non-stationary series. We further use ADF unit root to confirm the fact this is a non-stationary series. The correlogram interpretation for different time series variables is demonstrated in Pindyck and Rubinfeld (1981).

The ADF test shows LEXCR level series has unit root and it follows I(1) with significant trend and intercept. The statistical result has been documented in Table 10.4.

The unit root test (ADF) on the level series confirms that the series is non-stationary as we cannot reject the null (presence of unit root or

Table 10.4 Result of Unit Root Test-Level Series

Null Hypothesis: LEXR has a unit root
Exogenous: Constant, Linear Trend
Lag Length: 1 (Automatic - based on SIC, maxlag = 10)

		t-Statistic	Prob.*
Augmented Dickey-Fuller test statistic		−2.515321	0.3200
Test critical values:	1% level	−4.124265	
	5% level	−3.489228	
	10% level	−3.173114	

*MacKinnon (1996) one-sided *p*-values.

Augmented Dickey–Fuller Test Equation
Dependent Variable: D(LEXR)
Method: Least Squares
Date: 01/02/20 Time: 15:14
Sample (adjusted): 2004Q1 2018Q2
Included observations: 58 after adjustments

Variable	Coefficient	Std. Error	*t*-Statistic	Prob.
LEXR(-1)	−0.142426	0.056624	−2.515321	0.0149
D(LEXR(-1))	0.244588	0.128412	1.904713	0.0621
C	0.521621	0.207771	2.510560	0.0151
@TREND("2003Q3")	0.001475	0.000569	2.589830	0.0123
R-squared	0.150621	Mean dependent var		0.006682
Adjusted R-squared	0.103434	S.D. dependent var		0.034624
S.E. of regression	0.032785	Akaike info criterion		−3.931223
Sum squared resid	0.058042	Schwarz criterion		−3.789123
Log likelihood	118.0055	Hannan-Quinn criter.		−3.875872
F-statistic	3.191959	Durbin-Watson stat		2.071918
Prob(F-statistic)	0.030714			

non-stationarity). Note that in the above result, both trend and intercept are significant.

When we again perform the unit root ADF test on differenced series, we obtain stationarity. The unit root test on the 1st difference series shows that this series has become stationary (as we reject the null of unit root). The result has been shown in Table 10.4a.

Table 10.4a Augmented Dickey–Fuller Unit Root Test on Differenced Series: D(LEXR)

Null Hypothesis: D(LEXR) has a unit root
Exogenous: Constant, Linear Trend
Lag Length: 0 (Automatic - based on SIC, maxlag = 10)

		t-Statistic	Prob.*
Augmented Dickey-Fuller test statistic		−6.046731	0.0000
Test critical values:	1% level	−4.124265	
	5% level	−3.489228	
	10% level	−3.173114	

*MacKinnon (1996) one-sided *p*-values.

Augmented Dickey-Fuller Test Equation
Dependent Variable: D(LEXR,2)
Method: Least Squares
Date: 01/02/20 Time: 15:48
Sample (adjusted): 2004Q1 2018Q2
Included observations: 58 after adjustments

Variable	Coefficient	Std. Error	*t*-Statistic	Prob.
D(LEXR(-1))	−0.803966	0.132959	−6.046731	0.0000
C	−0.000504	0.009370	−0.053834	0.9573
@TREND('2003Q3')	0.000199	0.000271	0.733327	0.4665
R-squared	0.399413	Mean-dependent var		0.000909
Adjusted R-squared	0.377574	SD-dependent var		0.043522
S.E. of regression	0.034336	Akaike info criterion		−3.854913
Sum squared resid	0.064842	Schwarz criterion		−3.748338
Log likelihood	114.7925	Hannan-Quinn criter.		−3.813400
F-statistic	18.28857	Durbin-Watson stat		2.018448
Prob(F-statistic)	0.000001			

One can check that the Durbin–Watson statistic which is very close to 2 which means there is no serial autocorrelation between the residuals.

Thus, D(LEXCR) series becomes stationary after first difference. Hence, the LEXCR series follows I(1) process.

As a next step, we inspect the correlogram of difference series D(LEXCR) and identify AR and MA patterns through ACF and PACF

Sample: 2003Q3 2018Q3
Included observations: 59

<table>
<tr><th>Autocorrelation</th><th>Partial Correlation</th><th></th><th>AC</th><th>PAC</th><th>Q-Stat</th><th>Prob</th></tr>
<tr><td>.|*. |</td><td>.|*. |</td><td>1</td><td>0.202</td><td>0.202</td><td>2.5323</td><td>0.112</td></tr>
<tr><td>.|*. |</td><td>.|*. |</td><td>2</td><td>0.131</td><td>0.094</td><td>3.6114</td><td>0.164</td></tr>
<tr><td>.*|. |</td><td>.*|. |</td><td>3</td><td>−0.080</td><td>−0.129</td><td>4.0233</td><td>0.259</td></tr>
<tr><td>**|. |</td><td>**|. |</td><td>4</td><td>−0.268</td><td>−0.258</td><td>8.7092</td><td>0.069</td></tr>
<tr><td>.|. |</td><td>.|*. |</td><td>5</td><td>−0.020</td><td>0.112</td><td>8.7355</td><td>0.120</td></tr>
<tr><td>**|. |</td><td>**|. |</td><td>6</td><td>−0.286</td><td>−0.272</td><td>14.289</td><td>0.027</td></tr>
<tr><td>.|. |</td><td>.|*. |</td><td>7</td><td>0.053</td><td>0.125</td><td>14.482</td><td>0.043</td></tr>
<tr><td>.*|. |</td><td>.*|. |</td><td>8</td><td>−0.099</td><td>−0.165</td><td>15.180</td><td>0.056</td></tr>
<tr><td>.|. |</td><td>.|*. |</td><td>9</td><td>0.050</td><td>0.103</td><td>15.363</td><td>0.081</td></tr>
<tr><td>.|. |</td><td>**|. |</td><td>10</td><td>−0.016</td><td>−0.212</td><td>15.381</td><td>0.119</td></tr>
<tr><td>.|. |</td><td>.|*. |</td><td>11</td><td>−0.009</td><td>0.158</td><td>15.387</td><td>0.165</td></tr>
<tr><td>.|** |</td><td>.|** |</td><td>12</td><td>0.343</td><td>0.223</td><td>24.391</td><td>0.018</td></tr>
<tr><td>.|. |</td><td>.|. |</td><td>13</td><td>0.056</td><td>0.017</td><td>24.640</td><td>0.026</td></tr>
<tr><td>.|*. |</td><td>.|. |</td><td>14</td><td>0.173</td><td>−0.020</td><td>27.048</td><td>0.019</td></tr>
<tr><td>.*|. |</td><td>.|. |</td><td>15</td><td>−0.081</td><td>−0.014</td><td>27.581</td><td>0.024</td></tr>
<tr><td>.*|. |</td><td>.|. |</td><td>16</td><td>−0.134</td><td>−0.053</td><td>29.092</td><td>0.023</td></tr>
<tr><td>.|. |</td><td>.|. |</td><td>17</td><td>−0.024</td><td>0.064</td><td>29.143</td><td>0.033</td></tr>
<tr><td>.*|. |</td><td>.|. |</td><td>18</td><td>−0.129</td><td>0.043</td><td>30.610</td><td>0.032</td></tr>
<tr><td>.|*. |</td><td>.|*. |</td><td>19</td><td>0.122</td><td>0.094</td><td>31.946</td><td>0.032</td></tr>
<tr><td>.*|. |</td><td>.*|. |</td><td>20</td><td>−0.094</td><td>−0.151</td><td>32.763</td><td>0.036</td></tr>
<tr><td>.|. |</td><td>.|. |</td><td>21</td><td>0.024</td><td>−0.004</td><td>32.818</td><td>0.048</td></tr>
<tr><td>.*|. |</td><td>.*|. |</td><td>22</td><td>−0.158</td><td>−0.193</td><td>35.243</td><td>0.037</td></tr>
<tr><td>.*|. |</td><td>.|*. |</td><td>23</td><td>−0.107</td><td>0.075</td><td>36.393</td><td>0.038</td></tr>
<tr><td>.|*. |</td><td>.|. |</td><td>24</td><td>0.112</td><td>−0.019</td><td>37.683</td><td>0.037</td></tr>
</table>

Figure 10.4 Correlogram of D(LEXCR)

spikes. These rules are discussed already. The correlogram graph is presented in Figure 10.4.

Clearly, there is a spike in AC (or ACF) at 1st lag and 4th lag. Similarly, there is a significant spike in PACF at 6th lag. Accordingly, we choose the ARMA structure and run regression to fit the forecasting model.

We obtain following fitted regression equation:

D(LEXCR) C AR(6) MA(1) MA(4)

The regression result done in EVIEWS 10 econometric package is reported in Table 10.5.

The parameter estimation for one additional variable labelled as 'SIGMASQ' is obtained in Eviews10 which refers to estimate of the

Table 10.5 ARIMA Model for Quarterly Exchange Rate in India (Rupee vs. Dollar)

Dependent Variable: D(LEXR)
Method: ARMA Maximum Likelihood (BFGS)
Sample: 2003Q4 2018Q2
Included observations: 59
Convergence achieved after 7 iterations
Coefficient covariance computed using outer product of gradients

Variable	Coefficient	Std. Error	*t*-Statistic	Prob.
C	0.007130	0.003052	2.336445	0.0232
AR(6)	−0.327031	0.127906	−2.556804	0.0134
MA(1)	0.332012	0.110773	2.997242	0.0041
MA(4)	−0.370949	0.123290	−3.008759	0.0040
SIGMASQ	0.000849	0.000158	5.385675	0.0000
R-squared	0.269933	Mean-dependent var		0.006380
Adjusted R-squared	0.215854	SDdependent var		0.034403
S.E. of regression	0.030465	Akaike info criterion		-4.035331
Sum squared resid	0.050117	Schwarz criterion		-3.859269
Log likelihood	124.0423	Hannan−Quinn criter.		-3.966604
F-statistic	4.991453	Durbin−Watson stat		1.988442
Prob(F-statistic)	0.001695			
Inverted AR Roots	0.72−0.42i	0.72+0.42i	0.00+0.83i	−0.00−0.83i
	−0.72−0.42i	−0.72+0.42i		
Inverted MA Roots	0.71	−0.08+0.77i	−0.08−0.77i	−0.88

Source: Author's own, results generated from EVIEWS 10 package

residual variance. After the fitting the AR model to the data, the difference between the fitted values and the actual data yields the residuals. The variance of these residuals is SIGMASQ. It is not included in forecasting the dependent variable. The regressor coefficients for AR(6), MA(1), and MA(4) are less than one. EVIEWS provides several statistics that can be used as model selection criteria (e.g. R-square—the higher the better, Akaike Information—the lower the better, and Scwartz Bayesian Criterion—the lower values are better). The model is also invertible which is confirmed through inverted AR and MA roots.

In order to finalize the equation, a Ljung and Box Q test was conducted on the residual of the above regression results. The result is presented in

Sample: 2003Q3 2018Q3
Included observations: 59
Q-statistic probabilities adjusted for 3 ARMA terms

Autocorrelation	Partial Correlation		AC	PAC	Q-Stat	Prob
.|. |	.|. |	1	-0.001	-0.001	2.E-05	
.|*. |	.|*. |	2	0.077	0.077	0.3700	
.|. |	.|. |	3	0.006	0.006	0.3723	
.|. |	.|. |	4	0.003	-0.003	0.3729	0.541
.|. |	.|. |	5	0.057	0.056	0.5881	0.745
.|. |	.|. |	6	0.059	0.060	0.8261	0.843
.|*. |	.|*. |	7	0.124	0.117	1.8932	0.755
.|. |	.|. |	8	0.002	-0.006	1.8934	0.864
.|*. |	.|*. |	9	0.092	0.076	2.5076	0.868
.*|. |	.*|. |	10	-0.129	-0.134	3.7204	0.811
.|. |	.|. |	11	-0.006	-0.025	3.7227	0.881
.|** |	.|** |	12	0.216	0.227	7.2946	0.606
.|. |	.|. |	13	0.047	0.041	7.4667	0.681
.|*. |	.|. |	14	0.089	0.037	8.1066	0.704
.|. |	.|. |	15	-0.027	-0.035	8.1649	0.772
.*|. |	.*|. |	16	-0.142	-0.173	9.8412	0.707
.|. |	.|. |	17	-0.001	0.016	9.8413	0.774
.|. |	.|. |	18	-0.049	-0.058	10.053	0.816
.|. |	.|. |	19	0.050	0.021	10.280	0.852
.|. |	.|. |	20	-0.042	-0.064	10.441	0.884
.|. |	.|. |	21	0.018	0.038	10.473	0.915
.*|. |	.*|. |	22	-0.173	-0.106	13.367	0.819
.*|. |	.*|. |	23	-0.106	-0.076	14.482	0.805
.|*. |	.|*. |	24	0.105	0.127	15.626	0.790

Figure 10.5 Correlogram of Residual
Source: Generated in EVIEWS 10 software

Figure 10.5. If the ARIMA (p, q) process has been reasonably identified, the residuals should be white noise. Accordingly, the correlations up to any lag among the residuals should be zero. The Q-static enables us to test whether a group of autocorrelations (e.g. up to lag 8 or 16) is significantly different from zero. For each group size, EVIEWS gives the confidence intervals for the Q statistic. It was found that the residual has become stationary or white noise series. More detailed discussions on Q statistic and its application in financial variables forecasting are available in Box, Jenkins, Reinsel, and Ljung (2015).

Finally, the model estimated in Table 10.4 can be used to predict static (one period ahead) as well as dynamic (two or three periods ahead) forecast.

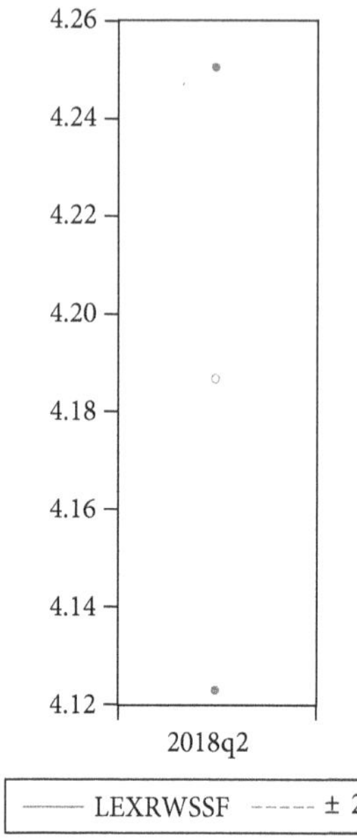

Forecast: LEXRWSSF	
Actual: LEXR	
Forecast sample: 2018Q2 2018Q2	
Included observations: 1	
Root Mean Squared Error	0.018678
Mean Absolute Error	0.018678
Mean Abs. Percent Error	0.444162
Symmetric MAPE	0.445151

Figure 10.6 Static Forecast Error for Log of Exchange Rate Series (Within Sample)

A static forecast is a one-period ahead forecast, and it will utilize all values of y_t for each subsequent forecast. Thus, in static forecasting y_T, the model will utilize all values of y_t, where $t \leq T$. A dynamic forecast on the other hand will take recursively previous forecasted values. Hence, a dynamic forecast of y_T, on the other hand, will only use values of y_t such that $t \leq T^* < T$.

The use of forecasting is becoming predominant in risk analysis across the world to address core objectives of obtaining early warning signals and estimate provisioning requirements. The forecasted values then compared with actual series to validate the forecast error. Both static and dynamic forecasts generated from the regression model estimated in Table 10.5 are presented in Figures 10.6 and 10.7.

Root-mean-square error, mean absolute error, and mean absolute percentage errors are checked to validate the forecasting models. It has been observed that the forecast error rate is < 1% for static and < 2% for dynamic ones. EVIEWS allows a forecast of both the level and the differenced variable. A lower model error confirms that this can be used to generate one/two/three period ahead static as well as dynamic forecasts.

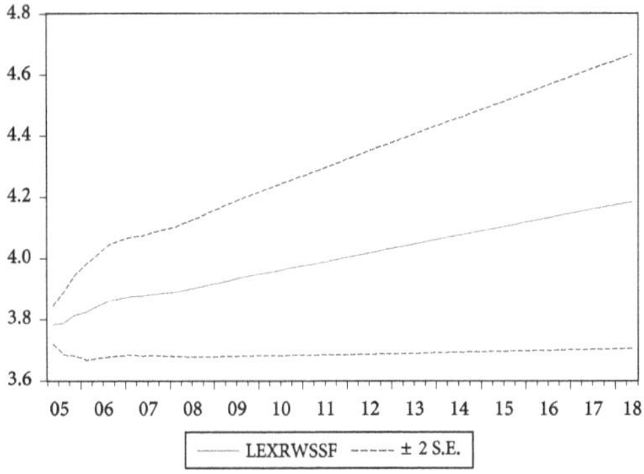

Forecast: LEXRDF	
Actual: LEXR	
Forecast sample: 2003Q3 2018Q2	
Adjusted sample: 2005Q2 2018Q2	
Included observations: 53	
Root Mean Squared Error	0.093534
Mean Absolute Error	0.072361
Mean Abs. Percent Error	1.866306
Theil Inequality Coefficient	0.011742
Bias Proportion	0.165924
Variance Proportion	0.450860
Covariance Proportion	0.383215
Theil U2 Coefficient	2.641289
Symmetric MAPE	1.843045

Figure 10.7 Dynamic Forecast Error (Within Sample)

This method has numerous applications in interest rate forecasting, probability of default forecasting, as well. These predictive models can be used to generate forecasts for loan loss provisions, default risk, non-performing assets, and also several macro-variables (GDP, index of industrial production, wholesale price index, etc.).

Multivariate Time-Series Model

Multivariate time-series models can be used to create forward-looking stress testing scenarios. Multivariate models have many advantages since it can factor interrelationship between the variables. Many forward-looking probability scenarios can be generated from multivariate time-series regressions. Forward-looking scenarios are 'what-if' scenarios. They may not have occurred before, but they can happen in the future as well. The trick is not to predict growth in business and apply historical shocks, but to create such unforeseen shocks which may hurt the existing portfolio as well. For credit risk, the shocks can arise due to increase in NPA, increase in restructured assets, depletion in collateral value, downgrade of borrowers-rated portfolio. Bank can use these shocks report and analyse the incremental capital requirement (due to increase in provision and rise in RWA). Moreover, the can use Macroeconomic stress testing methodology based on multivariate time-series models. For this, the following steps may be followed—first determine how default or loss indictors react to macroeconomic variable. In the next step, make aggregate forecasts under macroeconomic stress scenario (say 1 standard deviation change in marginal PD or slippage rate). In step 3, calculate stress results based on increase in RWA, higher NPA provision and loss of interest income (or ROA) and resultant impact on CRAR (depletion in the solvency ratio). From this, bank can further estimate their capital gap if they target certain minimum CRAR threshold (say 10.875%).

We have constructed a multivariate that may be used for stress testing.

We have used quarterly fresh slippage data of the bank and established a linkage with macroeconomic factors using a multivariate regression analysis:

$$MPD = 0.008399 \times CDR + 0.611589 \times GNPAR - 2.21E-06 \times NIFTYENERGY + 0.073589 \times LNWPI \qquad \text{Eq. 10.13}$$

Variable Definition:
MPD = marginal probability of default or quarterly fresh slippage ratio; GNPAR = gross NPA ratio of all SCBs, NIFTYENERGY = Nifty energy index values, and LNWPI = Long of wholesale price index.
The regression output produced in EVIEWS is documented in Table 10.6:

The overall R-square = 84.33% and Adjusted R Sq. = 81.39%. Further, the multivariate macro-model has been validated using unit root test and normality test on residual, Breusch-Godfrey serial correlation LM test, Breusch-Pagan-Godfrey heteroskedasticity test and found to be following the conditions of residual normality, no serial correlation, and no heteroskedasticity.

Hence, Equation 10.13 and the results reported in Table 10.5 can be used to study the impact of forecasted macroeconomic factors on fresh slippage ratio and based on that additional impact on NPA, RWA, Provisions and on capital adequacy ratio (CRAR) can be assessed.

Many simulated values for the independent variables can be taken for the calculation of the stressed marginal probability of default MPD (or fresh slippage rate) values. As a next step, different scenarios of low, medium, and severe stress were taken corresponding to 95%, 97.5%, and 99% worst scenarios. The MPD values for the scenarios, respectively, are obtained as 5.424%, 7.739%, and 8.592%. The impact of higher slippage on additional provisioning and risk weighted assets and their final effect

Table 10.6 Multivariate Time-Series Regression

Dependent Variable: MPD
Method: Least Squares
Sample (adjusted): 9/01/2013 6/01/2018
Included observations: 20 after adjustments

Variable	Coefficient	Std. Error	*t*-Statistic	Prob.
CDR	0.008399	0.001053	7.975316	0.0000
D(GNPA_RATIO)	0.611589	0.068215	8.965643	0.0000
D(NIFTENERGY)	−2.21E-06	9.14E-07	−2.421890	0.0277
LN_WPI	0.073589	0.018164	4.051258	0.0009
R-squared	0.843282	Mean dependent var		0.010638
Adjusted R-squared	0.813897	S.D. dependent var		0.005713
S.E. of regression	0.002465	Akaike info criterion		−8.996742
Sum squared resid	9.72E-05	Schwarz criterion		−8.797595
Log likelihood	93.96742	Hannan-Quinn criter.		−8.957866
Durbin-Watson stat	1.118749			

on capital adequacy ratio (CRAR) are generally examined in the stress testing exercise.

Note that stress testing measures are used to assess impacts of business plans, capital allocation, and capital lanning. It enables the top management to understand vulnerabilities.

A more sophisticated approach is to develop vector autoregressive (VAR) or a vector error correction (VEC) models by introducing appropriate time lags can provide more insightful risk estimates. EVIEWS 10 provides several alternative estimation methods for a multivariate time-series model like general least-square estimates as well as VAR and VECM models. The application of these multivariate models and their empirical interpretations are discussed in Brooks and Tsolacos (2010).

Summary

This chapter explains the nature and properties of time-series variables. It explains modelling techniques with hands-on examples that can be useful for risk analysts to forecast key risk factors (such as probability of default, exchange rate, etc.). Time-series forecasting techniques have numerous applications in deriving early warning signals, loss provisioning model, stress testing bank capital, etc. We have checked how polynomial trend fitting exercise, ARMA as well as ARIMA regression methods can be used to generate forward looking forecasts. A risk analyst can use these models to predict default rate, NPA slippage ratio etc. It can also be used to generate forecast of macroeconomic variables (both dynamic as well as static). To check the model accuracy, first within sample validation tests must be conducted. For diagnostic tests, model R-square, Akaike, Schwarz criterion should be tested. In within sample forecasting, root-mean-square error, mean absolute error, and mean absolute percentage errors are checked to validate the forecasting models.

We have also seen how multivariate time-series models can be constructed for the purpose of stress testing analysis. These types of forecasting models would also help banks/FIs to project their business as well as capital plan.

Review Questions

1. What is quadratic equation? How it can be used to generate risk forecasts?
2. What is the difference between 'trend' and 'seasonality' in time series?
3. Write quadratic polynomial regression equation. How a trend fitting can be done in EVIEWS? Why trend fitting is necessary?
4. What is the difference between ARMA and ARIMA models?
5. What is correlogram analysis? How ACF and PACF spikes help you to identify ARMA pattern?
6. What is ADF test statistic? How it can be interpreted?
7. What is the null hypothesis of augmented Dickey–Fuller test? What are the test criteria?
8. What is the difference between ACF and PACF? How they help a risk manager to predict risk?
9. What is the difference between static forecast and dynamic forecast?
10. How multivariate time-series model can be used for stress testing?

References

Box, G. E. P., and G. M. Jenkins (1976). 'Time Series Analysis: Forecasting and Control', Holden Day, San Francisco.

Box, G. E. P., G. M. Jenkins, G. C. Reinsel, and G. M. Ljung (2015). 'Time Series Analysis: Forecasting and Control', 5th Edition, Wiley.

Brooks, C., and S. Tsolacos (2010). 'Real Estate Modelling and Forecasting', Cambridge.

Enders, W. (2014). 'Applied Econometric Time Series', 4th Edition, Wiley.

Johnston, J., and J. DiNardo (1997). 'Econometric Methods', 4th Edition, The McGraw-Hill Companies, Inc.

Pindyck, R. S., and D. L. Rubinfeld (1981). 'Econometric Models and Economic Forecasts', 2nd Edition, McGraw-Hill International Editions.

Profillidis, V. A., and G. N. Botzoris (2019). 'Trend Projection and Time Series Methods', in *Modeling and Transport Demand*, Chapter 6, pp. 225–270, ScienceDirect. URL: https://www.sciencedirect.com/book/9780128115138/modeling-of-transport-demand

Tsay, R. S. (2014). 'Analysis of Financial Time Series', 3rd Edition, Wiley.

APPENDIX

Statistical Tables

Appendix A

Table of the Student's t-Distribution
The table gives the values of α where
$\Pr(T_v > t_{\alpha;\,v}) = \alpha$, with v degrees of freedom

v \ α	0.1	0.05	0.025	0.01	0.005	0.001	0.0005
1	3.078	6.314	12.076	31.821	63.657	318.310	636.620
2	1.886	2.920	4.303	6.965	9.925	22.326	31.598
3	1.638	2.353	3.182	4.541	5.841	10.213	12.924
4	1.533	2.132	2.776	3.747	4.604	7.173	8.610
5	1.476	2.015	2.571	3.365	4.032	5.893	6.869
6	1.440	1.943	2.447	3.143	3.707	5.208	5.959
7	1.415	1.895	2.365	2.998	3.499	4.785	5.408
8	1.397	1.860	2.306	2.896	3.355	4.501	5.041
9	1.383	1.833	2.262	2.821	3.250	4.297	4.781
10	1.372	1.812	2.228	2.764	3.169	4.144	4.587
11	1.363	1.796	2.201	2.718	3.106	4.025	4.437
12	1.356	1.782	2.179	2.681	3.055	3.930	4.318
13	1.350	1.771	2.160	2.650	3.012	3.852	4.221
14	1.345	1.761	2.145	2.624	2.977	3.787	4.140
15	1.341	1.753	2.131	2.602	2.947	3.733	4.073
16	1.337	1.746	2.120	2.583	2.921	3.686	4.015
17	1.333	1.740	2.110	2.567	2.898	3.646	3.965
18	1.330	1.734	2.101	2.552	2.878	3.610	3.922
19	1.328	1.729	2.093	2.539	2.861	3.579	3.883
20	1.325	1.725	2.086	2.528	2.845	3.552	3.850
21	1.323	1.721	2.080	2.518	2.831	3.527	3.819
22	1.321	1.717	2.074	2.508	2.819	3.505	3.792
23	1.319	1.714	2.069	2.500	2.807	3.485	3.767
24	1.318	1.711	2.064	2.492	2.797	3.467	3.745
25	1.316	1.708	2.060	2.485	2.787	3.450	3.725

ν \ α	**0.1**	**0.05**	**0.025**	**0.01**	**0.005**	**0.001**	**0.0005**
26	1.315	1.706	2.056	2.479	2.779	3.435	3.707
27	1.314	1.703	2.052	2.473	2.771	3.421	3.690
28	1.313	1.701	2.048	2.467	2.763	3.408	3.674
29	1.311	1.699	2.045	2.462	2.756	3.396	3.659
30	1.310	1.697	2.042	2.457	2.750	3.385	3.646
40	1.303	1.684	2.021	2.423	2.704	3.307	3.551
60	1.296	1.671	2.000	2.390	2.660	3.232	3.460
120	1.289	1.658	1.980	2.358	2.617	3.160	3.373
∞	1.282	1.645	1.960	2.326	2.576	3.090	3.291

Appendix B

Statistical Table of the Standard Normal Distribution Values ($z \leq 0$)

$-z$	0.00	0.01	0.02	0.03	0.04	0.05	0.06	0.07	0.08	0.09
0.0	0.50000	0.49601	0.49202	0.48803	0.48405	0.48006	0.47608	0.47210	0.46812	0.46414
0.1	0.46017	0.45621	0.45224	0.44828	0.44433	0.44038	0.43644	0.43251	0.42858	0.42466
0.2	0.42074	0.41683	0.41294	0.40905	0.40517	0.40129	0.39743	0.39358	0.38974	0.38591
0.3	0.38209	0.37828	0.37448	0.37070	0.36693	0.36317	0.35942	0.35569	0.35197	0.34827
0.4	0.34458	0.34090	0.33724	0.33360	0.32997	0.32636	0.32276	0.31918	0.31561	0.31207
0.5	0.30854	0.30503	0.30153	0.29806	0.29460	0.29116	0.28774	0.28434	0.28096	0.27760
0.6	0.27425	0.27093	0.26763	0.26435	0.26109	0.25785	0.25463	0.25143	0.24825	0.24510
0.7	0.24196	0.23885	0.23576	0.23270	0.22965	0.22663	0.22363	0.22065	0.21770	0.21476
0.8	0.21186	0.20897	0.20611	0.20327	0.20045	0.19766	0.19489	0.19215	0.18943	0.18673
0.9	0.18406	0.18141	0.17879	0.17619	0.17361	0.17106	0.16853	0.16602	0.16354	0.16109
1.0	0.15866	0.15625	0.15386	0.15151	0.14917	0.14686	0.14457	0.14231	0.14007	0.13786
1.1	0.13567	0.13350	0.13136	0.12924	0.12714	0.12507	0.12302	0.12100	0.11900	0.11702
1.2	0.11507	0.11314	0.11123	0.10935	0.10749	0.10565	0.10384	0.10204	0.10027	0.09853
1.3	0.09680	0.09510	0.09342	0.09176	0.09012	0.08851	0.08692	0.08534	0.08379	0.08226
1.4	0.08076	0.07927	0.07780	0.07636	0.07493	0.07353	0.07215	0.07078	0.06944	0.06811
1.5	0.06681	0.06552	0.06426	0.06301	0.06178	0.06057	0.05938	0.05821	0.05705	0.05592
1.6	0.05480	0.05370	0.05262	0.05155	0.05050	0.04947	0.04846	0.04746	0.04648	0.04551
1.7	0.04457	0.04363	0.04272	0.04182	0.04093	0.04006	0.03920	0.03836	0.03754	0.03673
1.8	0.03593	0.03515	0.03438	0.03363	0.03288	0.03216	0.03144	0.03074	0.03005	0.02938
1.9	0.02872	0.02807	0.02743	0.02680	0.02619	0.02559	0.02500	0.02442	0.02385	0.02330
2.0	0.02275	0.02222	0.02169	0.02118	0.02068	0.02018	0.01970	0.01923	0.01876	0.01831

-z	**0.00**	**0.01**	**0.02**	**0.03**	**0.04**	**0.05**	**0.06**	**0.07**	**0.08**	**0.09**
2.1	0.01786	0.01743	0.01700	0.01659	0.01618	0.01578	0.01539	0.01500	0.01463	0.01426
2.2	0.01390	0.01355	0.01321	0.01287	0.01255	0.01222	0.01191	0.01160	0.01130	0.01101
2.3	0.01072	0.01044	0.01017	0.00990	0.00964	0.00939	0.00914	0.00889	0.00866	0.00842
2.4	0.00820	0.00798	0.00776	0.00755	0.00734	0.00714	0.00695	0.00676	0.00657	0.00639
2.5	0.00621	0.00604	0.00587	0.00570	0.00554	0.00539	0.00523	0.00509	0.00494	0.00480
2.6	0.00466	0.00453	0.00440	0.00427	0.00415	0.00403	0.00391	0.00379	0.00368	0.00357
2.7	0.00347	0.00336	0.00326	0.00317	0.00307	0.00298	0.00289	0.00280	0.00272	0.00264
2.8	0.00256	0.00248	0.00240	0.00233	0.00226	0.00219	0.00212	0.00205	0.00199	0.00193
2.9	0.00187	0.00181	0.00175	0.00170	0.00164	0.00159	0.00154	0.00149	0.00144	0.00140
3.0	0.00135	0.00131	0.00126	0.00122	0.00118	0.00114	0.00111	0.00107	0.00104	0.00100
3.1	0.00097	0.00094	0.00090	0.00087	0.00085	0.00082	0.00079	0.00076	0.00074	0.00071
3.2	0.00069	0.00066	0.00064	0.00062	0.00060	0.00058	0.00056	0.00054	0.00052	0.00050
3.3	0.00048	0.00047	0.00045	0.00043	0.00042	0.00040	0.00039	0.00038	0.00036	0.00035
3.4	0.00034	0.00033	0.00031	0.00030	0.00029	0.00028	0.00027	0.00026	0.00025	0.00024
3.5	0.00023	0.00022	0.00022	0.00021	0.00020	0.00019	0.00019	0.00018	0.00017	0.00017

Appendix C

Table of the Standard Normal Distribution Values ($z \geq 0$)

z	0.00	0.01	0.02	0.03	0.04	0.05	0.06	0.07	0.08	0.09
0.0	0.50000	0.50399	0.50798	0.51197	0.51595	0.51994	0.52392	0.52790	0.53188	0.53586
0.1	0.53983	0.54380	0.54776	0.55172	0.55567	0.55962	0.56356	0.56749	0.57142	0.57535
0.2	0.57926	0.58317	0.58706	0.59095	0.59483	0.59871	0.60257	0.60642	0.61026	0.61409
0.3	0.61791	0.62172	0.62552	0.62930	0.63307	0.63683	0.64058	0.64431	0.64803	0.65173
0.4	0.65542	0.65910	0.66276	0.66640	0.67003	0.67364	0.67724	0.68082	0.68439	0.68793
0.5	0.69146	0.69497	0.69847	0.70194	0.70540	0.70884	0.71226	0.71566	0.71904	0.72240
0.6	0.72575	0.72907	0.73237	0.73565	0.73891	0.74215	0.74537	0.74857	0.75175	0.75490
0.7	0.75804	0.76115	0.76424	0.76730	0.77035	0.77337	0.77637	0.77935	0.78230	0.78524
0.8	0.78814	0.79103	0.79389	0.79673	0.79955	0.80234	0.80511	0.80785	0.81057	0.81327
0.9	0.81594	0.81859	0.82121	0.82381	0.82639	0.82894	0.83147	0.83398	0.83646	0.83891
1.0	0.84134	0.84375	0.84614	0.84849	0.85083	0.85314	0.85543	0.85769	0.85993	0.86214
1.1	0.86433	0.86650	0.86864	0.87076	0.87286	0.87493	0.87698	0.87900	0.88100	0.88298
1.2	0.88493	0.88686	0.88877	0.89065	0.89251	0.89435	0.89617	0.89796	0.89973	0.90147
1.3	0.90320	0.90490	0.90658	0.90824	0.90988	0.91149	0.91308	0.91466	0.91621	0.91774
1.4	0.91924	0.92073	0.92220	0.92364	0.92507	0.92647	0.92785	0.92922	0.93056	0.93189
1.5	0.93319	0.93448	0.93574	0.93699	0.93822	0.93943	0.94062	0.94179	0.94295	0.94408
1.6	0.94520	0.94630	0.94738	0.94845	0.94950	0.95053	0.95154	0.95254	0.95352	0.95449
1.7	0.95543	0.95637	0.95728	0.95818	0.95907	0.95994	0.96080	0.96164	0.96246	0.96327
1.8	0.96407	0.96485	0.96562	0.96638	0.96712	0.96784	0.96856	0.96926	0.96995	0.97062
1.9	0.97128	0.97193	0.97257	0.97320	0.97381	0.97441	0.97500	0.97558	0.97615	0.97670
2.0	0.97725	0.97778	0.97831	0.97882	0.97932	0.97982	0.98030	0.98077	0.98124	0.98169
2.1	0.98214	0.98257	0.98300	0.98341	0.98382	0.98422	0.98461	0.98500	0.98537	0.98574

z	**0.00**	**0.01**	**0.02**	**0.03**	**0.04**	**0.05**	**0.06**	**0.07**	**0.08**	**0.09**
2.2	0.98610	0.98645	0.98679	0.98713	0.98745	0.98778	0.98809	0.98840	0.98870	0.98899
2.3	0.98928	0.98956	0.98983	0.99010	0.99036	0.99061	0.99086	0.99111	0.99134	0.99158
2.4	0.99180	0.99202	0.99224	0.99245	0.99266	0.99286	0.99305	0.99324	0.99343	0.99361
2.5	0.99379	0.99396	0.99413	0.99430	0.99446	0.99461	0.99477	0.99492	0.99506	0.99520
2.6	0.99534	0.99547	0.99560	0.99573	0.99585	0.99598	0.99609	0.99621	0.99632	0.99643
2.7	0.99653	0.99664	0.99674	0.99683	0.99693	0.99702	0.99711	0.99720	0.99728	0.99736
2.8	0.99744	0.99752	0.99760	0.99767	0.99774	0.99781	0.99788	0.99795	0.99801	0.99807
2.9	0.99813	0.99819	0.99825	0.99831	0.99836	0.99841	0.99846	0.99851	0.99856	0.99861
3.0	0.99865	0.99869	0.99874	0.99878	0.99882	0.99886	0.99889	0.99893	0.99896	0.99900
3.1	0.99903	0.99906	0.99910	0.99913	0.99916	0.99918	0.99921	0.99924	0.99926	0.99929
3.2	0.99931	0.99934	0.99936	0.99938	0.99940	0.99942	0.99944	0.99946	0.99948	0.99950
3.3	0.99952	0.99953	0.99955	0.99957	0.99958	0.99960	0.99961	0.99962	0.99964	0.99965
3.4	0.99966	0.99968	0.99969	0.99970	0.99971	0.99972	0.99973	0.99974	0.99975	0.99976
3.5	0.99977	0.99978	0.99978	0.99979	0.99980	0.99981	0.99981	0.99982	0.99983	0.99983

Index

Lightning Source UK Ltd.
Milton Keynes UK
UKHW020020031122
411564UK00001B/1

9 780192 849014